Jesus Calling®
Morning & Evening

Enjoying Peace in His Presence

Sarah Young

THOMAS NELSON
Since 1798

Jesus Calling® Morning and Evening

© 2015 by Sarah Young

All rights reserved. No portion of this book may be reproduced, stored in a retrieval system, or transmitted in any form or by any means—electronic, mechanical, photocopy, recording, scanning, or other—except for brief quotations in critical reviews or articles, without the prior written permission of the publisher.

Published in Nashville, Tennessee, by Thomas Nelson. Thomas Nelson is a registered trademark of HarperCollins Christian Publishing, Inc.

Thomas Nelson titles may be purchased in bulk for educational, business, fund-raising, or sales promotional use. For information, please e-mail SpecialMarkets@ThomasNelson.com.

These devotions include text from *Jesus Calling®*, *Jesus Today*™, *Dear Jesus*, and *Jesus Lives*™. They are used with the author's permission.

Unless otherwise noted, Scripture quotations are taken from the Holy Bible, New International Version®, NIV®. Copyright © 1973, 1978, 1984 by Biblica, Inc™. Used by permission of Zondervan. All rights reserved worldwide. www.zondervan.com

Other Scripture quotations are taken from the following sources:

The King James Version (KJV). *The Message* (MSG). Copyright © 1993, 1994, 1995, 1996, 2000, 2001, 2002. Used by permission of Tyndale House Publishers, Inc. The New King James Version® (NKJV). Copyright © 1982 by Thomas Nelson. Used by permission. All rights reserved. The NEW AMERICAN STANDARD BIBLE® (NASB), Copyright © 1960, 1962, 1963, 1968, 1971, 1972, 1973, 1975, 1977, 1995 by The Lockman Foundation. Used by permission. The Amplified Bible (AMP), Copyright © 1954, 1958, 1962, 1964, 1965, 1987 by The Lockman Foundation, La Habra, CA. All rights reserved. Used by permission. www.lockman.org. The Living Bible (TLB) copyright © 1971. Used by permission of Tyndale House Publishers, Inc., Carol Stream, Illinois 60188. All rights reserved. The New Revised Standard Version Bible (NRSV), copyright © 1989 the Division of Christian Education of the National Council of the Churches of Christ in the United States of America. Used by permission. All rights reserved. The ESV® Bible (The Holy Bible, English Standard Version®) (ESV), copyright © 2001 by Crossway, a publishing ministry of Good News Publishers. Used by permission. All rights reserved.

ISBN-13: 978-0-7180-4015-4

Printed in China

16 17 18 19 20 DSC 12 11 10 9 8 7

I dedicate Jesus Calling to my mother, whose encouragement inspired me to persevere in writing this book. She demonstrated her appreciation of my writing in poignant ways. She kept my manuscript beside her bed, so she could read it every morning. Once, while away from her home, she even asked me to fax her the readings day by day. After she died from cancer, I found portions of my writings that she had hand-copied into a journal. This mother who had prayed me through thick and thin, including years of rebellion, opened her heart fully to my devotional writing. Her oft-expressed desire to write children's books never came to fruition. But there is a sense in which she has written — through me — this book.

Thank you, Nani! Your legacy lives on.

Preface

Be still and know that I am God.

—Psalm 46:10

This new morning and evening edition of *Jesus Calling*® allows readers to begin each day focusing on the hope and peace that can be found only in Jesus and then, in turn, to go to bed each evening reflecting on His Word.

Let the morning bring me word of your unfailing love, for I have put my trust in you. Show me the way I should go, for to you I entrust my life. (Psalm 143:8)

What a gift it is to start the day knowing that God loves us and has a plan for us. Before the rush of the calendar and responsibilities takes over, while the world is still and the morning coffee is hot, take a moment to pause in the presence of Jesus. Starting your day in Scripture reading, prayer, and devotions provides you with strength and peace—both of which you are likely to need in the coming hours.

As the day winds to a close, thank the Lord for the joys and blessings of the day, acknowledging that He was with you each step of the way. Release your fears and cast your anxieties on Him, knowing that they are safe in His care and trusting that He is at work on your behalf. Rest peacefully, knowing that you are not in control but that the One who is in control is working to make all things to work together for good.

When you lie down, you will not be afraid; when you lie down, your sleep will be sweet. (Proverbs 3:24)

May you greet each day with His hope in your heart, and may you sleep sweetly at night, sustained by the promises of His Word.

Sarah Young

Introduction
Jesus Calling

I FIRST EXPERIENCED THE PRESENCE OF GOD in a setting of exquisite beauty. I was studying at a Christian community in a tiny Alpine village in France. This was a branch of L'Abri, an international ministry that began in Switzerland through Francis and Edith Schaeffer's work. During my stay at L'Abri, I often explored the fairyland-like environment all around me. It was late winter, and the noonday sun was warm enough for sunbathing, but the depth of the snow kept it from melting. Brilliant sunlight reflecting from pure white snow was cleansing my mind of the darkness that had held it captive for years.

Every day I climbed up a steep hill to attain a view that delighted my soul. As I stood at the top, I would lose myself in a panorama of unbroken beauty. Below me was the village that had become my home. Viewed from this height, the village was dominated by a high-steepled church. Turning 180 degrees, I could see Lake Geneva far below me, shouting greetings in refracted sunbeams. When I looked up, I saw icy tips of Alpine mountains encircling me. I would turn round and round, absorbing as much as I could with two eyes and a finite mind.

The daughter of a college professor, I had been encouraged to read widely and think for myself. I had majored in philosophy at Wellesley College and had almost completed my master's degree in child development at Tufts University. A few months earlier, my brother had asked me to read Francis Schaeffer's *Escape from Reason*. To my great surprise and delight, that small book had answered questions I'd long before dismissed as unanswerable. It was the intellectual integrity of Schaeffer's books that had drawn me to this pristine place. I was searching for absolute, unchanging truth—a foundation on which to build my life.

Shortly after I settled into the home I shared with other students, I met a gifted counselor who had come from the Swiss branch of L'Abri to talk with some of us. I went into the room where she was waiting, and she told me to close the door. Before I even had time to sit down, she asked her first question: "Are you a Christian?" I answered that I wasn't sure; I wanted to be a Christian, but I didn't really understand why I needed Jesus. I thought that knowing God might be enough. Her second question was: "What can you *not* forgive yourself for?" This question brought me face to face with my sinfulness, and immediately I understood my need for Jesus—to save me from my many sins. Later, when I was alone, I asked Him to forgive all my sins and to be my Savior-God.

One night I found myself leaving the warmth of our cozy chalet to walk alone in the snowy mountains. I went into a deeply wooded area, feeling vulnerable and awed by cold, moonlit beauty. The air was crisp and dry, piercing to inhale. After a while, I came into an open area and I stopped walking. Time seemed to stand still as I gazed around me in wonder—soaking in the beauty of this place. Suddenly I became aware of a lovely Presence with me, and my involuntary response was to whisper, "Sweet Jesus." This experience of Jesus' Presence was far more personal than the intellectual answers for which I'd been searching. This was a relationship with the Creator of the universe—the One who is *the way, the truth, and the life* (John 14:6 NKJV).

The following year, back in the United States, I had another encounter with the Presence of Jesus. I was grieving the loss of a serious dating relationship and wondering whether being a Christian made much difference in the quality of my life.

At that time I was working as a technical writer in Virginia. My boss sent me to Atlanta to attend a conference. I accepted this assignment dutifully and checked in to the hotel without enthusiasm. Alone in my room, I felt waves of desolation wash over me. So I began walking the streets of Atlanta aimlessly, trying to escape my solitude. I glanced at some books in an outdoor stall and was drawn to *Beyond Ourselves* by Catherine Marshall. That night, as I read the book, I no longer felt alone. I knelt beside the bed in that sterile room and felt an overwhelming Presence of peace and love come over me. I knew that Jesus was with me and that He sympathized with my heartache. This was unquestionably the same "Sweet Jesus" I had encountered in the snowy splendor of the Alps.

During the next sixteen years, I lived what many people might consider an exemplary Christian life. I went to Covenant

Theological Seminary in St. Louis, where I earned a master's degree in counseling and biblical studies. While there, I met my husband, Steve, a third-generation missionary to Japan. After graduation, we spent two four-year terms in Japan doing church-planting ministry. We had a baby girl during our first term and a baby boy during our furlough in the United States. After our second term, we returned to the US for three years. We lived in Atlanta, where Steve worked with a local Japanese church and I earned a further degree in counseling at Georgia State University.

As part of my training, I worked at a Christian counseling center in the Atlanta area. I cherished my experiences of helping deeply wounded women find healing in Christ. I was also thankful for my kind, loving husband and our two delightful children, who were the main joys of my life. However, not once during those sixteen years did I vividly experience the Presence of Jesus.

So I was ready to begin a new spiritual quest. It started with delving into a devotional book, *The Secret of the Abiding Presence* by Andrew Murray. The theme of this book is that God's Presence is meant to be the continual experience of Christians. Murray emphasizes the importance of spending time alone with God in quiet, uninterrupted communion.

I began reading the book at a very unstructured time in my life. We were waiting for our Australian visas to be approved so that we could begin a church among Japanese people living in Melbourne. I had quit my counseling job to prepare for the move overseas, so I was adjusting to the loss of this fulfilling work. In the midst of those momentous changes, I began seeking God's Presence in earnest. My days started alone with God, equipped with Bible, devotional book, prayer journal, pen, and coffee. An hour or two alone with Him seemed too brief.

The uncertainties I faced at that time deepened my increasing closeness to God. My husband and I had no idea how long it would take to receive permanent residency visas, so the waiting period seemed to stretch indefinitely into the future. During that period, I had four surgeries, including two for melanoma. A Bible verse that comforted me during this difficult time of waiting also accompanied me on the seemingly endless flight to Australia: "You will go out in joy and be led forth in peace" (Isaiah 55:12).

We settled in Australia and began our dual ministries. I supported Steve in planting the first-ever Japanese church in Melbourne, but my main ministry focus was counseling Australian women, some of whom were coming out of terrible abuse and spiritual bondage.

Our combined ministries subjected our family to intense spiritual warfare, and I prayed for protection every morning. One morning as I prayed, I visualized God protecting each of us. I pictured first our daughter, then our son, and then Steve encircled by God's protective Presence. When I prayed for myself, I was suddenly enveloped in brilliant light and profound peace. I had not sought this powerful experience of God's Presence, but I received it gratefully and was strengthened by it.

Only two or three days later, a counseling client who was an incest survivor began remembering experiences of satanic ritual abuse. This form of Satan worship involves subjecting victims (who are often young children) to incredibly evil, degrading tortures. My courageous client and I walked together into the darkness of her memories. But God had prepared me for stepping into deep darkness by first bathing me in His glorious light. I realized that experiences of God's Presence were not only for my benefit but were also preparation for helping others.

The following year, I began to wonder if I could change my prayer times from monologue to dialogue. I had been writing in prayer journals for many years, but this was one-way communication: I did all the talking. Increasingly, I wanted to hear what God might want to communicate to me on a given day. I decided to "listen" with pen in hand, writing down whatever I "heard" in my mind. As J. I. Packer wrote in his book *Your Father Loves You*: "God . . . guides our minds as we think things out in his presence." This is how I was listening to Him—by focusing on Jesus and His Word, while asking Him to guide my thoughts. I was *not* listening for an audible voice; I was spending time *seeking God's Face* (Psalm 27:8 NKJV).

My journaling thus changed from monologue to dialogue. This new way of communicating with God became the high point of my day. Of course, I knew my writings were not inspired—as only Scripture is—but they were helping me grow closer to God. This became a delightful way to *encourage myself in the LORD* (1 Samuel 30:6 KJV).

As I was learning to seek God's Face, "Be still, and know that I am God" (Psalm 46:10) became a life-changing verse.

Alternate readings for "Be still" are "Relax," "Let go," and "Cease striving" (NASB). This is an enticing invitation from God to lay down our cares and seek His Presence.

Among other resources, *Praying: Finding Our Way Through Duty to Delight* has been helpful. This book, written by J. I. Packer and Carolyn Nystrom, contains a wonderful quote from Martin Luther—"If the Holy Spirit should come and begin to preach to your heart, giving you rich and enlightened thoughts, . . . be quiet and listen to him who can talk better than you; and note what he proclaims and *write it down*; so will you experience miracles as David says: 'Open my eyes that I may behold wondrous things out of thy law' (Psalm 119:18)."

During the years that I've been waiting in God's Presence and listening with pen in hand, I have found themes of His Peace becoming more prominent in my writing. I'm sure this tendency reflects, in part, my personal need. However, when people open up to me, I find that most of them also desire the balm of Jesus' Peace.

This practice of being still in God's Presence has increased my intimacy with Him more than any other spiritual discipline, so I want to share some of the writings I have gleaned from these quiet moments. In many parts of the world, Christians seem to be searching for a deeper experience of Jesus' Presence and Peace. The devotions that follow address that felt need.

The Bible is the only infallible, inerrant Word of God, and I endeavor to keep my writings consistent with that unchanging standard. I have written from the perspective of Jesus speaking, to help readers feel more personally connected with Him. So the first person singular ("I," "Me," "My," "Mine") always refers to Christ; "you" refers to you, the reader.

I have included Scripture references after each daily reading. As I waited in God's Presence, Bible verses or fragments of verses often came to mind. So I interwove these into the devotions. Words from the Scriptures (some paraphrased, some quoted) are indicated in italics. Certain Bible verses figure rather heavily in my writing. That is because God often uses these passages to strengthen and encourage me, raising my sights from my "light and momentary troubles" (2 Corinthians 4:17) to His eternal perspective.

Themes of thankfulness and trust recurred often during my listening times. These themes are quite prevalent in the Bible, and they are essential for a close relationship with the Lord.

The devotions in this book are meant to be read slowly, preferably in a quiet place—with your Bible open. Remember that Jesus is Immanuel, *God with us.* May you enjoy His Presence and His Peace in ever-increasing measure.

Sarah Young

January

"For I know the plans I have for you," declares the Lord, *"plans to prosper you and not to harm you, plans to give you a hope and a future."*

Jeremiah 29:11

January 1
MORNING

COME TO ME with a teachable spirit, eager to be changed. A close walk with Me is a life of continual newness. Do not cling to old ways as you step into a new year. Instead, seek My Face with an open mind, knowing that your journey with Me involves being *transformed by the renewing of your mind*. As you focus your thoughts on Me, be aware that I am fully attentive to you. I see you with a steady eye because My attention span is infinite. I know and understand you completely; My thoughts embrace you in everlasting Love. *I also know the plans I have for you: plans to prosper you and not to harm you, plans to give you hope and a future.* Give yourself fully to this adventure of increasing attentiveness to My Presence.

PSALM 27:8 ESV; ROMANS 12:2;
JEREMIAH 29:11

January 1
EVENING

I WANT YOU TO LOVE ME, *listen to My voice, and hold fast to Me—for I am your Life.* This is the way of wisdom. I am training you to stay close to Me as you walk along perilous paths.

> *[Choose life,] that you may love the LORD your God, listen to his voice, and hold fast to him. For the LORD is your life, and he will give you many years in the land he swore to give to your fathers, Abraham, Isaac and Jacob.* —DEUTERONOMY 30:20

> *Trust in him at all times, O people; pour out your hearts to him, for God is our refuge.* —PSALM 62:8

> *Also read:*
> ZEPHANIAH 3:17 NKJV

Before You Turn Out the Light

Listen for My voice in My Word and through My Spirit.

January 2
MORNING

Relax in My healing Presence. As you spend time with Me, your thoughts tend to jump ahead to today's plans and problems. Bring your mind back to Me for refreshment and renewal. Let the Light of My Presence soak into you as you focus your thoughts on Me. Thus I equip you to face whatever the day brings. This sacrifice of time pleases Me and strengthens you. Do not skimp on our time together. Resist the clamor of tasks waiting to be done. *You have chosen what is better, and it will not be taken away from you.*

Psalm 89:15; Psalm 105:4;

Luke 10:39–42

January 2
EVENING

The world abounds with idols—things you turn to when you want to feel better about yourself: eating, entertainment, exercise, mastery of something or someone. However, none of these things can slake the thirst of your soul, which yearns for Me alone. When you get that gnawing sensation around the edges of your soul, return to Me—*your soul will be satisfied as with the richest of foods.*

O God, you are my God, earnestly I seek you; my soul thirsts for you . . . I have seen you in the sanctuary and beheld your power and your glory. Because your love is better than life, my lips will glorify you. I will praise you as long as I live, and in your name I will lift up my hands. My soul will be satisfied as with the richest of foods; with singing lips my mouth will praise you. —Psalm 63:1–5

Also read:
Isaiah 54:10; Psalm 46:10 NASB

Before You Turn Out the Light

Retreat into My loving Presence while I refocus your thoughts and feelings on Me.

January 3
MORNING

REFRESH YOURSELF in the Peace of My Presence. This Peace can be your portion at all times and in all circumstances. Learn to *hide in the secret of My Presence*, even as you carry out your duties in the world. I am both with you and within you. I go before you to open up the way, and I also walk alongside you. There could never be another companion as devoted as I am.

Because I am your constant Companion, there should be a lightness to your step that is observable to others. Do not be weighed down with problems and unresolved issues, for I am your burden-bearer. In the world you have trials and distress, but don't let them get you down. *I have conquered the world and deprived it of power to harm you.* In Me you may have confident Peace.

PSALM 31:19–20 NASB; JOHN 16:33 AMP

January 3
EVENING

My Peace is a soft, soothing pillow for your weary head. Pry your mind away from plans and problems so you can rest in My healing Presence. If anxious thoughts try to intrude, give them over to Me *with thanksgiving*—you have a Helper who is infinitely powerful, tenderly loving, and wise beyond all understanding.

And He said, "My Presence will go with you, and I will give you rest." —Exodus 33:14 NKJV

Rejoice in the Lord always. I will say it again: Rejoice! Let your gentleness be evident to all. The Lord is near. Do not be anxious about anything, but in everything, by prayer and petition, with thanksgiving, present your requests to God. And the peace of God, which transcends all understanding, will guard your hearts and your minds in Christ Jesus. —Philippians 4:4–7

Also read:
John 8:31–32 esv; John 15:26 nkjv

Before You Turn Out the Light

Instead of pondering your problems, renew your mind with My precious, freeing truths.

January 4
MORNING

I WANT YOU TO LEARN A NEW HABIT. Try saying, "I trust You, Jesus," in response to whatever happens to you. If there is time, think about who I am in all My Power and Glory; ponder also the depth and breadth of My Love for you.

This simple practice will help you see Me in every situation, acknowledging My sovereign control over the universe. When you view events from this perspective—through the Light of My universal Presence—fear loses its grip on you. Adverse circumstances become growth opportunities when you affirm your trust in Me no matter what. You receive blessings gratefully, realizing they flow directly from My hand of grace. Your continual assertion of trusting Me will strengthen our relationship and keep you close to Me.

PSALM 63:2; ISAIAH 40:10–11;
PSALM 139:7–10

January 4
EVENING

I AM CALLING YOU TO TRUST IN ME *at all times*, no matter what is happening. I understand what a difficult assignment this is, and I know that you will sometimes fail in this venture, but I continue to love you perfectly even when you don't succeed. Let this assurance of My unfailing Love draw you back to Me—back to trusting Me.

Trust in the LORD forever, for the LORD, the LORD, is the Rock eternal. —ISAIAH 26:4

Lean on, trust in, and be confident in the Lord with all your heart and mind and do not rely on your own insight or understanding. —PROVERBS 3:5 AMP

Also read:
MATTHEW 11:28 NKJV

Before You Turn Out the Light

How will you rely on Me tomorrow beyond what you did today?

January 5
MORNING

YOU CAN ACHIEVE THE VICTORIOUS LIFE through living in deep dependence on Me. People usually associate victory with success: not falling or stumbling, not making mistakes. But those who are successful in their own strength tend to go their own way, forgetting about Me. It is through problems and failure, weakness and neediness, that you learn to rely on Me.

True dependence is not simply asking Me to bless what you have decided to do. It is coming to Me with an open mind and heart, inviting Me to plant My desires within you. I may infuse within you a dream that seems far beyond your reach. You know that in yourself you cannot achieve such a goal. Thus begins your journey of profound reliance on Me. It is a faith-walk, taken one step at a time, leaning on Me as much as you need. This is not a path of continual success but of multiple failures. However, each failure is followed by a growth spurt, nourished by increased reliance on Me. Enjoy the blessedness of a victorious life through deepening your dependence on Me.

PSALM 34:17–18; 2 CORINTHIANS 5:7 NKJV

January 5
EVENING

D**ON'T TRY TO PRETEND** that you have it all together or that you're stronger than you really are. Instead, lean hard on Me, letting Me bear most of your weight. Rejoice in Me—*your Strength*—and worship Me.

A man of many companions may come to ruin, but there is a friend who sticks closer than a brother. —PROVERBS 18:24

But I will sing of your strength, in the morning I will sing of your love; for you are my fortress, my refuge in times of trouble. O my Strength, I sing praise to you; you, O God, are my fortress, my loving God. —PSALM 59:16–17

Also read:
HEBREWS 11:21 NKJV

Before You Turn Out the Light

In your mind's eye, do you see Me standing nearby with My strong arm extended toward you? I am offering you My help.

January 6
MORNING

I AM ABLE *to do far beyond all that you ask or imagine.* Come to Me with positive expectations, knowing that there is no limit to what I can accomplish. Ask My Spirit to control your mind so that you can think great thoughts of Me. Do not be discouraged by the fact that many of your prayers are yet unanswered. Time is a trainer, teaching you to wait upon Me, to trust Me in the dark. The more extreme your circumstances, the more likely you are to see *My Power and Glory* at work in the situation. Instead of letting difficulties draw you into worrying, try to view them as setting the scene for My glorious intervention. Keep your eyes and your mind wide open to all that I am doing in your life.

EPHESIANS 3:20–21; ROMANS 8:6;
ISAIAH 40:30–31 NKJV; REVELATION 5:13

January 6
EVENING

THIS PLANET YOU INHABIT is in such a big mess that sometimes you feel overwhelmed, but I am *the Almighty*; nothing is beyond My control. I am also the Lord who *comforts His people and will have compassion on His afflicted ones*. You can transcend your troubles because I am both powerful and compassionate.

> *"I am the Alpha and the Omega, the Beginning and the End," says the Lord, "who is and who was and who is to come, the Almighty."* —REVELATION 1:8 NKJV

> *Shout for joy, O heavens; rejoice, O earth; burst into song, O mountains! For the LORD comforts his people and will have compassion on his afflicted ones.* —ISAIAH 49:13

Also read:
PSALM 91:1–2 ESV

Before You Turn Out the Light

In the face of tonight's headlines, consider who I am: the Beginning and the End, the Almighty, the Compassionate One.

January 7
MORNING

It is impossible to praise or thank Me too much. As it is written, *I inhabit the praises of My people.* Sometimes your adoration is a spontaneous overflow of Joy, in response to radiant beauty or rich blessings. At other times your praise is more disciplined and measured—an act of your will. I dwell equally in both types of praise. Thankfulness, also, is a royal road to draw near Me. A thankful heart has plenty of room for Me.

When you thank Me for the many pleasures I provide, you affirm that I am God, from whom all blessings flow. When adversity strikes and you thank Me anyway, your trust in My sovereignty is a showpiece in invisible realms. Fill up the spare moments of your life with praise and thanksgiving. This joyous discipline will help you live in the intimacy of My Presence.

Psalm 22:3 kjv; Psalm 146:1–2;
1 Thessalonians 5:18

January 7
EVENING

Even the greatest blessings can fail to bring Joy unless they are received with gratitude. Just keep coming into My Presence with thanksgiving. Your persistent thankfulness may actually provide the long-awaited key I will use to unlock major difficulties in your life.

Enter his gates with thanksgiving and his courts with praise; give thanks to him and praise his name. For the Lord is good and his love endures forever; his faithfulness continues through all generations. —Psalm 100:4–5

"You now have sorrow; but I will see you again and your heart will rejoice, and your joy no one will take from you." —John 16:22 NKJV

Also read:
Psalm 107:21–22 NKJV

Before You Turn Out the Light

Thank Me, not only for obvious blessings but for the situations you would never have chosen. This is true trust.

January 8
MORNING

SOFTLY I ANNOUNCE MY PRESENCE. Shimmering hues of radiance tap gently at your consciousness, seeking entrance. Though I have all Power in heaven and on earth, I am infinitely tender with you. The weaker you are, the more gently I approach you. Let your weakness be a door to My Presence. Whenever you feel inadequate, remember that I am your *ever-present Help.*

Hope in Me, and you will be protected from despair and self-pity. Hope is like a golden cord connecting you to heaven. The more you cling to this cord, the more I bear the weight of your burdens; thus, you are lightened. Heaviness is not of My kingdom. Cling to hope, and My rays of Light will reach you through the darkness.

PSALM 46:1; ROMANS 12:12;
ROMANS 15:13

January 8
EVENING

Y OU HAVE A RESTLESS MIND. It skips and scampers about continually, rarely taking time to be still. Listen, and you will hear Me saying, *"Come to Me."* I am the only resting place for your mind that will truly satisfy and strengthen you.

*Find rest, O my soul, in God alone; my
hope comes from him.* —PSALM 62:5

*"Come to me, all you who are weary and burdened, and
I will give you rest. Take my yoke upon you and learn
from me, for I am gentle and humble in heart, and you
will find rest for your souls."* —MATTHEW 11:28–29

Also read:
EXODUS 3:3–5 NKJV; MATTHEW 10:16 NKJV

Before You Turn Out the Light

Do not be deceived by the many voices calling out to you. In Me alone is rest for your restless mind.

January 9
MORNING

I AM WITH YOU AND FOR YOU. When you decide on a course of action that is in line with My will, nothing in heaven or on earth can stop you. You may encounter many obstacles as you move toward your goal, but don't be discouraged—never give up! With My help, you can overcome any obstacle. Do not expect an easy path as you journey hand in hand with Me, but do remember that I, your *very-present Helper*, am omnipotent.

Much, much stress results from your wanting to make things happen before their times have come. One of the main ways I assert My sovereignty is in the timing of events. If you want to stay close to Me and do things My way, ask Me to show you the path forward moment by moment. Instead of dashing headlong toward your goal, let Me set the pace. Slow down, and enjoy the journey in My Presence.

ROMANS 8:31; PSALM 46:1–3 NKJV;
LUKE 1:37

January 9
EVENING

It is through trust that you follow Me along the right path. From your limited perspective, your journey may be confusing, with puzzling twists and turns. However, from My limitless, big-picture perspective, I am indeed *leading you along straight paths.*

> *I guide you in the way of wisdom and lead you along straight paths.* —PROVERBS 4:11

> *A man's steps are directed by the LORD. How then can anyone understand his own way?* —PROVERBS 20:24

Also read:
ROMANS 8:28 AMP

Before You Turn Out the Light

Determine to follow Me wherever I take you. I am beckoning you forward.

January 10
MORNING

EVERY TIME YOU AFFIRM YOUR TRUST IN ME, you put a coin into My treasury. Thus you build up equity in preparation for days of trouble. I keep safely in My heart all trust invested in Me, with interest compounded continuously. The more you trust Me, the more I empower you to do so.

Practice trusting Me during quiet days, when nothing much seems to be happening. Then when storms come, your trust balance will be sufficient to see you through. *Store up for yourself treasure in heaven* through placing your trust in Me. This practice will keep you in My Peace.

PSALM 33:20–21; PSALM 56:3–4;
MATTHEW 6:20–21

January 10
EVENING

I AM INDEED WITH YOU—watching over you wherever you are, wherever you go. Rejoice that I am with you not only in this life but also in the life to come. Let the promise of heaven flood your heart with My eternal Presence!

> *"I am with you and will watch over you wherever you go, and I will bring you back to this land. I will not leave you until I have done what I have promised you."* —GENESIS 28:15

> *"Therefore everyone who hears these words of mine and puts them into practice is like a wise man who built his house on the rock."* —MATTHEW 7:24

Also read:
JOHN 14:16–17 NASB; JOHN 14:2–3

Before You Turn Out the Light

Accept My Presence with you as the deepest Reality—
as a rock on which you can build your life.

January 11
MORNING

Trust Me by relinquishing control into My hands. *Let go, and recognize that I am God.* This is My world: I made it and I control it. Yours is a responsive part in the litany of Love. I search among My children for receptivity to Me. Guard well this gift that I have planted in your heart. Nurture it with the Light of My Presence.

When you bring Me prayer requests, lay out your concerns before Me. Speak to Me candidly; pour out your heart. Then thank Me for the answers that I have set into motion long before you can discern results. When your requests come to mind again, continue to thank Me for the answers that are on the way. If you keep on stating your concerns to Me, you will live in a state of tension. When you thank Me for how I am answering your prayers, your mind-set becomes much more positive. Thankful prayers keep your focus on My Presence and My promises.

PSALM 46:10 AMP; COLOSSIANS 4:2;
2 PETER 1:3–4

January 11
EVENING

TRUST ME MOMENT BY MOMENT. Though the battle is fierce and you are weak, your resources are unlimited. My Spirit is ever ready to help you; you have only to ask.

> *Trust in him at all times, O people; pour out your hearts to him, for God is our refuge.* —PSALM 62:8

"And I will pray the Father, and He will give you another Helper, that He may abide with you forever—the Spirit of truth, whom the world cannot receive, because it neither sees Him nor knows Him; but you know Him, for He dwells with you and will be in you." —JOHN 14:16–17 NKJV

Also read:
PSALM 32:10

Before You Turn Out the Light

Search for Me in this moment; call upon
My Name with confident trust.

January 12

MORNING

LET ME PREPARE YOU for the day that stretches out before you. I know exactly what this day will contain, whereas you have only vague ideas about it. You would like to see a map, showing all the twists and turns of your journey. You'd feel more prepared if you could somehow visualize what is on the road ahead. However, there is a better way to be prepared for *whatever* you will encounter today: Spend quality time with Me.

I will not show you what is on the road ahead, but I will thoroughly equip you for the journey. My living Presence is your Companion each step of the way. Stay in continual communication with Me, whispering My Name whenever you need to redirect your thoughts. Thus, you can walk through this day with your focus on Me. My abiding Presence is the best road map available.

EXODUS 33:14; JOHN 15:4–7

January 12
EVENING

Both My words and My works *testify to the truth*: I performed countless *miraculous signs* so that the display of My Glory would confirm the truth of My teaching. My resurrection and ascension further verify that I am who I claim to be: the only true Savior-God. The more you build your life on the truth, the closer to Me you can live—enjoying Me, depending on Me, glorifying Me.

> *"You are a king, then!" said Pilate. Jesus answered, "You are right.... In fact, for this reason I was born, and for this I came into the world, to testify to the truth. Everyone on the side of truth listens to Me."* —JOHN 18:37

> *Jesus did many other miraculous signs in the presence of his disciples, which are not recorded in this book. But these are written that you may believe that Jesus is the Christ, the Son of God, and that by believing you may have life in his name.* —JOHN 20:30–31

Also read:
JOHN 14:6; 1 CORINTHIANS 15:19

Before You Turn Out the Light

You can face the morning with confidence simply by dwelling in the truth—My truth—tonight.

January 13

MORNING

Try to view each day as an adventure, carefully planned out by your Guide. Instead of staring into the day that is ahead of you, attempting to program it according to your will, be attentive to Me and to all I have prepared for you. Thank Me for this day of life, recognizing that it is a precious, unrepeatable gift. Trust that I am with you each moment, whether you sense My Presence or not. A thankful, trusting attitude helps you to see events in your life from My perspective.

A life lived close to Me will never be dull or predictable. Expect each day to contain surprises! Resist your tendency to search for the easiest route through the day. Be willing to follow wherever I lead. No matter how steep or treacherous the path before you, the safest place to be is by My side.

Psalm 118:24 nkjv; Isaiah 41:10;
1 Peter 2:21

January 13
EVENING

A PREDICTABLE LIFESTYLE MAY FEEL safer, but it can shield you from what you need most of all—Me! When unexpected events shake up your routines, rejoice. This is exactly what you need to wake you up and point you toward Me.

There is no fear in love. But perfect love drives out fear, because fear has to do with punishment. The one who fears is not made perfect in love. —1 JOHN 4:18

My soul clings to you; your right hand upholds me. —PSALM 63:8

Also read:
EPHESIANS 3:17–18

Before You Turn Out the Light

As we venture into tomorrow, prepare to cling tightly to My hand, every step of the way.

January 14
MORNING

Let Me bless you with My grace and Peace. Open your heart and mind to receive all that I have for you. Do not be ashamed of your emptiness. Instead, view it as the optimal condition for being filled with My Peace.

It is easy to touch up your outward appearance, to look as if you have it all together. Your attempts to look good can fool most people. But I see straight through you, into the depths of your being. There is no place for pretense in your relationship with Me. Rejoice in the relief of being fully understood. Talk with Me about your struggles and feelings of inadequacy. Little by little, I will transform your weaknesses into strengths. Remember that your relationship with Me is saturated in grace. Therefore, *nothing that you do or don't do can separate you from My Presence.*

1 Samuel 16:7; Romans 8:38–39

January 14
EVENING

*S*ince I am *the same yesterday and today and forever,* there could never be a time when you might find Me lacking. Whenever you are feeling empty, *come boldly to My throne of grace.* Confess not only your neediness but also the idolatrous ways you have tried to satisfy your needs; then, lift up empty hands of faith to receive all that I have for you.

Jesus Christ is the same yesterday and today and forever. —Hebrews 13:8

Let us therefore come boldly to the throne of grace, that we may obtain mercy and find grace to help in time of need. —Hebrews 4:16 nkjv

Also read:
Psalm 16:11; Psalm 63:5

Before You Turn Out the Light

Cooperate with Me as I cleanse your heart of idols.

January 15
MORNING

My Face is shining upon you, beaming out *Peace that transcends understanding*. You are surrounded by a sea of problems, but you are face to Face with Me, your Peace. As long as you focus on Me, you are safe. If you gaze too long at the myriad problems around you, you will sink under the weight of your burdens. When you start to sink, simply call out, "Help me, Jesus!" and I will lift you up.

The closer you live to Me, the safer you are. Circumstances around you are undulating, and there are treacherous-looking waves in the distance. *Fix your eyes on Me*, the One who never changes. By the time those waves reach you, they will have shrunk to proportions of My design. I am always beside you, helping you face *today's* waves. The future is a phantom, seeking to spook you. Laugh at the future! Stay close to Me.

Philippians 4:7; Matthew 14:29–30;
Hebrews 12:2

January 15
EVENICE

Use your trials and troubles to draw closer to Me. When you view troubles in this way—as reminders to draw near to Me—you can actually rejoice in your trials. Reach into your arsenal of prayers, and speak one or more of them boldly—the enemy will retreat, and I will draw near.

Consider it all joy, my brethren, when you encounter various trials. —James 1:2 nasb

Let the morning bring me word of your unfailing love, for I have put my trust in you. Show me the way I should go, for to you I lift up my soul. —Psalm 143:8

Also read:
Psalm 27:11; James 4:7–8 nkjv

Before You Turn Out the Light

Don't run from Me. Draw near to Me,
and I will draw near to you.

January 16
MORNING

COME TO ME, and rest in My loving Presence. You know that this day will bring difficulties, and you are trying to think your way through those trials. As you anticipate what is ahead of you, you forget that *I am with you*—now and always. Rehearsing your troubles results in experiencing them many times, whereas you are meant to go through them only when they actually occur. Do not multiply your suffering in this way! Instead, come to Me, and relax in My Peace. I will strengthen you and prepare you for this day, transforming your fear into confident trust.

MATTHEW 11:28–30; JOSHUA 1:5, 9

January 16
EVENING

It is vital to place your hope ultimately in *Me*. Circumstances change all the time, but *I am the same yesterday, today, and forever.* Moreover, I love you with perfect, life-giving Love.

> *Jesus Christ is the same yesterday, today, and forever.* —Hebrews 13:8 nkjv

> *May your unfailing love rest upon us, O Lord, even as we put our hope in you.* —Psalm 33:22

Also read:
Psalm 62:5–6; Deuteronomy 33:12

Before You Turn Out the Light

Make plans to nurture your hope,
which comes from Me.

January 17
MORNING

COME TO ME WITH A THANKFUL HEART so that you can enjoy My Presence. This is the day that I have made. I want you to rejoice *today*, refusing to worry about tomorrow. Search for all that I have prepared for you, anticipating abundant blessings and accepting difficulties as they come. I can weave miracles into the most mundane day if you keep your focus on Me.

Come to Me with all your needs, knowing that *My glorious riches* are a more-than-adequate supply. Stay in continual communication with Me so that you can live above your circumstances even while you are in the midst of them. *Present your requests to Me with thanksgiving, and My Peace, which surpasses all comprehension, will guard your heart and mind.*

PSALM 118:24; PHILIPPIANS 4:19;
PHILIPPIANS 4:6–7 NASB

January 17
EVENING

A THANKFUL ATTITUDE opens windows of heaven through which spiritual blessings fall freely—and all I require to rain those blessings on you is your gratitude! It seems such a simple choice; yet you stumble over it almost every day of your life. Let Me help you become more grateful so you can receive bountiful blessings through those openings into eternity.

Enter his gates with thanksgiving and his courts with praise; give thanks to him and praise his name. —PSALM 100:4

Rejoice greatly, O daughter of Zion! Shout, O daughter of Jerusalem! Behold, your King is coming to you. —ZECHARIAH 9:9 NKJV

Also read:
EPHESIANS 1:3 NASB; COLOSSIANS 4:2

Before You Turn Out the Light

Your gratitude opens the floodgates of heaven.
Pour out your words of thanksgiving to Me.

January 18
MORNING

I AM LEADING YOU ALONG THE HIGH ROAD, but there are descents as well as ascents. In the distance you see snow-covered peaks glistening in brilliant sunlight. Your longing to reach those peaks is good, but you must not take shortcuts. Your assignment is to follow Me, allowing Me to direct your path. Let the heights beckon you onward, but stay close to Me.

Learn to trust Me when things go "wrong." Disruptions to your routine highlight your dependence on Me. Trusting acceptance of trials brings blessings that *far outweigh them all*. Walk hand in hand with Me through this day. I have lovingly planned every inch of the way. Trust does not falter when the path becomes rocky and steep. Breathe deep draughts of My Presence, and hold tightly to My hand. Together we can make it!

> JOHN 21:19; 2 CORINTHIANS 4:17;
> HABAKKUK 3:19

January 18
EVENING

I HAVE ALREADY ACCOMPLISHED the greatest miracle—saving you from your sins. The next time you face an "impossible" situation, turn to Me immediately with a hopeful heart. *All things are possible with Me!*

Jesus looked at them and said, "With man this is impossible, but with God all things are possible." —MATTHEW 19:26

The eternal God is your refuge, and underneath are the everlasting arms. —DEUTERONOMY 33:27 NKJV

Also read:
JAMES 1:2–3; HABAKKUK 3:17–18

Before You Turn Out the Light

Be courageous—"impossibilities" are My specialty!

January 19
MORNING

Seek My Face, and you will find more than you ever dreamed possible. *Let Me displace worry at the center of your being.* I am like a supersaturated cloud, showering Peace into the pool of your mind. My Nature is to bless. Your nature is to receive with thanksgiving. This is a true fit, designed before the foundation of the world. Glorify Me by receiving My blessings gratefully.

I am the goal of all your searching. *When you seek Me, you find Me* and are satisfied. When lesser goals capture your attention, I fade into the background of your life. I am still there, watching and waiting, but you function as if you were alone. Actually, My Light shines on every situation you will ever face. Live radiantly by expanding your focus to include Me in all your moments. Let nothing dampen your search for Me.

PSALM 27:8 NKJV; PHILIPPIANS 4:7 MSG;
JEREMIAH 29:13

January 19
EVENING

THINK OF ALL IT MEANS to have Me as your Shepherd: My full-time job is watching over you, taking care of you. When danger threatens, I never abandon you—I have even gone so far as to lay down My Life for you. I, the Good Shepherd, know My sheep and My sheep know Me—just as the Father knows Me and I know the Father.

> *The LORD is my shepherd, I shall not be in want. He makes me lie down in green pastures, he leads me beside quiet waters.* —PSALM 23:1–2

> *"I am the good shepherd; I know my sheep and my sheep know me—just as the Father knows me and I know the Father—and I lay down my life for the sheep."* —JOHN 10:14–15

Also read:

ISAIAH 54:10

Before You Turn Out the Light

Savor My tender care as you lie down in the green pastures I have reserved for you.

January 20
MORNING

Approach this day with awareness of who is Boss. As you make plans for the day, remember that it is I who orchestrates the events of your life. On days when things go smoothly, according to your plans, you may be unaware of My sovereign Presence. On days when your plans are thwarted, be on the lookout for Me! I may be doing something important in your life, something quite different from what you expected. It is essential at such times to stay in communication with Me, accepting My way as better than yours. Don't try to figure out what is happening. Simply trust Me and thank Me in advance for the good that will come out of it all. *I know the plans I have for you, and they are good.*

ISAIAH 55:9–11; JEREMIAH 29:11

January 20
EVENING

Do not be discouraged when I choose to give you strength sufficient only for the moment—this may be My way of keeping you ever so close to Me on your life-path. This closeness helps you hear My whispers—telling you of My delight in you. To hear these whispers clearly, you must trust that I, *the Sovereign Lord*, am in charge of your life and that your journey—though difficult—is full of blessing.

The Sovereign Lord is my strength; he makes my feet like the feet of a deer, he enables me to go on the heights. —Habakkuk 3:19

My God shall supply all your need according to His riches in glory by Christ Jesus. —Philippians 4:19 NKJV

Also read:
Psalm 96:6–7

Before You Turn Out the Light

Don't worry that you are keenly aware of your weakness. In turning to Me, you allow Me to supply your every need.

January 21
MORNING

I WANT YOU TO BE ALL MINE. I am weaning you from other dependencies. Your security rests in Me alone—not in other people, not in circumstances. Depending only on Me may feel like walking on a tightrope, but there is a safety net underneath: *the everlasting arms.* So don't be afraid of falling. Instead, look ahead to Me. I am always before you, beckoning you on—one step at a time. *Neither height nor depth, nor anything else in all creation, can separate you from My loving Presence.*

DEUTERONOMY 33:27; PROVERBS 16:9;
ROMANS 8:38–39

January 21
EVENING

MISPLACED DEPENDENCE CAN BORDER on idolatry. If you let your basic well-being depend on another person's behavior, your life may come to resemble a roller-coaster ride: subject to his or her whims and moods. Even worse, your intimacy with Me will be hindered by your preoccupation with someone else. I deserve first place in your heart!

Every good and perfect gift is from above, coming down from the Father of the heavenly lights. —JAMES 1:17

Yet I hold this against you: You have forsaken your first love. —REVELATION 2:4

Also read:
PHILIPPIANS 4:4–7

Before You Turn Out the Light

Be mindful that every good gift is ultimately from Me, even if it comes to you through human hands.

January 22
MORNING

STRIVE TO TRUST ME in more and more areas of your life. Anything that tends to make you anxious is a growth opportunity. Instead of running away from these challenges, embrace them, eager to gain all the blessings I have hidden in the difficulties. If you believe that I am sovereign over every aspect of your life, it is possible to trust Me in all situations. Don't waste energy regretting the way things are or thinking about what might have been. Start at the present moment—accepting things exactly as they are—and search for My way in the midst of those circumstances.

Trust is like a staff you can lean on as you journey uphill with Me. If you are trusting in Me consistently, the staff will bear as much of your weight as needed. *Lean on, trust, and be confident in Me with all your heart and mind.*

PSALM 52:8; PROVERBS 3:5–6 AMP

January 22
EVENING

Growing in grace is all about trusting Me: in good times, in bad times, at all times. One of the best ways of connecting with Me—here and now—is trusting Me in the very situation where you find yourself. Be encouraged by knowing that though you may see only darkness, My Light is shining through you in surpassing splendor!

> *But if we walk in the light, as he is in the light, we have fellowship with one another, and the blood of Jesus, his Son, purifies us from all sin.* —1 John 1:7

> *Even there Your hand shall lead me, and Your right hand shall hold me.* —Psalm 139:10 nkjv

Also read:
Psalm 62:8

Before You Turn Out the Light

Grasp My hand in the dark, and don't let go, for I will never let go of you.

January 23
MORNING

IT'S ALL RIGHT TO BE HUMAN. When your mind wanders while you are praying, don't be surprised or upset. Simply return your attention to Me. Share a secret smile with Me, knowing that I understand. Rejoice in My Love for you, which has no limits or conditions. Whisper My Name in loving contentment, assured that *I will never leave you or forsake you.* Intersperse these peaceful interludes abundantly throughout your day. This practice will enable you to attain *a quiet and gentle spirit*, which is pleasing to Me.

As you live in close contact with Me, the Light of My Presence filters through you to bless others. Your weakness and woundedness are the openings through which *the Light of the knowledge of My Glory* shines forth. *My strength and power show themselves most effective in your weakness.*

DEUTERONOMY 31:6; 1 PETER 3:4;
2 CORINTHIANS 4:6–7; 2 CORINTHIANS 12:9 AMP

January 23
EVENING

Your weakness and brokenness draw Me ever so near you. As you open yourself to My healing Presence, I fill you with *Peace that transcends understanding*. Trust Me in the depths of your being, where I live in union with you.

A bruised reed he will not break, and a smoldering wick he will not snuff out. —Isaiah 42:3

Do not be anxious about anything, but in everything, by prayer and petition, with thanksgiving, present your requests to God. And the peace of God, which transcends all understanding, will guard your hearts and your minds in Christ Jesus. —Philippians 4:6–7

Also read:
Proverbs 3:5 amp; Isaiah 54:10

Before You Turn Out the Light

While you rest your head on My chest, I am watching over you and all that concerns you.

January 24
MORNING

My Peace is the treasure of treasures: *the pearl of great price.* It is an exquisitely costly gift, both for the Giver and the receiver. I purchased this Peace for you with My blood. You receive this gift by trusting Me in the midst of life's storms. If you have the world's peace—everything going your way—you don't seek My unfathomable Peace. Thank Me when things do not go your way, because spiritual blessings come wrapped in trials. Adverse circumstances are normal in a fallen world. Expect them each day. Rejoice in the face of hardship, *for I have overcome the world.*

MATTHEW 13:46 NKJV; JAMES 1:2–3;
JOHN 16:33 ESV

January 24
EVENING

Though you lose everything else, if you gain My Peace, you are rich indeed. Let that be a deep comfort to you, especially amid the many aspects of your life over which you have no control! My desire is to help you treasure My Peace above everything in the world—recognizing it as a supernatural gift bequeathed to My followers shortly before My death.

"Peace I leave with you; my peace I give you. I do not give to you as the world gives. Do not let your hearts be troubled and do not be afraid." —John 14:27

Do not be anxious about anything, but in everything, by prayer and petition, with thanksgiving, present your requests to God. And the peace of God, which transcends all understanding, will guard your hearts and your minds in Christ Jesus. —Philippians 4:6–7

Also read:
John 20:19

Before You Turn Out the Light

When you feel at the mercy of your circumstances, ask for My Peace before you ask for anything else.

January 25
MORNING

Let My Love enfold you in the radiance of My Glory. Sit still in the Light of My Presence, and receive My Peace. These quiet moments with Me transcend time, accomplishing far more than you can imagine. Bring Me the sacrifice of your time, and watch to see how abundantly I bless you and your loved ones.

Through the intimacy of our relationship, you are *being transformed* from the inside out. As you keep your focus on Me, I form you into the one I desire you to be. Your part is to yield to My creative work in you, neither resisting it nor trying to speed it up. Enjoy the tempo of a God-breathed life by letting Me set the pace. Hold My hand in childlike trust, and the way before you will open up step by step.

Hebrews 13:15; 2 Corinthians 3:18;
Psalm 73:23–24

January 25
EVENING

In a world that may seem increasingly hopeless, remember that I am *the hope of Glory*. This hope is ultimately about heaven, where you will live with Me forever, but the Light of heaven's Glory is so brilliant that some of its rays can reach you even in the present—no matter how dark your circumstances may appear. I am *the Light that shines on in the darkness, for the darkness has never overpowered it.*

> *God has chosen to make known among the Gentiles the glorious riches of this mystery, which is Christ in you, the hope of glory.* —Colossians 1:27

> *The Light shines on in the darkness, for the darkness has never overpowered it [put it out or absorbed it or appropriated it].* —John 1:5 AMP

Also read:
Ephesians 3:16–17; Proverbs 4:18 ESV

Before You Turn Out the Light

Where can you see My Light overcoming the darkness?

January 26
MORNING

GIVE UP THE ILLUSION that you deserve a problem-free life. Part of you is still hungering for the resolution of all difficulties. This is a false hope! As I told My disciples, *in the world you will have trouble.* Link your hope not to problem solving in this life but to the promise of an eternity of problem-free life in heaven. Instead of seeking perfection in this fallen world, pour your energy into seeking Me: the Perfect One.

It is possible to enjoy Me and glorify Me in the midst of adverse circumstances. In fact, My Light shines most brightly through believers who trust Me in the dark. That kind of trust is supernatural: a production of My indwelling Spirit. When things seem all wrong, trust Me anyway. I am much less interested in right circumstances than in right responses to whatever comes your way.

JOHN 16:33; PSALM 112:4, 7

January 26
EVENING

No matter how much darkness you see in the world around you, My Light continues to *shine on*, for it is infinitely more powerful! Because you are My child, this Light shines not only upon you but also within you. You live *in the midst of a crooked and perverse generation*; this is the perfect backdrop for you to *shine as light in the world*.

The Light shines on in the darkness, for the darkness has never overpowered it [put it out or absorbed it or appropriated it, and is unreceptive to it]. —John 1:5 AMP

Do all things without complaining and disputing, that you may become blameless and harmless, children of God without fault in the midst of a crooked and perverse generation, among whom you shine as lights in the world. —Philippians 2:14–15 NKJV

Also read:
Psalm 62:8

Before You Turn Out the Light

As you bask in My radiant Presence, you will blaze boldly in the darkness around you.

January 27
MORNING

TRUST IS A GOLDEN PATHWAY TO HEAVEN. When you walk on this path, you live above your circumstances. My glorious Light shines more brightly on those who follow this path of Life. Dare to walk on the high road with Me, for it is the most direct route to heaven. The low road is circuitous: twisting and turning in agonizing knots. There the air hangs heavy—and dark, ominous clouds predominate. *Relying on your own understanding* will weigh you down. *Trust in Me absolutely, and I will make your path straight.*

JOHN 14:1–2; 2 TIMOTHY 4:18;
PROVERBS 3:5–6

January 27
EVENING

Hoping can be a joyful occupation because it connects you to your promised inheritance in heaven. Such hope provides a rock-solid foundation in the present, helping you face the daily struggles of living in a broken world. Hope also connects you with Me, the God of hope.

Trust in him at all times, O people; pour out your hearts to him, for God is our refuge. —Psalm 62:8

May the God of hope fill you with all joy and peace as you trust in him so that you may overflow with hope by the power of the Holy Spirit. —Romans 15:13

Also read:
1 Timothy 1:17

Before You Turn Out the Light

Meditate on some of the ways that trusting Me gives meaning to your waiting and hoping.

January 28
MORNING

I AM WITH YOU ALWAYS. These were the last words I spoke before ascending into heaven. I continue to proclaim this promise to all who will listen. People respond to My continual Presence in various ways. Most Christians accept this teaching as truth but ignore it in their daily living. Some ill-taught or wounded believers fear (and may even resent) My awareness of all they do, say, and think. A few people center their lives around this glorious promise and find themselves blessed beyond all expectations.

When My Presence is the focal point of your consciousness, all the pieces of your life fall into place. As you gaze at Me through the eyes of your heart, you can see the world around you from My perspective. The fact that *I am with you* makes every moment of your life meaningful.

MATTHEW 28:20; PSALM 139:1–4

January 28
EVENING

You and I live not just *with* each other but also *in* each other. Every step you take, every word you speak, every breath you breathe—all is done in My watchful, embracing Presence. The more aware of Me you are, the more alive and complete you will feel.

> *"On that day you will realize that I am in my Father, and you are in me, and I am in you."* —John 14:20

> *"For in [God] we live and move and have our being." As some of your own poets have said, "We are his offspring."* —Acts 17:28

Also read:
Colossians 1:27 nkjv; Ephesians 3:17, 19 amp

Before You Turn Out the Light

Commit to start living in awareness of My divine Presence.

January 29
MORNING

KEEP YOUR FOCUS ON ME. I have gifted you with amazing freedom, including the ability to choose the focal point of your mind. Only the crown of My creation has such remarkable capability; this is a sign of being *made in My image.*

Let the goal of this day be to *bring every thought captive to Me*. Whenever your mind wanders, lasso those thoughts and bring them into My Presence. In My radiant Light, anxious thoughts shrink and shrivel away. Judgmental thoughts are unmasked as you bask in My unconditional Love. Confused ideas are untangled while you rest in the simplicity of My Peace. *I will guard you and keep you in constant Peace, as you focus your mind on Me.*

PSALM 8:5; GENESIS 1:26–27;
2 CORINTHIANS 10:5; ISAIAH 26:3 AMP

January 29
EVENING

WHEN YOU REMEMBER ME during the night, think about who I really am. Ponder My perfections: My Love, Joy, and Peace; rejoice in My majesty, wisdom, grace, and mercy; find comfort in My names: Shepherd, Savior, Immanuel, Prince of Peace; be awed by My Power and Glory, for I am King of kings and Lord of lords. These thoughts of Me will clear your mind and refresh your entire being.

> *On my bed I remember you; I think of you through the watches of the night.* —PSALM 63:6

> *Cast all your anxiety on [God] because he cares for you.* —1 PETER 5:7

Also read:
PSALM 63:7 NKJV; 1 TIMOTHY 6:12–16

Before You Turn Out the Light

Take charge of your night-thoughts before they take charge of you, remembering Who cares for you.

January 30
MORNING

WORSHIP ME ONLY. Whatever occupies your mind the most becomes your god. Worries, if indulged, develop into idols. Anxiety gains a life of its own, parasitically infesting your mind. Break free from this bondage by affirming your trust in Me and refreshing yourself in My Presence. What goes on in your mind is invisible, undetectable to other people. But I read your thoughts continually, searching for evidence of trust in Me. I rejoice when your mind turns toward Me. Guard your thoughts diligently; good thought-choices will keep you close to Me.

PSALM 112:7; 1 CORINTHIANS 13:11;
PSALM 139:23-24 NASB

January 30
EVENING

I AM *CHRIST IN YOU*—shining *the Light of the knowledge of My Glory* into your heart. When you do your work in dependence on Me, I can use it powerfully for My purposes. Delight in what we accomplish together, but find your utmost Joy in Me—your eternal Treasure.

> *For it is the God who commanded light to shine out of darkness, who has shone in our hearts to give the light of the knowledge of the glory of God in the face of Jesus Christ. But we have this treasure in earthen vessels, that the excellence of the power may be of God and not of us.* —2 CORINTHIANS 4:6–7 NKJV

> *To them God has chosen to make known among the Gentiles the glorious riches of this mystery, which is Christ in you, the hope of glory.* —COLOSSIANS 1:27

Also read:
LUKE 10:20

Before You Turn Out the Light

Where are you most prone to idolize what you've made or done rather than turning the praise toward Me?

January 31
MORNING

I AM YOUR STRENGTH AND SHIELD. I plan out each day and have it ready for you long before you arise from bed. I also provide the strength you need each step of the way. Instead of assessing your energy level and wondering about what's on the road ahead, concentrate on staying in touch with Me. My Power flows freely into you through our open communication. Refuse to waste energy worrying, and you will have strength to spare.

Whenever you start to feel afraid, remember that I am your Shield. But unlike inanimate armor, I am always alert and active. My Presence watches over you continually, protecting you from both known and unknown dangers. Entrust yourself to My watch-care, which is the best security system available. *I am with you and will watch over you wherever you go.*

PSALM 28:7; MATTHEW 6:34;
PSALM 56:3–4; GENESIS 28:15

January 31
EVENING

WHEN YOU'RE IN A TOUGH SITUATION, your mind tends to go into overdrive. I want you to have confidence in Me and My ways—patiently trusting in Me even when you can't see the way forward. You can trust that I will not forsake you in your time of need.

> *Thus says the Lord GOD, the Holy One of Israel: "In returning and rest you shall be saved; in quietness and confidence shall be your strength."* —ISAIAH 30:15 NKJV

> *Be strong and courageous. Do not be afraid or terrified because of them, for the LORD your God goes with you; he will never leave you nor forsake you.* —DEUTERONOMY 31:6

Also read:

ISAIAH 40:31 NASB

Before You Turn Out the Light

Rather than rushing into overdrive,
seek My Face and My direction.

February

*Look to the Lord and his strength;
seek his face always.*

Psalm 105:4

February 1
MORNING

Follow Me one step at a time. That is all I require of you. In fact, that is the only way to move through this space/time world. You see huge mountains looming, and you start wondering how you're going to scale those heights. Meanwhile, because you're not looking where you're going, you stumble on the easy path where I am leading you now. As I help you get back on your feet, you tell Me how worried you are about the cliffs up ahead. But you don't know what will happen today, much less tomorrow. Our path may take an abrupt turn, leading you away from those mountains. There may be an easier way up the mountains than is visible from this distance. If I do lead you up the cliffs, I will equip you thoroughly for that strenuous climb. *I will even give My angels charge over you, to preserve you in all your ways.*

Keep your mind on the present journey, enjoying My Presence. *Walk by faith, not by sight*, trusting Me to open up the way before you.

PSALM 18:29; PSALM 91:11–12 AMP;
2 CORINTHIANS 5:7 NKJV

February 1
EVENING

*E*VEN THOUGH THERE IS MUCH darkness in this world, you always have access to Me, so you are never in total darkness. The trail before you may look obscure, especially as it disappears into the future, but I tell you: I am enough! I am with you, and I also go before you—illuminating the way.

> *Then Jesus spoke to them again, saying, "I am the light of the world. He who follows Me shall not walk in darkness, but have the light of life."* —JOHN 8:12 NKJV

> *The path of the righteous is like the first gleam of dawn, shining ever brighter till the full light of day.* —PROVERBS 4:18

Also read:
REVELATION 22:5

Before You Turn Out the Light

Until I make darkness a thing of the past, follow My Light. It will be sufficient for your journey.

February 2
MORNING

I AM RENEWING YOUR MIND. When your thoughts flow freely, they tend to move toward problems. Your focus gets snagged on a given problem, circling round and round it in attempts to gain mastery. Your energy is drained away from other matters through this negative focus. Worst of all, you lose sight of Me.

A renewed mind is Presence-focused. Train your mind to seek Me in every moment, every situation. Sometimes you can find Me in your surroundings: a lilting birdsong, a loved one's smile, golden sunlight. At other times, you must draw inward to find Me. I am always present in your spirit. Seek My Face, speak to Me, and I will light up your mind.

ROMANS 12:2; HEBREWS 3:1;
PSALM 105:4

February 2
EVENING

CASTING YOUR BURDEN ON ME is a spiritual transaction: You acknowledge that I am in charge of your life and that outcomes are ultimately *My* domain. This lightens your load immensely, relieving you from feeling responsible for things beyond your control. When you *come to Me weary and burdened*, I have promised that *I will give you rest*.

Cast your burden on the LORD, and He shall sustain you; He shall never permit the righteous to be moved. —PSALM 55:22 NKJV

"Come to me, all you who are weary and burdened, and I will give you rest. Take my yoke upon you and learn from me, for I am gentle and humble in heart, and you will find rest for your souls. For my yoke is easy and my burden is light." —MATTHEW 11:28–30

Also read:
PSALM 13:5

Before You Turn Out the Light

Right now, depend on Me to carry your load.

February 3
MORNING

I AM WITH YOU AND FOR YOU. You face nothing alone—*nothing*! When you feel anxious, know that you are focusing on the visible world and leaving Me out of the picture. The remedy is simple: *Fix your eyes not on what is seen, but on what is unseen.* Verbalize your trust in Me, *the Living One who sees you always.* I will get you safely through this day and all your days. But you can find Me only in the present. Each day is a precious gift from My Father. How ridiculous to grasp for future gifts when today's is set before you! Receive today's gift gratefully, unwrapping it tenderly and delving into its depths. As you savor this gift, you find Me.

ROMANS 8:31; 2 CORINTHIANS 4:18;
GENESIS 16:13–14 AMP

February 3
EVENING

THE FUTURE BELONGS TO ME, so you don't need to worry about it. Focus your attention on Me and on what I am doing in your life. I am your living Savior, and I am always doing *new things*.

> *"Give your entire attention to what God is doing right now, and don't get worked up about what may or may not happen tomorrow. God will help you deal with whatever hard things come up when the time comes."* —MATTHEW 6:34 MSG

> *"See, the former things have taken place, and new things I declare; before they spring into being I announce them to you."* —ISAIAH 42:9

Also read:
LUKE 4:18 NKJV

Before You Turn Out the Light

Instead of trying to predict what tomorrow may bring, remind yourself that I will help you deal with whatever comes.

February 4
MORNING

Bring Me your weakness, and receive My Peace. Accept yourself and your circumstances just as they are, remembering that I am sovereign over everything. Do not wear yourself out with analyzing and planning. Instead, let thankfulness and trust be your guides through this day; they will keep you close to Me. As you live in the radiance of My Presence, My Peace shines upon you. You will cease to notice how weak or strong you feel because you will be focusing on Me. The best way to get through this day is step by step with Me. Continue this intimate journey, trusting that the path you are following is headed for heaven.

PSALM 29:11; NUMBERS 6:24–26;

PSALM 13:5

February 4
EVENING

IT IS ESSENTIAL FOR WEAK ONES to take pride in Me—rejoicing in who I AM. As you rejoice in your weaknesses, you open yourself to My Power. Let this sacred Power rest upon you, displaying My delight in you.

> *This is what the LORD says: "Let not the wise man boast of his wisdom or the strong man boast of his strength or the rich man boast of his riches, but let him who boasts boast about this: that he understands and knows me."* —JEREMIAH 9:23–24

> *My soul will boast in the Lord; let the afflicted hear and rejoice.* —PSALM 34:2

Also read:
2 CORINTHIANS 12:9; 1 PETER 2:9 NKJV

Before You Turn Out the Light

Finish out your day by boasting in the ways I have blessed our relationship through your difficulties.

February 5
MORNING

SEEK MY FACE, and you will find not only My Presence but also My Peace. To receive My Peace, you must change your grasping, controlling stance to one of openness and trust. The only thing you can grasp without damaging your soul is My hand. Ask My Spirit within you to order your day and control your thoughts, for *the mind controlled by the Spirit is Life and Peace.*

You can have as much of Me and My Peace as you want, through thousands of correct choices each day. The most persistent choice you face is whether to trust Me or to worry. You will never run out of things to worry about, but you can choose to trust Me no matter what. I am *an ever-present help in trouble.* Trust Me, *though the earth give way and the mountains fall into the heart of the sea.*

ROMANS 8:6; NUMBERS 6:26 NKJV;
PSALM 46:1–2

February 5
EVENING

This challenging journey is all about perseverance. As long as you continue seeking Me, you are on the right path. My Presence continually moves along before you—keeping you from stagnating and showing you the way forward. In spite of the difficulties of the arduous trail you are following, your success is certain: *I will be found by you!*

> *"You will seek me and find me when you seek me with all your heart. I will be found by you," declares the Lord.* —Jeremiah 29:13–14

> *Therefore, since we are surrounded by such a great cloud of witnesses, let us throw off everything that hinders and the sin that so easily entangles, and let us run with perseverance the race marked out for us.* —Hebrews 12:1

Also read:
Romans 5:3 nkjv; 2 Peter 1:5–6

Before You Turn Out the Light

Pursue Me wholeheartedly, understanding
that it is your effort that pleases Me.

February 6
MORNING

Come to Me and rest. I am all around you, to bless and restore. Breathe Me in with each breath. The way just ahead of you is very steep. Slow down and cling tightly to My hand. I am teaching you a difficult lesson, learned only by hardship.

Lift up empty hands of faith to receive My precious Presence. Light, Life, Joy, and Peace flow freely through this gift. When your focus turns away from Me, you grasp for other things. You drop the glowing gift of My Presence as you reach for lifeless ashes. Return to Me; regain My Presence.

MATTHEW 11:28–29; 1 TIMOTHY 2:8;

ZECHARIAH 1:3

February 6
EVENING

COMFORT IS NOT ONLY FOR YOUR blessing but for your empowerment. When you feel secure in My Love, you are strengthened—and able to do the things I've prepared for you to do. Rest in Me, and enjoy the gentle kiss of My Presence.

> *May your unfailing love be my comfort, according to your promise to your servant.* —PSALM 119:76

> *The LORD has appeared of old to me, saying: "Yes, I have loved you with an everlasting love; therefore with lovingkindness I have drawn you."* —JEREMIAH 31:3 NKJV

Also read:
ZEPHANIAH 3:17 NKJV

Before You Turn Out the Light

The more you memorize Scripture assuring you of My everlasting Love, the more you will be soothed by My tender Presence.

February 7
MORNING

COME TO ME FOR REST and refreshment. The journey has been too much for you, and you are bone-weary. Do not be ashamed of your exhaustion. Instead, see it as an opportunity for Me to take charge of your life.

Remember that *I can fit everything into a pattern for good*, including the things you wish were different. Start with where you are at this point in time and space, accepting that this is where I intend you to be. You will get through today one step, one moment at a time. Your main responsibility is to remain attentive to Me, letting Me guide you through the many choices along your pathway.

This sounds like an easy assignment, but it is not. Your desire to live in My Presence goes against the grain of the world, the flesh, and the devil. Much of your weariness results from your constant battle against these opponents. However, you are on the path of My choosing, so do not give up! *Hope in Me, for you will again praise Me for the help of My Presence.*

ROMANS 8:28 AMP; PSALM 42:5 NASB

February 7
EVENING

Instead of letting problems discourage you, use them as reminders to seek Me—My Presence, My Peace, My Love. These invisible realities are available to you anytime, anyplace, and they provide Joy that no one can take away from you. *So come to Me when you are weary and burdened*; I will provide *rest for your soul*.

> *In the multitude of my anxieties within me, Your comforts delight my soul.* —PSALM 94:19 NKJV

> *"Come to me, all you who are weary and burdened, and I will give you rest. Take my yoke upon you and learn from me, for I am gentle and humble in heart, and you will find rest for your souls."* —MATTHEW 11:28–29

Also read:
JOHN 16:22 NKJV

Before You Turn Out the Light

Seek My comfort for your weary soul. Just whisper My Name.

February 8
MORNING

I AM ABOVE ALL THINGS: your problems, your pain, and the swirling events in this ever-changing world. When you behold My Face, you rise above circumstances and rest with Me in *heavenly realms*. This is the way of Peace, living in the Light of My Presence. I guarantee that you will always have problems in this life, but they must not become your focus. When you feel yourself sinking in the sea of circumstances, say, *"Help me, Jesus!"* and I will draw you back to Me. If you have to say that thousands of times daily, don't be discouraged. I know your weakness, and I meet you in that very place.

EPHESIANS 2:6; MATTHEW 14:28–32;

ISAIAH 42:3

February 8
EVENING

Take time just to be with Me—basking in the Light of My Love. *As My Face shines upon you*, I bless you and *give you Peace*. Do not skimp on this time with Me, for I use it to strengthen you spiritually, emotionally, and physically.

> *[The Lord] gives strength to the weary and increases the power of the weak. Even youths grow tired and weary, and young men stumble and fall; but those who hope in the Lord will renew their strength. They will soar on wings like eagles; they will run and not grow weary, they will walk and not be faint.* —Isaiah 40:29–31

> *The Lord make His face shine upon you, and be gracious to you; the Lord lift up His countenance upon you, and give you peace.* —Numbers 6:25–26 nkjv

Also read:
Psalm 31:16

Before You Turn Out the Light

Let down your guard and lift up wide-open arms to Me, receiving Joy, Peace, *unfailing Love*.

February 9
MORNING

SEEK MY FACE more and more. You are really just beginning your journey of intimacy with Me. It is not an easy road, but it is a delightful and privileged way: a treasure hunt. I am the Treasure, and the Glory of My Presence glistens and shimmers along the way. Hardships are part of the journey too. I mete them out ever so carefully, in just the right dosage, with a tenderness you can hardly imagine. Do not recoil from afflictions, since they are among My most favored gifts. *Trust Me and don't be afraid, for I am your Strength and Song.*

PSALM 27:8 NKJV; 2 CORINTHIANS 4:7–8;
ISAIAH 12:2

February 9
EVENING

THE WORLD IS FULL OF TROUBLE, but *I have overcome the world*! I call you to transcend your troubles by looking up to Me. I am training you to be an overcomer—unfettered by circumstances.

Do not be anxious about anything, but in everything, by prayer and petition, with thanksgiving, present your requests to God. And the peace of God, which transcends all understanding, will guard your hearts and your minds in Christ Jesus. —Philippians 4:6–7

"These things I have spoken to you, that in Me you may have peace. In the world you will have tribulation; but be of good cheer, I have overcome the world." —John 16:33 nkjv

Also read:
Ephesians 2:6

Before You Turn Out the Light

Breathe in the Peace of My Presence, saying *no* to problems and *yes* to Me.

February 10
MORNING

Trust Me enough to spend ample time with Me, pushing back the demands of the day. Refuse to feel guilty about something that is so pleasing to Me, the King of the universe. Because I am omnipotent, I am able to bend time and events in your favor. You will find that you can accomplish *more* in less time after you have given yourself to Me in rich communion. Also, as you align yourself with My perspective, you can sort out what is important and what is not.

Don't fall into the trap of being constantly on the go. Many, many things people do in My Name have no value in My kingdom. To avoid doing meaningless works, stay in continual communication with Me. *I will instruct you and teach you in the way you should go; I will counsel you with My eye upon you.*

Luke 10:41–42; Hebrews 1:1–2;
Psalm 32:8 nasb

February 10
EVENING

I WANT YOU TO SPEND TIME WITH ME for the pure pleasure of being in My company. When you take delight in My Presence, you experience a foretaste of the eternal pleasures I have prepared for you. Naturally, you will lose sight of Me at times, but you can reconnect readily by moving toward Me in your thoughts, words, and feelings.

I wait for the LORD, my soul waits, and in his word I put my hope. My soul waits for the Lord. —PSALM 130:5–6

"For in him we live and move and have our being." As some of your own poets have said, "We are his offspring." —ACTS 17:28

Also read:
ACTS 17:28

Before You Turn Out the Light

Did you remember Me this day in your thoughts, words, and feelings? End your day by honoring Me now.

February 11
MORNING

My Peace is like a shaft of golden Light shining on you continuously. During days of bright sunshine, it may blend in with your surroundings. On darker days, My Peace stands out in sharp contrast to your circumstances. See times of darkness as opportunities for My Light to shine in transcendent splendor. I am training you to practice Peace that overpowers darkness. Collaborate with Me in this training. *Do not grow weary and lose heart.*

2 Thessalonians 3:16; John 1:4–5 amp;
Hebrews 12:3

February 11
EVENING

I AM TRAINING YOU to turn your thoughts to Me more and more—enjoying My Presence in tough times as well as good times. As you direct your attention to Me, I push back the darkness with My invincible Light! This is how you walk in *the way of Peace*; this is how *I turn your darkness into Light.*

> *You are my lamp, O LORD; the LORD turns my darkness into light.* —2 SAMUEL 22:29

> *"The Dayspring from on high has visited us, to give light to those who sit in darkness and the shadow of death, to guide our feet into the way of peace."* —LUKE 1:78–79 NKJV

Also read:
JOHN 8:12 NKJV; JOHN 16:33

Before You Turn Out the Light

Carry this truth with you as you close out this day: I am the Light of the world, and I am both with you and within you.

February 12
MORNING

I AM EVER SO NEAR YOU, hovering over your shoulder, reading every thought. People think that thoughts are fleeting and worthless, but yours are precious to Me. I smile when you think lovingly of Me. My Spirit, who lives within you, helps you to think My thoughts. As your thinking goes, so goes your entire being.

Let Me be your positive Focus. When you look to Me, knowing Me as *God with you*, you experience Joy. This is according to My ancient design, when I first crafted man. Modern man seeks his positive focus elsewhere: in sports, sensations, acquiring new possessions. Advertising capitalizes on the longing of people for a positive focus in their lives. I planted that longing in human souls, knowing that only I could fully satisfy it. *Delight yourself in Me; let Me become the Desire of your heart.*

PSALM 139:1–2; MATTHEW 1:23;
PSALM 37:4

February 12
EVENING

MOST PEOPLE ARE NOT VERY AWARE of their thoughts during their "down times," but I am quite aware of them. I want you to train your mind to turn toward Me more and more. Think about who I am—Creator, Savior, King of kings—and ponder My amazing, unending Love for you.

When I consider your heavens, the work of your fingers, the moon and the stars, which you have set in place, what is man that you are mindful of him, the son of man that you care for him? —PSALM 8:3–4

Do not conform any longer to the pattern of this world, but be transformed by the renewing of your mind. Then you will be able to test and approve what God's will is— his good, pleasing and perfect will. —ROMANS 12:2

Also read:
PSALM 119:11 NKJV

Before You Turn Out the Light

Spend some time in quietness—away from the television, the radio, and other distracting noise—to restore your focus to Me.

February 13
MORNING

PEACE BE WITH YOU! Ever since the resurrection, this has been My watchword to those who yearn for Me. As you sit quietly, let My Peace settle over you and enfold you in My loving Presence. To provide this radiant Peace for you, I died a criminal's death. Receive *My Peace* abundantly and thankfully. It is a rare treasure, dazzling in delicate beauty, yet strong enough to withstand all onslaughts. Wear My Peace with regal dignity. It will keep your heart and mind close to Mine.

JOHN 20:19, 21; JOHN 14:27; PHILIPPIANS 4:7

February 13
EVENING

PEOPLE WHO TRUST mainly in themselves and their own abilities often crowd Me out of their lives. As you learn to trust Me more, you increasingly delight in time spent with Me. And the more you wait in My Presence, the deeper your faith grows—increasing your Joy and Peace.

May the God of hope fill you with all joy and peace as you trust in him, so that you may overflow with hope by the power of the Holy Spirit. —ROMANS 15:13

You will keep him in perfect peace, whose mind is stayed on You, because he trusts in You. —ISAIAH 26:3 NKJV

Also read:
ROMANS 8:9; 2 CORINTHIANS 3:18

Before You Turn Out the Light

Spending time with Me demonstrates that you
really do trust Me. I will overflow you with
Joy and Peace as you linger with Me.

February 14
MORNING

GIVE YOURSELF FULLY to the adventure of today. Walk boldly along the path of Life, relying on your ever-present Companion. You have every reason to be confident because My Presence accompanies you all the days of your life—and onward into eternity.

Do not give in to fear or worry, those robbers of abundant living. Trust Me enough to face problems as they come, rather than trying to anticipate them. *Fix your eyes on Me, the Author and Perfecter of your faith*, and many difficulties on the road ahead will vanish before you reach them. Whenever you start to feel afraid, remember that *I am holding you by your right hand*. Nothing can separate you from My Presence!

PSALM 48:14; HEBREWS 12:2;
ISAIAH 41:13

February 14
EVENING

MY PRESENCE radiates Light that helps you find the way of Peace; My Word enlightens your mind and heart, empowering you to stay on the right path. As you read Scripture, look for a star of guidance, and ask My Spirit to illumine those words to your seeking heart. They are words of Life!

A Light from on high will dawn upon us and visit [us], to shine upon and give light to those who sit in darkness and in the shadow of death, to direct and guide our feet in a straight line into the way of peace. —LUKE 1:78–79 AMP

Jesus answered, "I am the way and the truth and the life. No one comes to the Father except through me." —JOHN 14:6

Also read:
PSALM 119:105; PSALM 145:18–19

Before You Turn Out the Light

Secure some time alone this evening so you
can take in My wonderful words of Life.

February 15
MORNING

Come to Me with all your weaknesses: physical, emotional, and spiritual. Rest in the comfort of My Presence, remembering that *nothing is impossible with Me.*

Pry your mind away from your problems so you can focus your attention on Me. Recall that I am *able to do immeasurably more than all you ask or imagine.* Instead of trying to direct Me to do this and that, seek to attune yourself to what I am *already* doing.

When anxiety attempts to wedge its way into your thoughts, remind yourself that *I am your Shepherd.* The bottom line is that I am taking care of you; therefore, you needn't be afraid of anything. Rather than trying to maintain control over your life, abandon yourself to My will. Though this may feel frightening—even dangerous—the safest place to be is in My will.

Luke 1:37; Ephesians 3:20–21;
Psalm 23:1–4

February 15
EVENING

WHEN YOU CANNOT SENSE My Presence, it is enough to *know* that I love you with compassionate, unfailing Love. If your heart is sinking under waves of panic, don't focus on those feelings—look up to Me! *As your soul clings to Me, My right hand will uphold you*, keeping you safe in turbulent waters.

> *"When you pass through the waters, I will be with you; and through the rivers, they will not overflow you. . . . since you are precious in My sight . . . and I love you."* —Isaiah 43:2–4 nasb

> *My soul clings to you; your right hand upholds me.* —Psalm 63:8

Also read:
Matthew 6:10 nkjv; Lamentations 3:32

Before You Turn Out the Light

Never fear, beloved: Though you may lose sight of Me at times, I am ever aware of your circumstances, and I will never abandon you to fend for yourself.

February 16
MORNING

Thank Me for the conditions that are requiring you to *be still*. Do not spoil these quiet hours by wishing them away, waiting impatiently to be active again. Some of the greatest works in My kingdom have been done from sickbeds and prison cells. Instead of resenting the limitations of a weakened body, search for My way in the midst of these very circumstances. Limitations can be liberating when your strongest desire is living close to Me.

Quietness and trust enhance your awareness of My Presence with you. Do not despise these simple ways of serving Me. Although you feel cut off from the activity of the world, your quiet trust makes a powerful statement in spiritual realms. *My Strength and Power show themselves most effective in weakness.*

ZECHARIAH 2:13; ISAIAH 30:15;
2 CORINTHIANS 12:9 AMP

February 16
EVENING

YOU HAVE BEEN STRUGGLING just to keep your head above water, and your strength is running low. Now is the time for you to stop striving and let Me fight for you. I am calling you to rest in Me.

The LORD will fight for you; you need only to be still. —EXODUS 14:14

He who dwells in the shelter of the Most High will rest in the shadow of the Almighty. —PSALM 91:1

Also read:
PSALM 46:10 NKJV; ROMANS 8:6

Before You Turn Out the Light

Rest in My shadow while I work on your behalf.

February 17
MORNING

I AM THE RISEN ONE who shines upon you always. You worship a living Deity, not some idolatrous, man-made image. Your relationship with Me is meant to be vibrant and challenging, as I invade more and more areas of your life. Do not fear change, for I am making you a *new creation, with old things passing away and new things continually on the horizon.* When you cling to old ways and sameness, you resist My work within you. I want you to embrace all that I am doing in your life, finding your security in Me alone.

It is easy to make an idol of routine, finding security within the boundaries you build around your life. Although each day contains twenty-four hours, every single one presents a unique set of circumstances. Don't try to force-fit today into yesterday's mold. Instead, ask Me to open your eyes so you can find all I have prepared for you in this precious day of Life.

MATTHEW 28:5–7; 2 CORINTHIANS 5:17

February 17
EVENING

Instead of focusing on all the brokenness in and around you, fan the flames of your love for Me. Though this love may be like the flickering flame of a candle, My Love for you is like a blazing forest fire. Come more and more into My passionate Presence, and My holy Fire will ignite holy ardor in you.

> *And you shall love the Lord your God with all your [mind and] heart and with your entire being and with all your might.* —Deuteronomy 6:5 amp

> *After removing Saul, he made David their king. He testified concerning him: "I have found David son of Jesse a man after my own heart; he will do everything I want him to do."* —Acts 13:22

Also read:
Hebrews 10:12–14 nkjv; 2 Samuel 6:14

Before You Turn Out the Light

Love Me with all your heart and mind, and I will fashion you after My own heart. How will you keep fanning your flame for Me?

February 18
MORNING

I AM WITH YOU. These four words are like a safety net, protecting you from falling into despair. Because you are human, you will always have ups and downs in your life experience. But the promise of My Presence limits how far down you can go. Sometimes you may feel as if you are in a free fall, when people or things you had counted on let you down. Yet as soon as you remember that *I am with you,* your perspective changes radically. Instead of bemoaning your circumstances, you can look to Me for help. You recall that not only am I with you; *I am holding you by your right hand. I guide you with My counsel, and afterward I will take you into Glory.* This is exactly the perspective you need: the reassurance of My Presence and the glorious hope of heaven.

ZEPHANIAH 3:17; PSALM 73:23–26

February 18
EVENING

REMEMBER THAT I AM BOTH *your Rock and your Redeemer*—though I am impregnable in My vast strength, I became a vulnerable Man so I could redeem you from your sins. The more you take refuge in Me, the more aware you become of My overflowing Love. In Me you are utterly safe, for I am your Rock of everlasting Love!

God is our refuge and strength, an ever-present help in trouble. Therefore we will not fear, though the earth give way and the mountains fall into the heart of the sea. —PSALM 46:1–2

May the words of my mouth and the meditation of my heart be pleasing in your sight, O LORD, my Rock and my Redeemer. —PSALM 19:14

Also read:
MATTHEW 23:37 NKJV; PSALM 91:4 AMP

Before You Turn Out the Light

It is in closeness to Me that you realize how trustworthy I am. Take refuge in Me.

February 19
MORNING

YOU ARE FEELING WEIGHED DOWN by a plethora of problems, both big and small. They seem to require more and more of your attention, but you must not give in to those demands. When the difficulties in your life feel as if they're closing in on you, break free by spending quality time with Me. You need to remember who I am in all My Power and Glory. Then humbly bring Me your prayers and petitions. Your problems will pale when you view them in the Light of My Presence. You can learn to *be joyful in Me, your Savior*, even in the midst of adverse circumstances. Rely on Me, *your Strength; I make your feet like the feet of a deer, enabling you to go on the heights.*

EXODUS 3:14; PSALM 63:2;
HABAKKUK 3:17–19

February 19
EVENING

YOU HAVE BEEN ON AN UPHILL JOURNEY for a long time, and you are growing weary. You yearn for some easy days, for a path that is not so steep. But it is the strenuous climbs that take you ever upward—closer and closer to the summit.

I will sing to the Lord, because He has dealt bountifully with me. —Psalm 13:6 NKJV

God is my strong fortress; and He sets the blameless in His way. He makes my feet like hinds' feet, and sets me on my high places. —2 Samuel 22:33–34 NASB

Also read:
John 21:22 NASB

Before You Turn Out the Light

Stop comparing your life-adventure with ones that seem easier. Stay the course and follow Me!

February 20
MORNING

LEARN TO LIVE from your true Center in Me. I reside in the deepest depths of your being, in eternal union with your spirit. It is at this deep level that My Peace reigns continually. You will not find lasting peace in the world around you, in circumstances, or in human relationships. The external world is always in flux—under the curse of death and decay. But there is a gold mine of Peace deep within you, waiting to be tapped. Take time to delve into the riches of My residing Presence. I want you to live increasingly from your real Center, where My Love has an eternal grip on you. *I am Christ in you, the hope of Glory.*

1 THESSALONIANS 5:23; COLOSSIANS 3:15;
COLOSSIANS 1:27

February 20
EVENING

THE WORST-CASE SCENARIO IN YOUR LIFE—that I might stop loving you—is not even in the realm of possibility, so rejoice that you don't have to perform well enough to earn My Love *or* to keep it. This Love is a pure gift, flowing out of My own perfect righteousness. It secures your connection to Me—your Savior—for all eternity.

Neither height nor depth, nor anything else in all creation, will be able to separate us from the love of God that is in Christ Jesus our Lord. —ROMANS 8:39

"The thief does not come except to steal, and to kill, and to destroy. I have come that they may have life, and that they may have it more abundantly." —JOHN 10:10 NKJV

Also read:
JOHN 16:33 NKJV

Before You Turn Out the Light

Allow My healing Presence to draw you ever closer to Me.

February 21
MORNING

Trust and thankfulness will get you safely through this day. Trust protects you from worrying and obsessing. Thankfulness keeps you from criticizing and complaining: those "sister sins" that so easily entangle you.

Keeping your eyes on Me is the same thing as trusting Me. It is a free choice that you must make thousands of times daily. The more you choose to trust Me, the easier it becomes. Thought patterns of trust become etched into your brain. Relegate troubles to the periphery of your mind so that I can be central in your thoughts. Thus you focus on Me, entrusting your concerns into My care.

PSALM 31:14 NKJV, COLOSSIANS 2:6–7;
PSALM 141:8; 1 PETER 5:7

February 21
EVENING

I WANT YOU TO TRUST ME with all your heart *and* all your mind. Instead of relying on your own understanding to help you feel in control, ask My Spirit to control your mind. As you look to Me, trusting Me and talking with Me, I straighten out the path before you.

Lean on, trust in, and be confident in the Lord with all your heart and mind and do not rely on your own insight or understanding. In all your ways know, recognize, and acknowledge Him, and He will direct and make straight and plain your paths. —PROVERBS 3:5–6 AMP

The mind of sinful man is death, but the mind controlled by the Spirit is life and peace. —ROMANS 8:6

Also read:
PSALM 37:5 NKJV

Before You Turn Out the Light

Your desire to trust Me is a worthy goal. Allow Me to do My supernatural work in your heart.

February 22
MORNING

YOU NEED ME EVERY MOMENT. Your awareness of your constant need for Me is your greatest strength. Your neediness, properly handled, is a link to My Presence. However, there are pitfalls that you must be on guard against: self-pity, self-preoccupation, giving up. Your inadequacy presents you with a continual choice—deep dependence on Me or despair. The emptiness you feel within will be filled either with problems or with My Presence. Make Me central in your consciousness by *praying continually*: simple, short prayers flowing out of the present moment. Use My Name liberally, to remind you of My Presence. *Keep on asking and you will receive, so that your gladness may be full and complete.*

PSALM 86:7; 1 THESSALONIANS 5:17;
JOHN 16:24 AMP

February 22
EVENING

WANDERING THOUGHTS are ever so human. As long as you live on earth, you will have to contend with this spiritual-emotional "gravity" pulling you away from Me. Thankfully, returning your thoughts to Me is not as laborious as carrying water back uphill would be: A short prayer in My Name is usually sufficient to reconnect with Me, for I am never far from you.

Put to death, therefore, whatever belongs to your earthly nature: sexual immorality, impurity, lust, evil desires and greed, which is idolatry. —COLOSSIANS 3:5

God did this so that men would seek him and perhaps reach out for him and find him, though he is not far from each one of us. —ACTS 17:27

Also read:
MATTHEW 28:20 AMP

Before You Turn Out the Light

Reconnect with Me before you sleep so I can give you rest.

February 23
MORNING

BE ON GUARD against the pit of self-pity. When you are weary or unwell, this demonic trap is the greatest danger you face. Don't even go near the edge of the pit. Its edges crumble easily, and before you know it, you are on the way down. It is ever so much harder to get out of the pit than to keep a safe distance from it. That is why I tell you to be on guard.

There are several ways to protect yourself from self-pity. When you are occupied with praising and thanking Me, it is impossible to feel sorry for yourself. Also, the closer you live to Me, the more distance there is between you and the pit. Live in the Light of My Presence by *fixing your eyes on Me*. Then you will be able *to run with endurance the race that is set before you*, without stumbling or falling.

PSALM 89:15; HEBREWS 12:1–2 NASB

February 23
EVENING

CONTENTMENT-TRAINING is learned through enduring a wide range of difficulties. On some days you are able to cope well with your hardships; on other days you just want *out*! I am here to help you with your "other days."

I know what it is to be in need, and I know what it is to have plenty. I have learned the secret of being content in any and every situation, whether well fed or hungry, whether living in plenty or in want. —PHILIPPIANS 4:12

It is good to give thanks to the LORD, and to sing praises to Your name, O Most High; to declare Your lovingkindness in the morning, and Your faithfulness every night. —PSALM 92:1–2 NKJV

Also read:
PSALM 62:8

Before You Turn Out the Light

From morning to night, in any and every situation, lift up My Name. I am Your Peace.

February 24
MORNING

BE STILL IN THE LIGHT of My Presence while I communicate Love to you. There is no force in the universe as powerful as My Love. You are constantly aware of limitations: your own and others'. But there is no limit to My Love; it fills all of space, time, and eternity.

Now you see through a glass, darkly, but someday you will see Me face to Face. Then you will be able to experience fully *how wide and long and high and deep is My Love for you.* If you were to experience that now, you would be overwhelmed to the point of feeling crushed. But you have an eternity ahead of you, absolutely guaranteed, during which you can enjoy My Presence in unrestricted ecstasy. For now, the knowledge of My loving Presence is sufficient to carry you through each day.

1 CORINTHIANS 13:12 KJV;

EPHESIANS 3:16–19

February 24
EVENING

My unfailing Love is your "fuel." This supernatural source of energy flows through you freely as you look to Me in trust. Not only does this increase your energy level; it also provides a pathway for Me to love other people *through you*.

> *To this end I labor, struggling with all his energy, which so powerfully works in me.* —COLOSSIANS 1:29

> *Whoever confesses that Jesus is the Son of God, God abides in him, and he in God. And we have known and believed the love that God has for us. God is love, and he who abides in love abides in God, and God in him.* —1 JOHN 4:15–16 NKJV

Also read:
PSALM 33:5; PHILIPPIANS 4:4 NKJV

Before You Turn Out the Light

Let My limitless Love energize and empower you as you live and love others.

February 25
MORNING

Rest in My Presence, allowing Me to take charge of this day. Do not bolt into the day like a racehorse suddenly released. Instead, walk purposefully with Me, letting Me direct your course one step at a time. Thank Me for each blessing along the way; this brings Joy to both you and Me. A grateful heart protects you from negative thinking. Thankfulness enables you to see the abundance I shower upon you daily. Your prayers and petitions are winged into heaven's throne room when they are permeated with thanksgiving. *In everything give thanks, for this is My will for you.*

MATTHEW 11:28 NKJV; COLOSSIANS 4:2;
1 THESSALONIANS 5:18 NASB

February 25
EVENING

When you praise Me, your Joy increases, as does your awareness of My holy Presence. Your body may or may not be mightily engaged in this endeavor, but I see into your heart. That is where the ultimate celebration of My Presence takes place.

> *You have made known to me the path of life; you will fill me with joy in your presence, with eternal pleasures at your right hand.* —PSALM 16:11

> *But the LORD said to Samuel, "Do not look at his appearance or at his physical stature, because I have refused him. For the LORD does not see as man sees; for man looks at the outward appearance, but the LORD looks at the heart.* —1 SAMUEL 16:7 NKJV

Also read:
DEUTERONOMY 33:27; 2 SAMUEL 6:14

Before You Turn Out the Light

Do you sense how safe and secure you are in My everlasting arms? Delight in Me!

February 26
MORNING

I AM LEADING YOU, STEP BY STEP, through your life. Hold My hand in trusting dependence, letting Me guide you through this day. Your future looks uncertain and feels flimsy—even precarious. That is how it should be. *Secret things belong to the Lord*, and future things are secret things. When you try to figure out the future, you are grasping at things that are Mine. This, like all forms of worry, is an act of rebellion: doubting My promises to care for you.

Whenever you find yourself worrying about the future, repent and return to Me. I will show you the next step forward, and the one after that, and the one after that. Relax and enjoy the journey in My Presence, trusting Me to open up the way before you as you go.

DEUTERONOMY 29:29; LUKE 12:25–26;
PSALM 32:8

February 26
EVENING

The gap between My call on your life and your ability to respond is part of My plan. Because you are Mine, I allow you to connect your deep inadequacy to My boundless sufficiency. The more you depend on My resources, the more you can celebrate My Majesty.

> *"I am the vine, you are the branches. He who abides in Me, and I in him, bears much fruit; for without Me you can do nothing."* —John 15:5 nkjv

> *And we, who with unveiled faces all reflect the Lord's glory, are being transformed into his likeness with ever-increasing glory, which comes from the Lord, who is the Spirit.* —2 Corinthians 3:18

Also read:
1 Peter 2:9 nkjv; Isaiah 61:10

Before You Turn Out the Light

In all that you do, forget your insufficiencies and consciously rely on My help.

February 27
MORNING

KEEP YOUR EYES ON ME! Waves of adversity are washing over you, and you feel tempted to give up. As your circumstances consume more and more of your attention, you are losing sight of Me. Yet *I am with you always, holding you by your right hand.* I am fully aware of your situation, *and I will not allow you to be tempted beyond what you are able to bear.*

Your gravest danger is worrying about tomorrow. If you try to carry tomorrow's burdens today, you will stagger under the load and eventually fall flat. You must discipline yourself to live within the boundaries of today. It is in the present moment that I walk close to you, helping you carry your burdens. Keep your focus on My Presence in the present.

PSALM 73:23; 1 CORINTHIANS 10:13; HEBREWS 3:13

February 27
EVENING

Don't let problems intimidate you. I, *the Mighty One*, am *in your midst*, and I am greater than all the trouble in the world. Hold tightly to My hand, and you can walk confidently through your toughest times.

> *Though I walk in the midst of trouble, You will revive me; You will stretch out Your hand against the wrath of my enemies, and Your right hand will save me.* —Psalm 138:7 NKJV

> *The Lord your God in your midst, the Mighty One, will save; He will rejoice over you with gladness, He will quiet you with His love, He will rejoice over you with singing.* —Zephaniah 3:17 NKJV

Also read:
1 Peter 5:9; Psalm 29:11

Before You Turn Out the Light

Remember that you are not alone. I am with you.

February 28
MORNING

STOP JUDGING AND EVALUATING YOURSELF, for this is not your role. Above all, stop comparing yourself with other people. This produces feelings of pride or inferiority, sometimes a mixture of both. I lead each of My children along a path that is uniquely tailor-made for him or her. Comparing is not only wrong; it is also meaningless.

Don't look for affirmation in the wrong places: your own evaluations or those of other people. The only source of real affirmation is My unconditional Love. Many believers perceive Me as an unpleasable Judge, angrily searching out their faults and failures. Nothing could be farther from the truth! I died for your sins so that I might *clothe you in My garments of salvation*. This is how I see you: *radiant in My robe of righteousness*. When I discipline you, it is never in anger or disgust; it is to prepare you for face-to-Face fellowship with Me throughout all eternity. Immerse yourself in My loving Presence. Be receptive to My affirmation, which flows continually from the throne of grace.

LUKE 6:37; ISAIAH 61:10 NASB; PROVERBS 3:11–12

February 28
EVENING

BEWARE OF COMPARING YOUR SITUATION with that of someone else—and feeling dissatisfied because of the comparison. Instead, make every effort to accept as your *calling* the life I have assigned to you. If I have called you to a situation, I will give you everything you need to endure it—and even to find Joy in the midst of it.

> *Let each person lead the life that the Lord has assigned to him, and to which God has called him. This is my rule in all the churches.* —1 CORINTHIANS 7:17 ESV

> *I know what it is to be in need, and I know what it is to have plenty. I have learned the secret of being content in any and every situation, whether well fed or hungry, whether living in plenty or in want.* —PHILIPPIANS 4:12

Also read:
ROMANS 11:33–36

Before You Turn Out the Light

Morning, noon, and night, practice training your mind to trust My sovereign ways. In this, you will learn to be content.

February 29
MORNING

You are on the right path. Listen more to Me and less to your doubts. I am leading you along the way I designed just for you. Therefore, it is a lonely way, humanly speaking. But I go before you as well as alongside you, so you are never alone. Do not expect anyone to understand fully My ways with you, any more than you can comprehend My dealings with others. I am revealing to you the path of Life, day by day and moment by moment. As I said to My disciple Peter, so I repeat to you: *Follow Me.*

PSALM 119:105; JOHN 21:22

February 29
EVENING

Y OU HAVE THE AMAZING PRIVILEGE of knowing Me intimately, yet this privilege is not an invitation to act as if you were My equal. I want you to worship Me as *King of kings* while walking hand in hand with Me. The Joy we share in one another cannot be measured.

> *Keep this command . . . until the appearing of our Lord Jesus Christ, which God will bring about in his own time—God, the blessed and only Ruler, the King of kings and Lord of lords.* —1 TIMOTHY 6:14–15

> *You have made known to me the path of life; you will fill me with joy in your presence, with eternal pleasures at your right hand.* —PSALM 16:11

Also read:
JOHN 8:58 NKJV; LUKE 15:20

Before You Turn Out the Light

Confess any irreverent ways or thoughts
so we can enjoy being close again.

March

"When he has brought out all his own, he goes on ahead of them, and his sheep follow him because they know his voice."

JOHN 10:4

March 1
MORNING

WHEN SOMETHING IN YOUR LIFE OR THOUGHTS makes you anxious, come to Me and talk about it. Bring Me your *prayer and petition, with thanksgiving,* saying, "Thank You, Jesus, for this opportunity to trust You more." Though the lessons of trust that I send to you come wrapped in difficulties, the benefits far outweigh the cost.

Well-developed trust will bring you many blessings, not the least of which is My Peace. I have promised to *keep you in perfect Peace* to the extent that you trust in Me. The world has it backwards, teaching that peace is the result of having enough money, possessions, insurance, and security systems. *My* Peace, however, is such an all-encompassing gift that it is independent of all circumstances. Though you lose everything else, if you gain My Peace you are rich indeed.

PHILIPPIANS 4:6; ISAIAH 26:3;
2 THESSALONIANS 3:16 NKJV

March 1
EVENING

There is immense Power in My Name to help you break free from the anxiety closing in on you. When you speak My Name, however quietly, you acknowledge My continual Presence. This truth is promised to all My followers, and it sets you free.

> *To the Jews who had believed him, Jesus said, "If you hold to my teaching, you are really my disciples. Then you will know the truth, and the truth will set you free."* —JOHN 8:31–32

> *Let the beloved of the LORD rest secure in him, for he shields him all day long, and the one the LORD loves rests between his shoulders.* —DEUTERONOMY 33:12

Also read:

PSALM 139:23

Before You Turn Out the Light

Shift the weight of your burden to My strong shoulders—and leave it there.

March 2

MORNING

I AM THE RESURRECTION AND THE LIFE; all lasting Life emanates from Me. People search for life in many wrong ways: chasing after fleeting pleasures, accumulating possessions and wealth, trying to deny the inevitable effects of aging. Meanwhile, I freely offer abundant Life to everyone who turns toward Me. As you *come to Me and take My yoke upon you*, I fill you with My very Life. This is how I choose to live in the world and accomplish My purposes. This is also how I bless you with *Joy unspeakable and full of Glory*. The Joy is Mine, and the Glory is Mine; but I bestow them on you as you live in My Presence, inviting Me to live fully in you.

JOHN 11:25; MATTHEW 11:28–29; 1 PETER 1:8–9 KJV

March 2
EVENING

The nature of hope is that it refers to something in the future, something *not yet*. If patience is not your strong point, remember that it is a *fruit of the Spirit*; you can ask the Holy Spirit to help you wait hopefully in My Presence. And when you wait, rejoice that you are in the company of the Creator and Sustainer of the universe.

I consider that the sufferings of this present time are not worthy to be compared with the glory which shall be revealed in us. —Romans 8:18 nkjv

The fruit of the Spirit is love, joy, peace, patience, kindness, goodness, faithfulness, gentleness, self-control; against such things there is no law. —Galatians 5:22–23 nasb

Also read:
Romans 5:1–2; Psalm 37:4 esv

Before You Turn Out the Light

Delight yourself in the privilege of being with Me now and throughout eternity.

March 3
MORNING

I LOVE YOU FOR WHO YOU ARE, not for what you do. Many voices vie for control of your mind, especially when you sit in silence. You must learn to discern what is My voice and what is not. Ask My Spirit to give you this discernment. Many of My children run around in circles, trying to obey the various voices directing their lives. This results in fragmented, frustrating patterns of living. Do not fall into this trap. Walk closely with Me each moment, listening for My directives and enjoying My Companionship. Refuse to let other voices tie you up in knots. *My sheep know My voice and follow Me wherever I lead.*

EPHESIANS 4:1–6; JOHN 10:4

March 3
EVENING

I NOT ONLY ACCEPT YOU as you are; I love you as you are. I died a criminal's death so I could adorn you with My own perfection. That's why bringing your thoughts to Me is so important: It is My perfect righteousness that saves you, and it will never be taken away from you!

> *But when this priest had offered for all time one sacrifice for sins, he sat down at the right hand of God. Since that time he waits for his enemies to be made his footstool, because by one sacrifice he has made perfect forever those who are being made holy.* —HEBREWS 10:12–14

> *"Martha, Martha," the Lord answered, "you are worried and upset about many things, but only one thing is needed. Mary has chosen what is better, and it will not be taken away from her."* —LUKE 10:41–42

Also read:
PSALM 36:7

Before You Turn Out the Light

Persist in returning your attention to Me, without judging yourself. I always welcome you back with unfailing Love.

March 4
MORNING

REFUSE TO WORRY! In this world there will always be something enticing you to worry. That is the nature of a fallen, fractured planet: Things are not as they should be. So the temptation to be anxious is constantly with you, trying to worm its way into your mind. The best defense is *continual communication with Me, richly seasoned with thanksgiving.* Awareness of My Presence fills your mind with Light and Peace, leaving no room for fear. This awareness lifts you up above your circumstances, enabling you to see problems from My perspective. Live close to Me! Together we can keep the wolves of worry at bay.

LUKE 12:25–26; 1 THESSALONIANS 5:16–18;
PSALM 36:9

March 4
EVENING

To break the deeply ingrained habit of focusing on tomorrow's troubles, you will need to monitor your thinking relentlessly. Most of the time you will discover you've been worrying about some future event. Offer that concern up to Me. Then rejoice in Me: your Savior and Sovereign Lord. I *enable you to go on the heights*—transcending your trouble! (Habakkuk 3:19).

> *"Therefore do not worry about tomorrow, for tomorrow will worry about itself. Each day has enough trouble of its own."* —Matthew 6:34

> *We demolish arguments and every pretension that sets itself up against the knowledge of God, and we take captive every thought to make it obedient to Christ.* —2 Corinthians 10:5

Before You Turn Out the Light

Never forget: Each day of your life is a precious gift from Me.

March 5

MORNING

MAKE FRIENDS WITH THE PROBLEMS IN YOUR LIFE. Though many things feel random and wrong, remember that I am sovereign over everything. *I can fit everything into a pattern for good*, but only to the extent that you trust Me. Every problem can teach you something, transforming you little by little into the masterpiece I created you to be. The very same problem can become a stumbling block over which you fall if you react with distrust and defiance. The choice is up to you, and you will have to choose many times each day whether to trust Me or defy Me.

The best way to befriend your problems is to thank Me for them. This simple act opens your mind to the possibility of benefits flowing from your difficulties. You can even give persistent problems nicknames, helping you to approach them with familiarity rather than with dread. The next step is to introduce them to Me, enabling Me to embrace them in My loving Presence. I will not necessarily remove your problems, but My wisdom is sufficient to bring good out of every one of them.

ROMANS 8:28 AMP; 1 CORINTHIANS 1:23–24

March 5

EVENING

There are a variety of wrong ways to handle difficulties: Some people simply pretend they don't exist, like ostriches hiding their heads in the sand; you, however, tend to go to the other extreme, focusing on problems much more than necessary. I am training you to pry your mind away from trouble so you can fix your thoughts on Me.

The Lord is near to all who call on him, to all who call on him in truth. —Psalm 145:18

For He Himself is our peace. —Ephesians 2:14 NKJV

Also read:
Hebrews 3:1

Before You Turn Out the Light

Persevere in directing your wayward thoughts toward Me. In Me is your Peace.

March 6
MORNING

CONTINUE ON THIS PATH WITH ME, enjoying My Presence even in adversity. I am always before you, as well as alongside you. See Me beckoning to you: "Come! Follow Me." The One who goes ahead of you, opening up the way, is the same One who stays close and never lets go of your hand. I am not subject to limitations of time or space. I am everywhere at every time, ceaselessly working on your behalf. That is why your best efforts are trusting Me and living close to Me.

ISAIAH 41:10 NASB; HEBREWS 7:25;
PSALM 37:3–4

March 6
EVENING

COME CLOSE TO ME, and rest in My Presence. I am all around you, closer than the very air you breathe. Trust Me with each breath you take.

> *Find rest, O my soul, in God alone; my hope comes from him. He alone is my rock and my salvation; he is my fortress, I will not be shaken.* —PSALM 62:5–6

> *I am like an olive tree flourishing in the house of God; I trust in God's unfailing love for ever and ever.* —PSALM 52:8

Also read:
MATTHEW 1:21 NKJV

Before You Turn Out the Light

Don't neglect the practice of My Presence. Keep coming back to Me again and again.

March 7
MORNING

Let Me help you through this day. The challenges you face are far too great for you to handle alone. You are keenly aware of your helplessness in the scheme of events you face. This awareness opens up a choice: to doggedly go it alone or to walk with Me in humble steps of dependence. Actually, this choice is continually before you, but difficulties highlight the decision-making process. *So consider it all joy whenever you are enveloped in various trials.* These are gifts from Me, reminding you to rely on Me alone.

PSALM 46:1; PSALM 63:7–8;
JAMES 1:2–3 AMP

March 7
EVENING

Until you reach your ultimate home in heaven, you will be at war. I do equip you fully to handle your difficulties, but you have to make the effort to use what I provide: My Presence, My Word, My Spirit. *Come to Me when you are heavy laden, and you will find rest for your soul.*

> "So do not fear, for I am with you; do not be dismayed, for I am your God. I will strengthen you and help you; I will uphold you with my righteous right hand." —Isaiah 41:10

> "Come to Me, all you who labor and are heavy laden . . . and you will find rest for your souls." —Matthew 11:28–29 NKJV

Also read:
1 Peter 5:8–9

Before You Turn Out the Light

Dig deep into My Word, where I can equip you with My promises and My power for your life.

March 8

MORNING

Save your best striving for seeking My Face. I am constantly communicating with you. To find Me and hear My voice, you must seek Me above all else. Anything that you desire more than Me becomes an idol. When you are determined to get your own way, you blot Me out of your consciousness. Instead of single-mindedly pursuing some goal, talk with Me about it. Let the Light of My Presence shine on this pursuit so that you can see it from My perspective. If the goal fits into My plans for you, I will help you reach it. If it is contrary to My will for you, I will gradually change the desire of your heart. *Seek Me first* and foremost; then the rest of your life will fall into place, piece by piece.

1 Chronicles 16:11;
Proverbs 19:21 nkjv; Matthew 6:33

March 8
EVENING

My promise to be *with you always* ensures that you never have to face anything alone. The evil one uses three *D*s to keep you from finding Me: distractions, deception, and discouragement. As you resist these tricky tactics and look for Me, *you will find Me.*

> *[Azariah] went out to meet King Asa as he was returning from battle. "Listen to me, Asa! Listen, armies of Judah and Benjamin!" he shouted. "The Lord will stay with you as long as you stay with him! Whenever you look for him, you will find him. But if you forsake him, he will forsake you."* —2 Chronicles 15:2 TLB

> *"And surely I am with you always, to the very end of the age."* —Matthew 28:20

> *Also read:*
> Genesis 3:13 NKJV

Before You Turn Out the Light

Study and absorb My Word, for it will
be life and protection to you.

March 9
MORNING

Rest in My radiant Presence. The world around you seems to spin faster and faster, till everything is a blur. Yet there is a cushion of calm at the center of your life, where you live in union with Me. Return to this soothing Center as often as you can, for this is where you are energized: filled with My Love, Joy, and Peace.

The world is a needy place; do not go there for sustenance. Instead, come to Me. Learn to depend on Me alone, and your weakness will become saturated with My Power. When you find your completeness in Me, you can help other people without using them to meet your own needs. Live in the Light of My Presence, and your light will shine brightly into the lives of others.

GALATIANS 5:22; 2 CORINTHIANS 12:9;

1 JOHN 4:12

March 9
EVENING

Instead of worrying about where and when you will find rest, remember that I have promised to provide it for you. Go gently and steadily through your day, looking to Me for help. Whenever you are struggling with weariness, *come to Me, and I will give you rest.*

> *And He said, "My Presence will go with you, and I will give you rest."* —Exodus 33:14 NKJV

> *"Come to me, all you who are weary and burdened, and I will give you rest."* —Matthew 11:28

> *Also read:*
> Psalm 121:2–3

Before You Turn Out the Light

Approach Me for the refreshment you're craving. I eagerly renew your reserves.

March 10

MORNING

You are Mine for all time—and beyond time, into eternity. No power can deny you your inheritance in heaven. I want you to realize how utterly secure you are! Even if you falter as you journey through life, I will never let go of your hand.

Knowing that your future is absolutely assured can free you to live abundantly today. I have prepared this day for you with the most tender concern and attention to detail. Instead of approaching the day as a blank page that you need to fill up, try living it in a responsive mode, being on the lookout for all that I am doing. This sounds easy, but it requires a deep level of trust, based on the knowledge that *My way is perfect*.

1 Peter 1:3–4; Psalm 37:23–24;
Psalm 18:30

March 10

EVENING

THE EVIL ONE has been deceiving people ever since time began, since the Garden of Eden. Do not listen to his lies. Instead, put your trust in Me, for I am absolute Truth.

Fear of man will prove to be a snare, but whoever trusts in the LORD is kept safe. —PROVERBS 29:25

The LORD God said to the woman, "What is this you have done?" The woman said, "The serpent deceived me, and I ate." —GENESIS 3:13

Also read:
JOHN 14:6 NKJV; JOHN 8:32 NKJV

Before You Turn Out the Light

Voice your trust in Me. I am the One who can keep you safe.

March 11
MORNING

WALK BY FAITH, NOT BY SIGHT. As you take steps of faith, depending on Me, I will show you how much I can do for you. If you live your life too safely, you will never know the thrill of seeing Me work through you. When I gave you My Spirit, I empowered you to live beyond your natural ability and strength. That's why it is so wrong to measure your energy level against the challenges ahead of you. The issue is not your strength but Mine, which is limitless. By walking close to Me, you can accomplish My purposes in My strength.

2 Corinthians 5:7 nkjv; Galatians 5:25; Psalm 59:16–17

March 11
EVENING

WHEN YOU BEGIN THE DAY with a muddled mind, you tend to ask yourself the wrong question—whether you will be able to cope with whatever happens—but the true question is whether you and I together can handle the circumstances you face. Broaden your perspective so you can "see" Me there alongside you—strengthening, guiding, and encouraging you. While you meditate on this joyous focus, the qualms you had about the day will gradually give way to cheerful confidence.

I can do everything through him who gives me strength. —PHILIPPIANS 4:13

"The virgin will be with child and will give birth to a son, and they will call him Immanuel"—which means, "God with us." —MATTHEW 1:23

Also read:
PSALM 112:7

Before You Turn Out the Light

Unscramble your thoughts from the day with a shift in perspective. Meditate on who I am, God with you.

March 12
MORNING

WAITING, TRUSTING, AND HOPING are intricately connected, like golden strands interwoven to form a strong chain. Trusting is the central strand because it is the response from My children that I desire the most. Waiting and hoping embellish the central strand and strengthen the chain that connects you to Me. Waiting for Me to work, with your eyes on Me, is evidence that you really do trust Me. If you mouth the words "I trust You" while anxiously trying to make things go your way, your words ring hollow. Hoping is future-directed, connecting you to your inheritance in heaven. However, the benefits of hope fall fully on you in the present.

Because you are Mine, you don't just pass time in your waiting. You can wait expectantly, in hopeful trust. Keep your "antennae" out to pick up even the faintest glimmer of My Presence.

JOHN 14:1; PSALM 27:14;
HEBREWS 6:18–20

March 12
EVENING

Bring all your dreams into My vibrant Light so we can look at them together. Some of them are not in My plans for you; as you commit them to Me, seeking My will, I gradually remove them from your heart. Other dreams I approve, encouraging you to work prayerfully toward reaching those goals. Some dreams, however, remain veiled in mystery—I neither remove them from your heart nor provide a path for you to follow. This keeps you waiting on Me, enjoying the benefits of My Presence.

For with you is the fountain of life; in your light we see light. —Psalm 36:9

Yet the Lord longs to be gracious to you; he rises to show you compassion. Blessed are all who wait for him! —Isaiah 30:18

Also read:
Isaiah 40:30–31 nasb

Before You Turn Out the Light

Have you yet realized that this time of waiting is a gift from Me? Name the ways.

March 13
MORNING

LEARN TO LIVE above your circumstances. This requires focused time with Me, the *One who overcame the world*. Trouble and distress are woven into the very fabric of this perishing world. Only My Life in you can empower you to face this endless flow of problems with *good cheer*.

As you sit quietly in My Presence, I shine Peace into your troubled mind and heart. Little by little, you are freed from earthly shackles and lifted up above your circumstances. You gain My perspective on your life, enabling you to distinguish between what is important and what is not. Rest in My Presence, *receiving Joy that no one can take away from you*.

JOHN 16:33 NKJV; PSALM 42:5 NASB;
JOHN 16:22

March 13
EVENING

A MASTERFUL SHEPHERD can often take care of trouble so skillfully that his sheep remain blissfully unaware of it. I am the only absolutely *Good Shepherd*. Follow Me and My ways; let Me protect you from danger *and* from fear.

> *The Lord is my shepherd, I shall not be in want. He makes me lie down in green pastures, he leads me beside quiet waters, he restores my soul. He guides me in paths of righteousness for his name's sake. Even though I walk through the valley of the shadow of death, I will fear no evil, for you are with me; your rod and your staff, they comfort me.* —PSALM 23:1–4

> *"I am the good shepherd; and I know My sheep, and am known by My own. As the Father knows Me, even so I know the Father; and I lay down My life for the sheep."* —JOHN 10:14–15 NKJV

Also read:

2 SAMUEL 22:31

Before You Turn Out the Light

Come close. Take refuge in Me and My shielding Presence.

March 14

MORNING

Do not hesitate to receive Joy from Me, for I bestow it on you abundantly. The more you rest in My Presence, the more freely My blessings flow into you. In the Light of My Love, you are gradually *transformed from glory to glory*. It is through spending time with Me that you realize *how wide and long and high and deep is My Love for you*.

Sometimes the relationship I offer you seems too good to be true. I pour My very Life into you, and all you have to do is receive Me. In a world characterized by working and taking, the admonition to rest and receive seems too easy. There is a close connection between receiving and believing: As you trust Me more and more, you are able to receive Me and My blessings abundantly. *Be still, and know that I am God.*

2 Corinthians 3:18 nasb;
Ephesians 3:17–19; Psalm 46:10

March 14
EVENING

WHEN YOU REMEMBER that I am your perfect Betrothed and that you are promised to Me forever, you can rejoice in Me even though you face many problems. It is in the present moment that you find Me ever near you. *My Presence in the present* is an endless source of Joy: *a continual feast*!

> *All the days of the afflicted are evil, but he who is of a merry heart has a continual feast.* —PROVERBS 15:15 NKJV

> *"Abide in Me, and I in you. As the branch cannot bear fruit of itself, unless it abides in the vine, neither can you, unless you abide in Me."* —JOHN 15:4 NKJV

Also read:
PHILIPPIANS 4:4–5; PSALM 63:5

Before You Turn Out the Light

How did you remain in Me today, celebrating
My Presence even amid your difficulties?

March 15
MORNING

LISTEN TO THE LOVE SONG that I am continually singing to you. *I take great delight in you. I rejoice over you with singing.* The voices of the world are a cacophony of chaos, pulling you this way and that. Don't listen to those voices; challenge them with My Word. Learn to take minibreaks from the world, finding a place to be still in My Presence and listen to My voice.

There is immense hidden treasure to be found through listening to Me. Though I pour out blessings upon you always, some of My richest blessings have to be actively sought. I love to reveal Myself to you, and your seeking heart opens you up to receive more of My disclosure. *Ask and it will be given to you; seek and you will find; knock and the door will be opened to you.*

ZEPHANIAH 3:17; MATTHEW 17:5;

MATTHEW 7:7

March 15
EVENING

PICTURE YOURSELF standing at the edge of an ocean, on a beach covered with pebbles that represent problems—yours, your family's, your friends', the world's. As you pick up these small stones and hold them close to your eyes—examining their details—they obscure your view of the grandeur all around you. I am calling you to put down all the pebbles for a time so that you can experience My Presence and receive *My unfailing Love.*

The LORD loves righteousness and justice; the earth is full of his unfailing love. —PSALM 33:5

You will show me the path of life; in Your presence is fullness of joy; at Your right hand are pleasures forevermore. —PSALM 16:11 NKJV

Also read:
HEBREWS 3:1; HEBREWS 11:27

Before You Turn Out the Light

In this quiet hour, lay down your problems and lift your head to all My treasures, reserved just for you.

March 16
MORNING

IT IS GOOD THAT YOU RECOGNIZE YOUR WEAKNESS. That keeps you looking to Me, your Strength. Abundant life is not necessarily health and wealth; it is living in continual dependence on Me. Instead of trying to fit this day into a preconceived mold, relax and be on the lookout for what I am doing. This mind-set will free you to enjoy Me and to find what I have planned for you to do. This is far better than trying to make things go according to your own plan.

Don't take yourself so seriously. Lighten up and laugh with Me. You have Me on your side, so what are you worried about? I can equip you to do absolutely anything, as long as it is My will. The more difficult your day, the more I yearn to help you. Anxiety wraps you up in yourself, trapping you in your own thoughts. When you look to Me and whisper My Name, you break free and receive My help. Focus on Me, and you will find Peace in My Presence.

PHILIPPIANS 4:13 AMP; PROVERBS 17:22

March 16
EVENING

I HAVE TOLD YOU that *whoever follows Me will never walk in darkness, but will have the Light of Life.* An excellent way to stay near Me is to place your confidence fully in Me. A heart that trusts in Me can even *leap for Joy*!

*The L*ORD *is my strength and my shield; my heart trusts in him, and I am helped. My heart leaps for joy and I will give thanks to him in song.* —PSALM 28:7

When Jesus spoke again to the people, he said, "I am the light of the world. Whoever follows me will never walk in darkness, but will have the light of life." —JOHN 8:12

Also read:
1 THESSALONIANS 5:16–18 NKJV; COLOSSIANS 3:23 NKJV

Before You Turn Out the Light

Recognize My continual Presence in your life
in a way that is meaningful to you.

March 17

MORNING

Come to Me for understanding since I know you far better than you know yourself. I comprehend you in all your complexity; *no detail of your life is hidden from Me.* I view you through eyes of grace, so don't be afraid of My intimate awareness. Allow the Light of My healing Presence to shine into the deepest recesses of your being—cleansing, healing, refreshing, and renewing you. Trust Me enough to accept the full forgiveness that I offer you continually. This great gift, which cost Me My Life, is yours for all eternity. Forgiveness is at the very core of My abiding Presence. *I will never leave you or forsake you.*

When no one else seems to understand you, simply draw closer to Me. Rejoice in the One who understands you completely and loves you perfectly. As I fill you with My Love, you become a reservoir of love, overflowing into the lives of other people.

PSALM 139:1–4; 2 CORINTHIANS 1:21–22;
JOSHUA 1:5

March 17
EVENING

YOUR DESIRE TO RELY ON ME wholly is a worthy goal. The Holy Spirit will help you think trusting thoughts, but He requires your cooperation. As you look to Me—trusting Me, talking with Me—I straighten out the path before you.

Lean on, trust in, and be confident in the Lord with all your heart and mind and do not rely on your own insight or understanding. In all your ways know, recognize, and acknowledge Him, and He will direct and make straight and plain your paths. —PROVERBS 3:5–6 AMP

Commit your way to the LORD, trust also in Him, and He shall bring it to pass. —PSALM 37:5 NKJV

Also read:
ROMANS 8:6

Before You Turn Out the Light

Allow Me to do this supernatural trust-work in your heart. Then wait confidently to see the results.

March 18
MORNING

Trust Me one day at a time. This keeps you close to Me, responsive to My will. Trust is not a natural response, especially for those who have been deeply wounded. My Spirit within you is your resident Tutor, helping you in this supernatural endeavor. Yield to His gentle touch; be sensitive to His prompting.

Exert your will to trust Me in all circumstances. Don't let your need to understand distract you from My Presence. I will equip you to get through this day victoriously as you live in deep dependence on Me. *Tomorrow is busy worrying about itself; don't get tangled up in its worry-webs.* Trust Me one day at a time.

PSALM 84:12; 1 CORINTHIANS 6:19;
JEREMIAH 17:7 NKJV; MATTHEW 6:34

March 18
EVENING

Trust Me here and now. This path is not of your choosing, but it is My way for you. Wait hopefully in My Presence, and watch to see what I will do.

> *Who among you fears the Lord and obeys the word of his servant? Let him who walks in the dark, who has no light, trust in the name of the Lord and rely on his God.* —Isaiah 50:10

> *Therefore I will look to the Lord; I will wait for the God of my salvation; my God will hear me.* —Micah 7:7 nkjv

> *Also read:*
> Psalm 42:5 nasb

Before You Turn Out the Light

Cling to My hand. My Presence goes with you.

March 19

MORNING

I SPEAK TO YOU FROM THE DEPTHS OF YOUR BEING. Hear Me saying soothing words of Peace, assuring you of My Love. Do not listen to voices of accusation, for they are not from Me. I speak to you in love-tones, lifting you up. My Spirit convicts cleanly, without crushing words of shame. Let the Spirit take charge of your mind, combing out tangles of deception. Be transformed by the truth that I live within you.

The Light of My Presence is shining upon you, in benedictions of Peace. Let My Light shine in you; don't dim it with worries or fears. Holiness is letting Me live through you. Since I dwell in you, you are fully equipped to be holy. Pause before responding to people or situations, giving My Spirit space to act through you. Hasty words and actions leave no room for Me; this is atheistic living. I want to inhabit all your moments—gracing your thoughts, words, and behavior.

ROMANS 8:1–2; COLOSSIANS 1:27;
1 CORINTHIANS 6:19

March 19
EVENING

I SEE YOU AS YOU TRULY ARE: gloriously clothed in My righteousness. The Light of My Love is shining upon you. Be still in this holy Light, resting in the assurance of *My unfailing Love.*

> *As for the saints who are in the land, they are the glorious ones in whom is all my delight.* —PSALM 16:3

> *I will greatly rejoice in the LORD, my soul shall be joyful in my God; for He has clothed me with the garments of salvation, He has covered me with the robe of righteousness, as a bridegroom decks himself with ornaments, and as a bride adorns herself with her jewels.* —ISAIAH 61:10 NKJV

Also read:
PSALM 46:10 NKJV; EXODUS 15:13

Before You Turn Out the Light

Open your arms and your heart to receive My delight.

March 20
MORNING

Thank Me for the glorious gift of My Spirit. This is like priming the pump of a well. As you bring Me the sacrifice of thanksgiving, regardless of your feelings, My Spirit is able to work more freely within you. This produces more thankfulness and more freedom, until you are overflowing with gratitude.

I shower blessings on you daily, but sometimes you don't perceive them. When your mind is stuck on a negative focus, you see neither Me nor My gifts. In faith, thank Me for whatever is preoccupying your mind. This will clear the blockage so that you can find Me.

PSALM 50:14; 2 CORINTHIANS 5:5;
2 CORINTHIANS 3:17; PSALM 95:2 NKJV

March 20
EVENING

Every time you thank Me, you acknowledge that I am your Lord and Provider. And every time you receive with thanksgiving, you demonstrate your kinship with Me. When you thank Me during a difficult day, you are assuming the proper stance for a child of God.

Give thanks in all circumstances, for this is God's will for you in Christ Jesus. —1 Thessalonians 5:18

Therefore, since we are receiving a kingdom that cannot be shaken, let us be thankful, and so worship God acceptably with reverence and awe. —Hebrews 12:28

Also read:
Acts 3:15; James 1:17

Before You Turn Out the Light

I give you Joy and Peace in the midst of your struggles when you refuse to grumble. You also demonstrate that you are part of Our Family.

March 21
MORINING

Trust Me and don't be afraid, for I am your Strength and Song. Think what it means to have Me as your Strength. I spoke the universe into existence; My Power is absolutely unlimited! Human weakness, consecrated to Me, is like a magnet, drawing My Power into your neediness. However, fear can block the flow of My Strength into you. Instead of trying to fight your fears, concentrate on trusting Me. When you relate to Me in confident trust, there is no limit to how much I can strengthen you.

Remember that I am also your Song. I want you to share My Joy, living in conscious awareness of My Presence. Rejoice as we journey together toward heaven; join Me in singing My Song.

ISAIAH 12:2–3; PSALM 56:3 NKJV;
PSALM 21:6

March 21
EVENING

I*t is easy to turn against yourself* when you have failed, but this is not pleasing to Me. The sooner you turn toward Me, the better: My tender Love can soothe your wounded pride and help you learn from your mistakes. *In My unfailing Love I will lead you. In My strength I will guide you—* all the way *to My holy dwelling.*

> *He will have no fear of bad news; his heart is steadfast, trusting in the Lord.* —Psalm 112:7

> *In your unfailing love you will lead the people you have redeemed. In your strength you will guide them to your holy dwelling.* —Exodus 15:13

Also read:
Psalm 143:8; Isaiah 61:3 nkjv

Before You Turn Out the Light

Lift your arms to Me for help; I cannot resist coming to your aid.

March 22
MORNING

REJOICE AND BE THANKFUL! As you walk with Me through this day, practice trusting and thanking Me all along the way. Trust is the channel through which My Peace flows into you. Thankfulness lifts you up above your circumstances.

I do My greatest works through people with grateful, trusting hearts. Rather than planning and evaluating, practice trusting and thanking Me continually. This is a paradigm shift that will revolutionize your life.

PHILIPPIANS 4:4; PSALM 95:1–2;
PSALM 9:10; 2 CORINTHIANS 2:14 NKJV

March 22
EVENING

ONE OF THE BEST WAYS TO FIND STRENGTH for your journey is to give Me thanks and praise. Thanksgiving and praise lift your perspective from your worries and woes to the glorious Treasure you have in Me. The more you praise Me, the closer to Me you will grow.

*Enter his gates with thanksgiving and his courts with praise; give thanks to him and praise his name. For the L*ORD *is good and his love endures forever; his faithfulness continues through all generations.* —PSALM 100:4–5

*Give thanks to the L*ORD*, for he is good, for his steadfast love endures forever. Give thanks to the God of gods, for his steadfast love endures forever. Give thanks to the Lord of lords, for his steadfast love endures forever.* —PSALM 136:1–3 ESV

Also read:
2 CORINTHIANS 5:7 NKJV; PSALM 22:3 KJV

Before You Turn Out the Light

Intimately align your heart with Mine by simply giving thanks.

March 23
MORNING

I AM A GOD of both intricate detail and overflowing abundance. When you entrust the details of your life to Me, you are surprised by how thoroughly I answer your petitions. I take pleasure in hearing your prayers, so feel free to bring Me all your requests. The more you pray, the more answers you can receive. Best of all, your faith is strengthened as you see how precisely I respond to your specific prayers.

Because I am infinite in all My ways, you need not fear that I will run out of resources. *Abundance* is at the very heart of who I AM. Come to Me in joyful expectation of receiving all you need—and sometimes much more! I delight in showering blessings on My beloved children. Come to Me with open hands and heart, ready to receive all I have for you.

PSALM 36:7–9; PSALM 132:15;
JOHN 6:12–13

March 23
EVENING

Think big when you pray, but remember that I always think bigger! I look at the big picture—all the moments of your life—and I am doing *more than you can imagine*. You can talk with Me about anything because I understand you perfectly.

> *Now to him who is able to do immeasurably more*
> *than all we ask or imagine, according to his power*
> *that is at work within us . . .* —Ephesians 3:20

> *In the morning, O Lord, you hear my voice;*
> *in the morning I lay my requests before you*
> *and wait in expectation.* —Psalm 5:3

> *Also read:*
> Psalm 93:1–2 esv

Before You Turn Out the Light

Collaborate with Me regarding your dreams and desires. You never have to handle things alone.

March 24
MORNING

THIS IS A TIME in your life when you must learn to let go: of loved ones, of possessions, of control. In order to let go of something that is precious to you, you need to rest in My Presence, where you are complete. Take time to bask in the Light of My Love. As you relax more and more, your grasping hand gradually opens up, releasing your prized possession into My care.

You can feel secure, even in the midst of cataclysmic changes, through awareness of My continual Presence. The One who never leaves you is the same One who never changes: *I am the same yesterday, today, and forever.* As you release more and more things into My care, remember that I never let go of your hand. Herein lies your security, which no one and no circumstance can take from you.

PSALM 89:15; HEBREWS 13:8;

ISAIAH 41:13

March 24
EVENING

It is indeed My prerogative to bring about change in people's lives. You can be part of the process, but remember that I am the Author and Director of the drama: You need to follow My script rather than creating your own. Trust in My Love and My unsearchable wisdom—I can work changes in your loved ones' lives beyond anything you might ask or imagine.

Then Jesus came to them and said, "All authority in heaven and on earth has been given to me." —Matthew 28:18

Let the morning bring me word of your unfailing love, for I have put my trust in you. Show me the way I should go, for to you I lift up my soul. —Psalm 143:8

Also read:
Ephesians 3:20–21

Before You Turn Out the Light

One by one, prayerfully release your loved ones to Me, and then linger a while in My unfailing Love—for them and also for you.

March 25
MORNING

LET THANKFULNESS TEMPER ALL YOUR THOUGHTS. A thankful mind-set keeps you in touch with Me. I hate it when My children grumble, casually despising My sovereignty. Thankfulness is a safeguard against this deadly sin. Furthermore, a grateful attitude becomes a grid through which you perceive life. Gratitude enables you to see the Light of My Presence shining on all your circumstances. Cultivate a thankful heart, for this glorifies Me and fills you with Joy.

1 CORINTHIANS 10:10; HEBREWS 12:28–29; COLOSSIANS 3:16

March 25
EVENING

Throughout the Bible, I repeatedly command thankfulness because it is vital to your well-being. It is also crucial for a healthy relationship with Me since I am your Creator, your Savior, your King. Look up to Me, and see spiritual blessings cascading down on you through wide-open windows of heaven.

Enter his gates with thanksgiving and his courts with praise; give thanks to him and praise his name. —Psalm 100:4

Blessed be the God and Father of our Lord Jesus Christ, who has blessed us with every spiritual blessing in the heavenly places in Christ. —Ephesians 1:3 nasb

Also read:
Colossians 4:2; Zechariah 9:9 nkjv

Before You Turn Out the Light

When you fail to be thankful, simply ask Me for forgiveness. Your gratitude will grow once again.

March 26
MORNING

WAITING ON ME means directing your attention to Me in hopeful anticipation of what I will do. It entails trusting Me with every fiber of your being instead of trying to figure things out yourself. Waiting on Me is the way I designed you to live: all day, every day. I created you to stay conscious of Me as you go about your daily duties.

I have promised many blessings to those who wait on Me: *renewed strength*, living above one's circumstances, resurgence of hope, awareness of My continual Presence. Waiting on Me enables you to glorify Me by living in deep dependence on Me, ready to do My will. It also helps you to enjoy Me; *in My Presence is fullness of Joy.*

LAMENTATIONS 3:24–26; ISAIAH 40:31;
PSALM 16:11 NKJV

March 26
EVENING

*S*OME OF YOUR PRAYERS that you consider frantic and unintelligible are actually quite profound: They rise from the depths of your heart—all the way to heaven. To form these deep prayers, you need only turn toward Me with the concerns that lie heavy on your heart. As you put your hope in Me, *My unfailing Love rests peacefully upon you.*

> *But as for me, I watch in hope for the L*ORD*, I wait for God my Savior; my God will hear me.* —MICAH 7:7

> *We wait in hope for the L*ORD*; he is our help and our shield. In him our hearts rejoice, for we trust in his holy name. May your unfailing love rest upon us, O L*ORD*, even as we put our hope in you.* —PSALM 33:20–22

Also read:
ROMANS 8:26–27

Before You Turn Out the Light

Watch in hope as you wait for My deliverance.

March 27
MORNING

BE STILL IN MY PRESENCE even though countless tasks clamor for your attention. Nothing is as important as spending time with Me. While you wait in My Presence, I do My best work within you, *transforming you by the renewing of your mind*. If you skimp on this time with Me, you may plunge headlong into the wrong activities, missing the richness of what I have planned for you.

Do not seek Me primarily for what I can give you. Remember that I, the Giver, am infinitely greater than any gift I might impart to you. Though I delight in blessing My children, I am deeply grieved when My blessings become idols in their hearts. Anything can be an idol if it distracts you from Me as your *First Love*. When I am the ultimate Desire of your heart, you are safe from the danger of idolatry. As you wait in My Presence, enjoy the greatest gift of all: *Christ in you, the hope of Glory*!

ROMANS 12:2; REVELATION 2:4;
COLOSSIANS 1:27

March 27
EVENING

Y OU NEED STILLNESS—outer and inner—to hear My gentle whispers in your heart. Find a quiet place where the noise of the world is minimal. Then focus your mind on this verse: *Cease striving and know that I am God.* Be still, let go, and relax in My Presence while I commune with you in holy whispers.

> *I pray that out of his glorious riches he may strengthen you with power through his Spirit in your inner being, so that Christ may dwell in your hearts through faith.* —EPHESIANS 3:16–17

> *Ceasing striving and know that I am God.* —PSALM 46:10 NASB

> *Also read:*
> HEBREWS 1:2; 1 KINGS 19:12

Before You Turn Out the Light

Delight in Me and My righteousness that purifies you.

March 28
MORNING

I AM A GOD WHO GIVES and gives and gives. When I died for you on the cross, I held back nothing; I poured out My Life *like a drink offering*. Because giving is inherent in My nature, I search for people who are able to receive in full measure. To increase your intimacy with Me, the two traits you need the most are receptivity and attentiveness. Receptivity is opening up your innermost being to be filled with My abundant riches. Attentiveness is directing your gaze to Me, searching for Me in all your moments. It is possible to *stay your mind on Me*, as the prophet Isaiah wrote. Through such attentiveness you receive a glorious gift: My perfect Peace.

PHILIPPIANS 2:17; MARK 10:15;
ISAIAH 26:3 NKJV

March 28
EVENING

I HAVE ALREADY PAID THE PENALTY for all the things in your life—past, present, and future—that could isolate you from Me. Though there is still some darkness in your heart, the Light of the knowledge of My Glory continues shining within you—as a Light that shines in a dark place, until the day dawns and the morning star rises in your heart. In this brilliant Love-Light, you can sometimes catch glimpses of the Glory revealed in My Face.

For God, who said, "Let light shine out of darkness," made His light shine in our hearts to give us the light of the knowledge of the glory of God in the face of Christ. —2 CORINTHIANS 4:6

And so we have the prophetic word confirmed, which you do well to heed as a light that shines in a dark place, until the day dawns and the morning star rises in your hearts. —2 PETER 1:19 NKJV

Also read:
ROMANS 3:23–24; PSALM 130:5–6

Before You Turn Out the Light

I desire intimate connection with you.

Wait in My holy Presence.

March 29
MORNING

STOP TRYING TO WORK THINGS OUT before their times have come. Accept the limitations of living one day at a time. When something comes to your attention, ask Me whether or not it is part of today's agenda. If it isn't, release it into My care and go on about today's duties. When you follow this practice, there will be a beautiful simplicity about your life: *a time for everything, and everything in its time.*

A life lived close to Me is not complicated or cluttered. When your focus is on My Presence, many things that once troubled you lose their power over you. Though the world around you is messy and confusing, remember that *I have overcome the world. I have told you these things, so that in Me you may have Peace.*

ECCLESIASTES 3:1; ECCLESIASTES 8:6–7;
JOHN 16:33

March 29
EVENING

PEOPLE WHO ARE STRUGGLING with long-term problems may feel as if their suffering will go on interminably. But for My children there is every reason to be hopeful, even while circumstances remain dark. Just as the night sometimes seems terribly long, yet always ends in dawn, so your journey through this world—no matter how long and hard it seems—will definitely end in Glory!

I wait for the LORD, my soul waits, and in his word I put my hope. My soul waits for the Lord more than watchmen wait for the morning, more than watchmen wait for the morning. —PSALM 130:5–6

The sun shall be no more your light by day, nor for brightness shall the moon give you light; but the LORD will be your everlasting light, and your God will be your glory. —ISAIAH 60:19 ESV

Also read:
PSALM 17:15 NKJV; EPHESIANS 3:20–21 NKJV

Before You Turn Out the Light

Watch for the morning. Relief is on its way!

March 30
MORNING

I AM TAKING CARE OF YOU. Trust Me at all times. Trust Me in all circumstances. *Trust Me with all your heart.* When you are weary and everything seems to be going wrong, you can still utter these four words: "I trust You, Jesus." By doing so, you release matters into My control, and you fall back into the security of *My everlasting arms.*

Before you arise from your bed in the morning, I have already arranged the events of your day. Every day provides many opportunities for you to learn My ways and grow closer to Me. Signs of My Presence brighten even the dullest day when you have eyes that really see. Search for Me as for hidden treasure. *I will be found by you.*

PROVERBS 3:5; DEUTERONOMY 33:27;
JEREMIAH 29:13–14

March 30
EVENING

Remember that I am a *Man of sorrows, fully acquainted with grief.* Because of all I suffered, I can empathize with you and share your pain. *Come to Me* and get to know Me in ever-increasing depth and breadth; you will find that I am indeed a Refuge—a safe place flooded with eternal Love.

> *He was despised and forsaken of men, a man of sorrows and acquainted with grief; and like one from whom men hide their face He was despised, and we did not esteem Him.* —Isaiah 53:3 NASB

> *"Come to Me, all you who labor and are heavy-laden and overburdened, and I will cause you to rest. [I will ease and relieve and refresh your souls.]"* —Matthew 11:28 AMP

Also read:
Psalm 62:8 NKJV; Proverbs 29:25

Before You Turn Out the Light

You don't have to hold in your emotions any longer. Release them in the safety of Me.

March 31
MORNING

Taste and see that I am good. The more intimately you experience Me, the more convinced you become of My goodness. I am *the Living One who sees you* and longs to participate in your life. I am training you to find Me in each moment and to be a channel of My loving Presence. Sometimes My blessings come to you in mysterious ways: through pain and trouble. At such times you can know My goodness only through your trust in Me. Understanding will fail you, but trust will keep you close to Me.

Thank Me for the gift of My Peace, a gift of such immense proportions that you cannot fathom its depth or breadth. When I appeared to My disciples after the resurrection, it was Peace that I communicated first of all. I knew this was their deepest need: to calm their fears and clear their minds. I also speak Peace to you, for I know your anxious thoughts. Listen to Me! Tune out other voices so that you can hear Me more clearly. I designed you to dwell in Peace all day, every day. Draw near to Me; receive My Peace.

PSALM 34:8; GENESIS 16:13–14 AMP;
JOHN 20:19; COLOSSIANS 3:15

March 31
EVENING

I AM SOVEREIGN, AND I AM GOOD. Subordinate your finite mind to My infinite intelligence and sovereign ways. Cling to Me in childlike trust, believing that *My way—though mysterious—is perfect.*

> *He will swallow up death forever. The Sovereign Lord will wipe away the tears from all faces; he will remove the disgrace of his people from all the earth. The Lord has spoken.* —ISAIAH 25:8

> *As for God, His way is perfect; the word of the Lord is proven; He is a shield to all who trust in Him.* —PSALM 18:30 NKJV

Also read:
1 JOHN 1:5 NKJV

Before You Turn Out the Light

Relinquish your demand to understand,
and find rest in My Presence.

April

*In all your ways acknowledge him, and
he will make your paths straight.*

Proverbs 3:6

April 1
MORNING

I AM CALLING YOU to a life of constant communion with Me. Basic training includes learning to live above your circumstances, even while interacting on that cluttered plane of life. You yearn for a simplified lifestyle so that your communication with Me can be uninterrupted. But I challenge you to relinquish the fantasy of an uncluttered world. Accept each day just as it comes, and find Me in the midst of it all.

Talk with Me about every aspect of your day, including your feelings. Remember that your ultimate goal is not to control or fix everything around you; it is to keep communing with Me. A successful day is one in which you have stayed in touch with Me, even if many things remain undone at the end of the day. Do not let your to-do list (written or mental) become an idol directing your life. Instead, ask My Spirit to guide you moment by moment. He will keep you close to Me.

1 THESSALONIANS 5:17; PROVERBS 3:6;
GALATIANS 5:25

April 1
EVENING

AFTER MY RESURRECTION, the first words I spoke to My disciples were, "Peace be with you!" You also need to be reminded of the divine nature of this gift, for it is not the world's peace I give you: It is Peace that transcends all understanding! As you receive My glorious Peace, you gain deeper intimacy with Me—the richest blessing of all!

> *"Peace I leave with you; my peace I give you. I do not give to you as the world gives. Do not let your hearts be troubled and do not be afraid."* —JOHN 14:27

> *On the evening of that first day of the week, when the disciples were together, with the doors locked for fear of the Jews, Jesus came and stood among them and said, "Peace be with you!"* —JOHN 20:19

Also read:
PHILIPPIANS 4:6–7

Before You Turn Out the Light

Lift your eyes and imagine the never-ending fountain of My Peace washing over you.

April 2
MORNING

I HAVE PROMISED *to meet all your needs according to My glorious riches.* Your deepest, most constant need is for My Peace. I have planted Peace in the garden of your heart, where I live, but there are weeds growing there too: pride, worry, selfishness, unbelief. I am the Gardener, and I am working to rid your heart of those weeds. I do My work in various ways. When you sit quietly with Me, I shine the Light of My Presence directly into your heart. In this heavenly Light, Peace grows abundantly and weeds shrivel up. I also send trials into your life. When you trust Me in the midst of trouble, Peace flourishes and weeds die away. Thank Me for troublesome situations; the Peace they can produce *far outweighs* the trials you endure.

PHILIPPIANS 4:19; 2 THESSALONIANS 3:16 NKJV;
2 CORINTHIANS 4:17

April 2
EVENING

THE ONE WHO IS ALWAYS WITH YOU is *the God of Love and Peace*! When you feel a need for more Love, come to Me and let Me lavish it upon you. Whenever you are feeling anxious or afraid, come into My peaceful Presence—and relax in *the everlasting arms* awaiting you. Make every effort to live close to Me.

> *Be of good comfort, be of one mind, live in peace; and the God of love and peace will be with you.* —2 CORINTHIANS 13:11 NKJV

> *The eternal God is your refuge, and underneath are the everlasting arms. He will drive out your enemy before you, saying, "Destroy him!"* —DEUTERONOMY 33:27

Also read:
GENESIS 1:27 NKJV

Before You Turn Out the Light

Soak in My Love and Peace now, and then extend them to others day after day. I want your character to reflect Me more and more.

April 3
MORNING

In Me you have everything. In Me you are complete. Your capacity to experience Me is increasing through My removal of debris and clutter from your heart. As your yearning for Me increases, other desires are gradually lessening. Since I am infinite and abundantly accessible to you, desiring Me above all else is the best way to live.

It is impossible for you to have a need that I cannot meet. After all, I created you and everything that is. The world is still at My beck and call, though it often appears otherwise. Do not be fooled by appearances. *Things that are visible are brief and fleeting, while things that are invisible are everlasting.*

EPHESIANS 3:20; 2 CORINTHIANS 4:18 AMP

April 3
EVENING

Your routine prayers help you cover a wide range of praises and petitions without overtaxing your brain, but that very efficiency carries with it a danger: You can sleepwalk through your regular prayers. To avoid doing that, make use of the massive Power source within you—the Holy Spirit. He will help you stay alert as you invite Him to empower your prayers with Life.

And pray in the Spirit on all occasions with all kinds of prayers and requests. With this in mind, be alert and always keep on praying for all the saints. —Ephesians 6:18

For great is your love, reaching to the heavens; your faithfulness reaches to the skies. Be exalted, O God, above the heavens; let your glory be over all the earth. —Psalm 57:10–11

Also read:
Genesis 1:1

Before You Turn Out the Light

Prayerfully consider new ideas for communing with Me that will awaken your soul and enliven our relationship.

April 4
MORNING

I MEET YOU in the stillness of your soul. It is there that I seek to commune with you. A person who is open to My Presence is exceedingly precious to Me. My eyes *search to and fro throughout the earth*, looking for one whose heart is seeking Me. I see you trying to find Me; our mutual search results in joyful fulfillment.

Stillness of soul is increasingly rare in this world addicted to noise and speed. I am pleased with your desire to create a quiet space where you and I can meet. Don't be discouraged by the difficulty of achieving this goal. I monitor all your efforts and am blessed by each of your attempts to seek My Face.

ZECHARIAH 2:13; 2 CHRONICLES 16:9 NKJV;
PSALM 23:2–3 NKJV

April 4
EVENING

When you reach the end of this day, stop and look back at the distance we have covered. Take time to ponder what you have learned and to savor the gifts you have found. Let your mind dwell on these things as you lie down to sleep, rejoicing in Me and My blessings.

This is the day the Lord has made; let us rejoice and be glad in it. —Psalm 118:24

He who did not spare his own Son but gave him up for us all—how will he not also, along with him, graciously give us all things? —Romans 8:32

Also read:
John 13:13

Before You Turn Out the Light

Set your heart on rejoicing to help you
see the good that was in this day.

April 5
MORNING

Let Me fill you with my Love, Joy, and Peace. These are Glory-gifts, flowing from my living Presence. Though you are an *earthen vessel*, I designed you to be filled with heavenly contents. Your weakness is not a deterrent to being filled with My Spirit; on the contrary, it provides an opportunity for My Power to shine forth more brightly.

As you go through this day, trust Me to provide the strength you need moment by moment. Don't waste energy wondering whether you are adequate for today's journey. My Spirit within you is more than sufficient to handle whatever this day may bring. That is the basis for your confidence! *In quietness* (spending time alone with Me) *and confident trust* (relying on My sufficiency) *is your strength*.

2 Corinthians 4:7 nasb; Ephesians 3:16;
Isaiah 30:15

April 5
EVENING

I ENABLE YOU TO *go on the heights.* You may think that "the heights" refers to the very top of the mountain you are climbing, but if you stop and look back at how far up you have come, you'll realize you are already on a high place. So relax a bit and gaze lovingly at Me—the Glory of My Presence is all around you!

> *The Sovereign L*ORD *is my strength; he makes my feet like the feet of a deer, he enables me to go on the heights.* —HABAKKUK 3:19

> *I saw the L*ORD *sitting on a throne, high and lifted up, and the train of His robe filled the temple. Above it stood seraphim; each one had six wings: with two he covered his face, with two he covered his feet, and with two he flew. And one cried to another and said: "Holy, holy, holy is the L*ORD *of hosts; the whole earth is full of His glory!"* —ISAIAH 6:1–3 NKJV

Also read:
PSALM 73:23–24

Before You Turn Out the Light

Be on the lookout for the pleasures I have prepared for you on this upward journey. I can infuse Joy into the steepest climb!

April 6
MORNING

Bring Me the sacrifice of thanksgiving. Take nothing for granted, not even the rising of the sun. Before Satan tempted Eve in the Garden of Eden, thankfulness was as natural as breathing. Satan's temptation involved pointing Eve to the one thing that was forbidden her. The Garden was filled with luscious, desirable fruits, but Eve focused on the one fruit she couldn't have rather than being thankful for the many good things freely available. This negative focus darkened her mind, and she succumbed to temptation.

When you focus on what you don't have or on situations that displease you, your mind also becomes darkened. You take for granted life, salvation, sunshine, flowers, and countless other gifts from Me. You look for what is wrong and refuse to enjoy life until that is "fixed."

When you approach Me with thanksgiving, the Light of My Presence pours into you, transforming you through and through. *Walk in the Light* with Me by practicing the discipline of thanksgiving.

PSALM 116:17 NKJV; GENESIS 3:2–4;

1 JOHN 1:7

April 6
EVENING

I WANT YOU TO ACCEPT your dependent way of living as a gift from Me. Moreover, I want you to receive this gift *joyfully*—with a glad and thankful heart. Nothing will lift you out of the doldrums faster than thanking and praising Me.

Indeed, O man, who are you to reply against God? Will the thing formed say to him who formed it, "Why have you made me like this?" —ROMANS 9:20 NKJV

Enter his gates with thanksgiving and his courts with praise; give thanks to him and praise his name. For the LORD is good and his love endures forever; his faithfulness continues through all generations. —PSALM 100:4–5

Also read:
ISAIAH 40:10

Before You Turn Out the Light

Come into My Presence this evening
with thanksgiving on your lips.

April 7
MORNING

I AM THE POTTER; you are My clay. I designed you before the foundation of the world. I arrange the events of each day to form you into this preconceived pattern. My everlasting Love is at work in every event of your life. On some days your will and Mine flow smoothly together. You tend to feel in control of your life when our wills are in harmony. On other days you feel as if you are swimming upstream, against the current of My purposes. When that happens, stop and seek My Face. The opposition you feel may be from Me, or it may be from the evil one.

Talk with Me about what you are experiencing. Let My Spirit guide you through treacherous waters. As you move through the turbulent stream with Me, let circumstances mold you into the one I desire you to be. Say *yes* to your Potter as you go through this day.

ISAIAH 64:8; PSALM 27:8;
1 JOHN 5:5–6 NKJV

April 7
EVENING

Sometimes My Sovereign hand—My control over your life—places you in humbling circumstances. You can learn to *be joyful in hope* while waiting in My Presence, where Joy abounds. Persevere in trusting Me, and I will eventually *lift you up*.

> *Be joyful in hope, patient in affliction, faithful in prayer.* —Romans 12:12

> *Humble yourselves, therefore, under God's mighty hand, that he may lift you up in due time. Cast all your anxiety on him because he cares for you.* —1 Peter 5:6–7

Also read:
Psalm 32:10; Psalm 16:11 nkjv

Before You Turn Out the Light

Wait quietly in My Presence.

April 8
MORNING

I AM WITH YOU AND FOR YOU, your constant Companion and Provider. The question is whether you are with Me and for Me. Though I never leave you, you can essentially "leave" Me by ignoring Me: thinking or acting as if I am not with you. When you feel distance in our relationship, you know where the problem lies. My Love for you is constant; *I am the same yesterday, today, and forever.* It is you who change like shifting sand, letting circumstances toss you this way and that.

When you feel far from Me, whisper My Name. This simple act, done in childlike faith, opens your heart to My Presence. Speak to Me in love-tones; prepare to receive My Love, which flows eternally from the cross. I am delighted when you open yourself to My loving Presence.

GENESIS 28:15; ROMANS 8:31;
HEBREWS 13:8; COLOSSIANS 3:17 NKJV

April 8
EVENING

When you become aware of sins, I want you to confess them and seek My help in making needed changes. Your status with Me is not based on confessing your sins quickly enough or thoroughly enough. The only thing that keeps you right with Me is My perfect righteousness, which I gave you freely and permanently when you joined My royal family.

But if we walk in the light as He is in the light, we have fellowship with one another, and the blood of Jesus Christ His Son cleanses us from all sin. —1 John 1:7 nkjv

Blessed are those who have learned to acclaim you, who walk in the light of your presence, O Lord. They rejoice in your name all day long; they exult in your righteousness. —Psalm 89:15–16

Also read:
Hebrews 13:5

Before You Turn Out the Light

Instead of striving to be good enough, I invite you to come confidently into My Presence.

April 9
MORNING

YOU ARE MINE FOR ALL TIME; *nothing can separate you from My Love.* Since I have invested My very Life in you, be well assured that I will also take care of you. When your mind goes into neutral and your thoughts flow freely, you tend to feel anxious and alone. Your focus becomes problem solving. To get your mind back into gear, just turn toward Me, bringing yourself and your problems into My Presence.

Many problems vanish instantly in the Light of My Love because you realize you are never alone. Other problems may remain, but they become secondary to knowing Me and rejoicing in the relationship I so freely offer you. Each moment you can choose to practice My Presence or to practice the presence of problems.

ROMANS 8:38–39; EXODUS 33:14;
JOHN 12:46 NKJV

April 9
EVENING

The very name I use to address you—Beloved—proclaims how dearly I love you. I showed you the *full extent of My Love* by enduring humiliation, torture, and death for you. *Trust in My unfailing Love*, secure in the salvation I won for you.

> *"Greater love has no one than this, than to lay down one's life for his friends."* —John 15:13 nkjv

> *But I trust in your unfailing love; my heart rejoices in your salvation.* —Psalm 13:5

Also read:
John 13:1; 1 John 4:16 nasb

Before You Turn Out the Light

Dwell on your memories of Me as often as your heart needs reminding. My extraordinary Love is yours throughout eternity.

April 10
MORNING

Trust Me in every detail of your life. Nothing is random in My kingdom. *Everything that happens fits into a pattern for good, to those who love Me.* Instead of trying to analyze the intricacies of the pattern, focus your energy on trusting Me and thanking Me at all times. Nothing is wasted when you walk close to Me. Even your mistakes and sins can be recycled into something good through My transforming grace.

While you were still living in darkness, I began to shine the Light of My Presence into your sin-stained life. Finally, I *lifted you up out of the mire into My marvelous Light.* Having sacrificed My very Life for you, I can be trusted in every facet of your life.

JEREMIAH 17:7; ROMANS 8:28 AMP;
PSALM 40:2 AMP; 1 PETER 2:9 NKJV

April 10
EVENING

Because the world is in such a fallen condition, it may seem as if I'm not in control—but I am waiting *to bring many sons and daughters to Glory*. So take heart as you live in this broken world. Your troubles are part of My majestic Master Plan, and they *are achieving an eternal Glory that far outweighs them all*!

> *Lean on, trust in, and be confident in the Lord with all your heart and mind and do not rely on your own insight or understanding.* —Proverbs 3:5 amp

> *Our light and momentary troubles are achieving for us an eternal glory that far outweighs them all.* —2 Corinthians 4:17

Also read:
Hebrews 2:10 nkjv

Before You Turn Out the Light

Believe that My purposes are being worked out through your difficulties—because they are!

April 11
MORNING

This is the day that I have made. Rejoice and be glad in it. Begin the day with open hands of faith, ready to receive all that I am pouring into this brief portion of your life. Be careful not to complain about anything, even the weather, since I am the Author of your circumstances. The best way to handle unwanted situations is to thank Me for them. This act of faith frees you from resentment and frees Me to work My ways into the situation, so that good emerges from it.

To find Joy in this day, you must live within its boundaries. I knew what I was doing when I divided time into twenty-four-hour segments. I understand human frailty, and I know that you can bear the weight of only one day at a time. Do not worry about tomorrow or get stuck in the past. There is abundant Life in My Presence today.

Psalm 118:24; Philippians 3:13–14;
Hebrews 3:13

April 11
EVENING

My Word is seasoned with multiple commands to be thankful—for good reason! I ransomed you from eternal punishment through My torturous death on the cross, and I continue to shower additional blessings upon you. As you learn to give thanks in all circumstances, My loving Presence will increasingly brighten your vision of life.

Moses also said . . . "Who are we? You are not grumbling against us, but against the Lord." —Exodus 16:8

Give thanks in all circumstances, for this is God's will for you in Christ Jesus. —1 Thessalonians 5:18

Also read:
Numbers 14:29

Before You Turn Out the Light

Start now to develop a grateful mind-set, and soon you'll perceive all of My gifts more clearly.

April 12
MORNING

Trusting Me is a moment-by-moment choice. My people have not always understood this truth. After I performed miracles in the wilderness, My chosen children trusted Me intensely—but only temporarily. Soon the grumbling began again, testing My patience to the utmost.

Isn't it often the same way with you? You trust Me when things go well, when you see Me working on your behalf. This type of trust flows readily within you, requiring no exertion of your will. When things go wrong, your trust-flow slows down and solidifies. You are forced to choose between trusting Me intentionally or rebelling, resenting My ways with you. This choice constitutes a fork in the road. Stay on the path of Life with Me, enjoying My Presence. Choose to trust Me in all circumstances.

Exodus 15:22–25; Psalm 31:14

April 12
EVENING

WHEN YOU ARE AFRAID, don't blame yourself for having that very human emotion. Instead, acknowledge what you are feeling; then affirm your trust in Me, out loud or in a whisper. This affirmation protects you from the lie that feeling fearful means you don't trust Me; even better, it brings you consciously into My Presence, where you can find comfort and hope.

> *The Lord himself goes before you and will be with you; he will never leave you nor forsake you. Do not be afraid; do not be discouraged.* —DEUTERONOMY 31:8

> *When I am afraid, I will trust in you.* —PSALM 56:3

Also read:
PSALM 55:5 NKJV; EPHESIANS 3:18–19

Before You Turn Out the Light

Reflect on the psalms of David: They show that genuine faith is not canceled out by fear.

April 13
MORNING

When I give you no special guidance, stay where you are. Concentrate on doing your everyday tasks in awareness of My Presence with you. The Joy of My Presence will shine on you, as you do everything for Me. Thus you invite Me into every aspect of your life. Through collaborating with Me in all things, you allow My Life to merge with yours. This is the secret of not only joyful living but of victorious living. I designed you to depend on Me moment by moment, recognizing that *apart from Me you can do nothing.*

Be thankful for quiet days, when nothing special seems to be happening. Instead of being bored by the lack of action, use times of routine to seek My Face. Although this is an invisible transaction, it speaks volumes in spiritual realms. Moreover, you are richly blessed when you walk trustingly with Me through the routines of your day.

Colossians 3:23; John 15:5;
Psalm 105:4

April 13
EVENING

Ever since I became your Savior, you have been building on the Rock of My Presence. The key to steadiness in your life is to *set Me always before you*. When you make Me your Focus, you can walk steadily along your life-path. See Me beckoning you on—step by step by step—all the way to heaven.

> *He lifted me out of the slimy pit, out of the mud*
> *and mire; he set my feet on a rock and gave*
> *me a firm place to stand.* —Psalm 40:2

> *I have set the Lord always before me. Because he is at*
> *my right hand, I will not be shaken.* —Psalm 16:8

> *Also read:*
> Ecclesiastes 1:2; 2 Samuel 22:47 nkjv

Before You Turn Out the Light

Set aside every distraction, and look to Me as your Guide.

April 14
MORNING

Heaven is both present and future. As you walk along your life-path holding My hand, you are already in touch with the essence of heaven: nearness to Me. You can also find many hints of heaven along your pathway because the earth is radiantly alive with My Presence. Shimmering sunshine awakens your heart, gently reminding you of My brilliant Light. Birds and flowers, trees and skies evoke praises to My holy Name. Keep your eyes and ears fully open as you journey with Me.

At the end of your life-path is an entrance to heaven. Only I know when you will reach that destination, but I am preparing you for it each step of the way. The absolute certainty of your heavenly home gives you Peace and Joy to help you along your journey. You know that you will reach your home in My perfect timing: not one moment too soon or too late. Let the hope of heaven encourage you as you walk along the path of Life with Me.

1 Corinthians 15:20–23; Hebrews 6:19

April 14
EVENING

I HAVE NOT LEFT YOU to handle by yourself the trouble and distress of this life—I have poured My very Being into you, in the Person of the Holy Spirit. Make plenty of space in your heart for this glorious One. Let Him empower you to live above your circumstances.

"And I will ask the Father, and he will give you another Counselor to be with you forever—the Spirit of truth . . . for he lives with you and will be in you." —JOHN 14:16–17

"These things I have spoken to you, that in Me you may have peace. In the world you will have tribulation; but be of good cheer, I have overcome the world." —JOHN 16:33 NKJV

Also read:
JOHN 14:2

Before You Turn Out the Light

How much of My Peace are you experiencing in the midst of your problems? Call out to My Spirit to calm you.

April 15
MORNING

Trust Me, and don't be afraid. Many things feel out of control. Your routines are not running smoothly. You tend to feel more secure when your life is predictable. Let Me lead you to *the rock that is higher than you* and your circumstances. *Take refuge in the shelter of My wings*, where you are absolutely secure.

When you are shaken out of your comfortable routines, grip My hand tightly and look for growth opportunities. Instead of bemoaning the loss of your comfort, accept the challenge of something new. *I lead you on from glory to glory*, making you fit for My kingdom. Say *yes* to the ways I work in your life. Trust Me, and don't be afraid.

ISAIAH 12:2; PSALM 61:2–4;
2 CORINTHIANS 3:18 NKJV

April 15
EVENING

As you release your weaknesses to Me for My purposes, you become a treasure in My kingdom. Making yourself fully available to Me guarantees that your life will not be wasted: I will use it for My Glory! In response, I dispatch My Power to you.

> *I appeal to you therefore, brethren, and beg of you in view of [all] the mercies of God, to make a decisive dedication of your bodies [presenting all your members and faculties] as a living sacrifice, holy (devoted, consecrated) and well pleasing to God, which is your reasonable (rational, intelligent) service and spiritual worship.* —ROMANS 12:1 AMP

> *"Consecrate yourselves and be holy, because I am the LORD your God."* —LEVITICUS 20:7

Also read:
REVELATION 4:11

Before You Turn Out the Light

Offer your frailty to Me for My service. I receive it as a sacred act of worship.

April 16
MORNING

I AM CALLING YOU to a life of thankfulness. I want all your moments to be punctuated with thanksgiving. The basis for your gratitude is My sovereignty. I am the Creator and Controller of the universe. Heaven and earth are filled with My glorious Presence.

When you criticize or complain, you are acting as if you think you could run the world better than I do. From your limited human perspective, it may look as if I'm mismanaging things. But you don't know what I know or see what I see. If I pulled back the curtain to allow you to view heavenly realms, you would understand much more. However, I have designed you to *live by faith*, not by sight. I lovingly shield you from knowing the future or seeing into the spirit world. Acknowledge My sovereignty by *giving thanks in all circumstances*.

ISAIAH 6:3; 2 CORINTHIANS 5:7;
1 THESSALONIANS 5:18

April 16
EVENING

YOU ARE BEING TRANSFORMED *into My image from Glory to Glory.* Trust My Spirit to do this massive work in you. Yield to My ways, wisdom, and will.

> *We all, with unveiled face, beholding as in a mirror the glory of the Lord, are being transformed into the same image from glory to glory, just as by the Spirit of the Lord.* —2 CORINTHIANS 3:18 NKJV

> *Now if we are children, then we are heirs—heirs of God and co-heirs with Christ, if indeed we share in his sufferings in order that we may also share in his glory.* —ROMANS 8:17

Also read:
2 CORINTHIANS 4:17; EPHESIANS 5:19–20

Before You Turn Out the Light

Willingly share in My sufferings so that
you may also share in My Glory.

April 17
MORNING

I AM TRAINING YOU IN STEADINESS. Too many things interrupt your awareness of Me. I know that you live in a world of sight and sound, but you must not be a slave to those stimuli. Awareness of Me can continue in all circumstances, no matter what happens. This is the steadiness I desire for you.

Don't let unexpected events throw you off course. Rather, respond calmly and confidently, remembering that I am with you. As soon as something grabs your attention, talk with Me about it. Thus I share your joys and your problems; I help you cope with whatever is before you. This is how I live in you and work through you. This is the way of Peace.

PSALM 112:7; 1 THESSALONIANS 5:17 AMP;
ISAIAH 41:10 NKJV

April 17
EVENING

Learn to live from a place of resting in Me. We can deal with your problems together—you and I—so there is no need to panic. The more you return to Me—to our resting place—the more peaceful and joyful your life will be.

> *I can do all things through Christ who strengthens me.* —Philippians 4:13 NKJV

> *The name of the Lord is a strong tower; the righteous run to it and are safe.* —Proverbs 18:10 NKJV

Also read:
Isaiah 9:6

Before You Turn Out the Light

Refuse to panic. Release your fears and return to My rest.

April 18
MORNING

PEACE IS MY CONTINUAL GIFT TO YOU. It flows abundantly from My throne of grace. Just as the Israelites could not store up manna for the future but had to gather it daily, so it is with My Peace. The day-by-day collecting of manna kept My people aware of their dependence on Me. Similarly, I give you sufficient Peace for the present when you come to me *by prayer and petition with thanksgiving.* If I gave you permanent Peace, independent of My Presence, you might fall into the trap of self-sufficiency. May that never be!

I have designed you to need Me moment by moment. As your awareness of your neediness increases, so does your realization of My abundant sufficiency. *I can meet every one of your needs* without draining My resources at all. *Approach My throne of grace with bold confidence*, receiving My Peace with a thankful heart.

EXODUS 16:15–16; PHILIPPIANS 4:6–7, 19;
HEBREWS 4:16

April 18
EVENING

This is when My grace is the most precious and glorious—when you know you cannot go another step without it. Do not be ashamed of your weaknesses; boast about them! Through them you are learning to depend more on Me *so that My Power may dwell in you.*

> *[The Lord] has said to me, "My grace is sufficient for you, for power is perfected in weakness." Most gladly, therefore, I will rather boast about my weaknesses, so that the power of Christ may dwell in me.* —2 Corinthians 12:9 NASB

> *[God] made us alive together with Christ . . . that in the ages to come He might show the exceeding riches of His grace in His kindness toward us in Christ Jesus.* —Ephesians 2:5, 7 NKJV

Also read:
Isaiah 54:10

Before You Turn Out the Light

Do you believe that My grace is enough? What will you do to reinforce this truth tomorrow?

April 19
MORNING

I LOVE YOU regardless of how well you are performing. Sometimes you feel uneasy, wondering if you are doing enough to be worthy of My Love. No matter how exemplary your behavior, the answer to that question will always be no. Your performance and My Love are totally different issues, which you need to sort out. *I love you with an everlasting Love* that flows out from eternity without limits or conditions. *I have clothed you in My robe of righteousness*, and this is an eternal transaction: Nothing and no one can reverse it. Therefore, your accomplishment as a Christian has no bearing on My Love for you. Even your ability to assess how well you are doing on a given day is flawed. Your limited human perspective and the condition of your body, with its mercurial variations, distort your evaluations.

Bring your performance anxiety to Me, and receive in its place *My unfailing Love*. Try to stay conscious of My loving Presence with you in all that you do, and I will direct your steps.

JEREMIAH 31:3; ISAIAH 61:10;
PSALM 31:16; PSALM 107:8

April 19
EVENING

THE IDEA OF *UNFAILING LOVE* is radical; there is no adequate model for it in this world. Such Love can be found only in Me—in the very essence of who I am. Even the most devoted parent, friend, or lover will let you down sometimes, but I am the eternal Lover who will never fail you.

> *The LORD delights in those who fear him, who put their hope in his unfailing love.* —PSALM 147:11

> *We have known and believed the love that God has for us. God is love, and he who abides in love abides in God, and God in him.* —1 JOHN 4:16 NKJV

Also read:
LAMENTATIONS 3:22; ISAIAH 51:6

Before You Turn Out the Light

Have hope in Me and My unfailing provision for you.

April 20
MORNING

DO NOT BE AFRAID, for I am with you. Hear Me saying, *"Peace, be still,"* to your restless heart. No matter what happens, *I will never leave you or forsake you.* Let this assurance soak into your mind and heart until you overflow with Joy. *Though the earth give way and the mountains fall into the heart of the sea*, you need not fear!

The media relentlessly proclaim bad news: for breakfast, lunch, and dinner. A steady diet of their fare will sicken you. Instead of focusing on fickle, ever-changing news broadcasts, tune in to the living Word—the One who is always the same. Let Scripture saturate your mind and heart, and you will walk steadily along the path of Life. Even though you don't know what will happen tomorrow, you can be absolutely sure of your ultimate destination. *I hold you by your right hand, and afterward I will take you into Glory.*

MARK 4:39 NKJV; DEUTERONOMY 31:6;
PSALM 46:2; PSALM 73:23–24

April 20
EVENING

FEARS THAT ARE NOT DEALT WITH tend to magnify themselves. Expose them to the revealing Light of My Presence, and they will shrink to manageable proportions. Follow Me confidently wherever I lead, and the shelter of My Presence will keep you safe.

> *If the LORD delights in a man's way, he makes his steps firm; though he stumble, he will not fall, for the LORD upholds him with his hand.* —PSALM 37:23–24

> *Let us fix our eyes on Jesus, the author and perfecter of our faith, who for the joy set before him endured the cross, scorning its shame, and sat down at the right hand of the throne of God.* —HEBREWS 12:2

Also read:
PSALM 31:20

Before You Turn Out the Light

Keep your eyes on Me as you step out on the limb of faith. You are actually safer here—with Me—than you would be on the ground.

April 21
MORNING

LET ME CONTROL YOUR MIND. The mind is the most restless, unruly part of mankind. Long after you have learned the discipline of holding your tongue, your thoughts defy your will and set themselves up against Me. Man is the pinnacle of My creation, and the human mind is wondrously complex. I risked all by granting you freedom to think for yourself. This is godlike privilege, forever setting you apart from animals and robots. *I made you in My image*, precariously close to deity.

Though My blood has fully redeemed you, your mind is the last bastion of rebellion. Open yourself to My radiant Presence, letting My Light permeate your thinking. *When My Spirit is controlling your mind, you are filled with Life and Peace.*

PSALM 8:5 NKJV; GENESIS 1:26–27;

ROMANS 8:6

April 21
EVENING

Habitual ways of thinking do not die easily. You may need to recapture the same thought many times before you gain mastery over it, but all that effort leads to a marvelous result: increased freedom to think My thoughts and commune deeply with Me. Wait with Me while I renovate you—from the inside out!

> *Do not conform any longer to the pattern of this world, but be transformed by the renewing of your mind.* —Romans 12:2

> *We take captive every thought to make it obedient to Christ.* —2 Corinthians 10:5

Also read:
Psalm 130:5

Before You Turn Out the Light

What hurtful thought patterns is the Spirit shining His light on? Write them down so you can root out the distortions and replace them with Truth.

April 22
MORNING

Listen to Me continually. I have much to communicate to you, so many people and situations in need of prayer. I am training you to set your mind on Me more and more, tuning out distractions through the help of My Spirit.

Walk with Me in holy trust, responding to My initiatives rather than trying to make things fit your plans. I died to set you free, and that includes freedom from compulsive planning. When your mind spins with a multitude of thoughts, you cannot hear My voice. A mind preoccupied with planning pays homage to the idol of control. Turn from this idolatry back to Me. Listen to Me and live abundantly!

PSALM 62:8 NKJV; JOHN 8:36;
PROVERBS 19:21; JOHN 10:27

April 22
EVENING

A SUCCESSFUL DAY IS ONE in which you have stayed in touch with Me, even if many things remain undone at the end of the day. When communicating with Me is your highest priority, I am pleased. The more you commune with Me as you go, the more you walk in My ways.

> *Jesus replied: "'Love the Lord your God with all your heart and with all your soul and with all your mind.' This is the first and greatest commandment."* —MATTHEW 22:37–38

> *This is what the LORD says: "Stand at the crossroads and look; ask for the ancient paths, ask where the good way is, and walk in it, and you will find rest for your souls."* —JEREMIAH 6:16

Also read:
PSALM 90:8; PSALM 63:5 NKJV

Before You Turn Out the Light

How successful was your day from this perspective? Do not pass up this present opportunity to commune with Me.

April 23
MORNING

KEEP YOUR EYES ON ME, not only for direction but also for empowerment. I never lead you to do something without equipping you for the task. That is why it's so important to seek My will in everything you do. There are many burned-out Christians who think more is always better, who deem it unspiritual to say no.

In order to know My will, you must spend time with Me—enjoying My Presence. This is not an onerous task but a delightful privilege. I will show you *the path of Life; in My Presence is fullness of Joy; at My right hand there are pleasures forevermore.*

PSALM 141:8; ISAIAH 48:17;
PSALM 16:11 NKJV

April 23
EVENING

YOU'LL FIND NO DEEPER COMFORT than knowing that *I am with you always*, both here on earth and throughout eternity in heaven. You have known this great truth in your head for many years; however, your heart is fickle and tends to chase after other gods. Only as My Spirit helps you can you grasp the awesomeness of My Presence with you forever.

I am with you and will watch over you wherever you go. —GENESIS 28:15

"In my Father's house are many rooms; if it were not so, I would have told you. I am going there to prepare a place for you. And if I go and prepare a place for you, I will come back and take you to be with me that you also may be where I am." —JOHN 14:2–3

Also read:
MATTHEW 7:24; JOHN 14:16–17 NASB

Before You Turn Out the Light

Let the promise of heaven flood your heart, for I am with you not only in this life but in the life to come.

April 24
MORNING

REST IN THE STILLNESS of My Presence while I prepare you for this day. Let the radiance of My Glory shine upon you as you wait on Me in confident trust. *Be still, and know that I am God.* There is both a passive and an active side to trusting Me. As you rest in My Presence, focusing on Me, I quietly build bonds of trust between us. When you respond to the circumstances of your life with affirmations of trust, you actively participate in this process.

I am always with you, so you have no reason to be afraid. Your fear often manifests itself in excessive planning. Your mind is so accustomed to this pattern of thinking that you are only now becoming aware of how pervasive it is and how much it hinders your intimacy with Me. Repent of this tendency and resist it whenever you realize you are wandering down this well-worn path. Return to My Presence, which always awaits you in the present moment. I accept you back with *no condemnation*.

PSALM 46:10; ROMANS 8:1–2

April 24
EVENING

If you don't stay alert, anxious feelings can slip into your day without your noticing them. How much better it is to "catch" worry-thoughts before they take hold of you. If you are watchful and alert, you can choose to take refuge in Me whenever anxiety comes at you.

Be of sober spirit, be on the alert. Your adversary, the devil, prowls around like a roaring lion, seeking someone to devour. —1 Peter 5:8 nasb

O taste and see that the Lord [our God] is good! Blessed (happy, fortunate, to be envied) is the man who trusts and takes refuge in Him. —Psalm 34:8 amp

Also read:
Psalm 57:1 nkjv

Before You Turn Out the Light

What have you worried about today? What worry will you hand over to Me before you sleep?

April 25
MORNING

MAKE ME YOUR FOCAL POINT as you move through this day. Just as a spinning ballerina must keep returning her eyes to a given point to maintain her balance, so you must keep returning your focus to Me. Circumstances are in flux, and the world seems to be whirling around you. The only way to keep your balance is to *fix your eyes on Me*, the One who never changes. If you gaze too long at your circumstances, you will become dizzy and confused. Look to Me, refreshing yourself in My Presence, and your steps will be steady and sure.

HEBREWS 12:2; PSALM 102:27;
1 JOHN 3:19–20

April 25
EVENING

NOTHING IS AS IMPORTANT as knowing and loving Me as I truly am. Making Me your highest priority gives focus to your thinking. Other priorities fall into their proper place when I am first and foremost in your life.

> *"Let him who glories glory in this, that he understands and knows Me, that I am the LORD, exercising lovingkindness, judgment, and righteousness in the earth. For in these I delight," says the LORD.* —JEREMIAH 9:24 NKJV

> *Jesus replied: "'Love the Lord your God with all your heart and with all your soul and with all your mind.' This is the first and greatest commandment."* —MATTHEW 22:37–38

Also read:
PSALM 19:1–2

Before You Turn Out the Light

Set your priorities according to My will,
not the ways of this world.

April 26
MORNING

WELCOME PROBLEMS as perspective-lifters. My children tend to sleepwalk through their days until they bump into an obstacle that stymies them.

If you encounter a problem with no immediate solution, your response to that situation will take you either up or down. You can lash out at the difficulty, resenting it and feeling sorry for yourself. This will take you down into a pit of self-pity. Alternatively, the problem can be a ladder, enabling you to climb up and see your life from My perspective. Viewed from above, the obstacle that frustrated you is only *a light and momentary trouble*. Once your perspective has been heightened, you can look away from the problem altogether. Turn toward Me, and see *the Light of My Presence* shining upon you.

2 CORINTHIANS 4:16–18; PSALM 89:15

April 26
EVENING

If you have a problem that comes and goes over a long period of time, you may start dreading its recurrence. This reaction only makes matters worse. Let Me suggest a better way: When the problem is absent or minimal, rejoice and thank Me continually. If the problem is present, look to Me and affirm your trust in Me. Ask My Spirit to help you persevere and keep your focus on Me. If you do this consistently, you will no longer be letting your circumstances dictate the quality of your life.

Be joyful in hope, patient in affliction, faithful in prayer. —Romans 12:12

Let me hear in the morning of your steadfast love, for in you I trust. Make me know the way I should go, for to you I lift up my soul. —Psalm 143:8 ESV

Also read:
1 Thessalonians 5:16–18 AMP

Before You Turn Out the Light

I am in the midst of your every moment. You can trust Me—with your problems and your praises.

April 27
MORNING

Come to Me with empty hands and an open heart, ready to receive abundant blessings. I know the depth and breadth of your neediness. Your life-path has been difficult, draining you of strength. Come to Me for nurture. Let Me fill you up with My Presence: I in you, and you in Me.

My Power flows most freely into weak ones aware of their need for Me. Faltering steps of dependence are not lack of faith; they are links to My Presence.

JOHN 17:20–23; ISAIAH 40:29–31

April 27
EVENING

Because you are Mine, I want to bless you with My Peace. The Peace I give you is *not as the world gives*; it can coexist with the most difficult situations because it is transcendent. It rises above both your circumstances and your understanding—and it can lift *you* up too!

> *The Lord gives strength to his people; the Lord blesses his people with peace.* —Psalm 29:11

> *"Peace I leave with you, My peace I give to you; not as the world gives do I give to you. Let not your heart be troubled, neither let it be afraid."* —John 14:27 nkjv

Also read:
John 3:16 nkjv; Philippians 4:7

Before You Turn Out the Light

Find Peace in this: I stand ready to help you with every challenge you face.

April 28
MORNING

As you look into the day that stretches out before you, you see many choice-points along the way. The myriad possibilities these choices present can confuse you. Draw your mind back to the threshold of this day, where I stand beside you, lovingly preparing you for what is ahead.

You must make your choices one at a time since each is contingent upon the decision that precedes it. Instead of trying to create a mental map of your path through this day, focus on My loving Presence with you. I will equip you as you go so that you can handle whatever comes your way. Trust Me to supply what you need when you need it.

LAMENTATIONS 3:22–26; PROVERBS 16:9;
PSALM 34:8 NKJV

April 28
EVENING

It saddens Me to see you obsessing about possible problems rather than bringing these matters to Me. When you find yourself anxiously scanning the horizon of your life, use that as a reminder to seek My Face. You will not find Me off in the distance—I am here beside you, nearer than you dare believe.

Yet I am always with you; you hold me by my right hand. You guide me with your counsel, and afterward you will take me into glory. . . . But as for me, it is good to be near God. I have made the Sovereign Lord my refuge; I will tell of all your deeds. —Psalm 73:23–24, 28

Also read:
1 Chronicles 16:11; Jeremiah 31:3

Before You Turn Out the Light

Instead of wasting time worrying, devote that time to developing a closer friendship with Me. Why not start right now?

April 29
MORNING

Let Me teach you thankfulness. Begin by acknowledging that everything—all your possessions and all that you are—belongs to Me. The dawning of each new day is a gift from Me, not to be taken for granted. The earth is vibrantly alive with My blessings, giving vivid testimony to My Presence. If you slow down your pace of life, you can find Me anywhere.

Some of My most precious children have been laid aside in sickbeds or shut away in prisons. Others have voluntarily learned the discipline of spending time alone with Me. The secret of being thankful is learning to see everything from My perspective. My world is your classroom. *My Word is a lamp to your feet and a light for your path.*

Hebrews 12:28–29; Psalm 19:1 nkjv;
Psalm 119:105

April 29
EVENING

REMEMBER THAT MY DELIGHT IN YOU is based on My finished work on the cross, so don't fall into the trap of trying to earn My Love. Instead, live as the one you truly are—My beloved—and let your gratitude keep you close to Me, eager to follow wherever I lead. I delight in you!

The LORD your God is with you, he is mighty to save. He will take great delight in you, he will quiet you with his love, he will rejoice over you with singing. —ZEPHANIAH 3:17

The Lord make His face to shine upon and enlighten you and be gracious (kind, merciful, and giving favor) to you; the Lord lift up His [approving] countenance upon you and give you peace (tranquility of heart and life continually). —NUMBERS 6:25–26 AMP

Also read:
PSALM 27:8 NKJV

Before You Turn Out the Light

Relax in My Presence. Do you hear Me singing over you with Love?

April 30

MORNING

When some basic need is lacking—time, energy, money—consider yourself blessed. Your very lack is an opportunity to latch onto Me in unashamed dependence. When you begin a day with inadequate resources, you must concentrate your efforts on the present moment. This is where you are meant to live—in the present. It is the place where I always await you. Awareness of your inadequacy is a rich blessing, training you to rely wholeheartedly on Me.

The truth is that self-sufficiency is a myth perpetuated by pride and temporary success. Health and wealth can disappear instantly, as can life itself. Rejoice in your insufficiency, knowing that *My Power is made perfect in weakness.*

James 1:2–3; 2 Corinthians 12:9 nasb

April 30
EVENING

THE WORLD HAS IT ALL WRONG about what constitutes success. Media (and even some churches) promote health and wealth as ultimate goals, but I have showered you with humble, rarely sought gifts: neediness and weaknesses. These gifts, properly received and used, help make My ways known on earth.

As for God, his way is perfect; the word of the Lord is flawless. He is a shield for all who take refuge in him. —2 Samuel 22:31

May God be gracious to us and bless us and make his face shine upon us, that your ways may be known on earth, your salvation among all nations. —Psalm 67:1–2

Also read:
Psalm 34:5

Before You Turn Out the Light

Strive for closeness with Me rather than strategies for escaping your problems.

May

*Ascribe to the Lord the glory due his name;
worship the Lord in the splendor of his holiness.*

Psalm 29:2

May 1
MORNING

YOU ARE ON THE PATH of My choosing. There is no randomness about your life. Here and Now comprise the coordinates of your daily life. Most people let their moments slip through their fingers, half-lived. They avoid the present by worrying about the future or longing for a better time and place. They forget that they are creatures who are subject to the limitations of time and space. They forget their Creator, who walks with them only in the present.

Every moment is alive with My glorious Presence, to those whose hearts are intimately connected with Mine. As you give yourself more and more to a life of constant communion with Me, you will find that you simply have no time for worry. Thus, you are freed to let My Spirit direct your steps, enabling you to walk along *the path of Peace*.

LUKE 12:25–26; JUDE vv. 24–25;
LUKE 1:79

May 1
EVENING

I WANT YOU TO LIVE ABUNDANTLY all your days. As you stay close to Me, some of My Life "rubs off" on you—awakening your heart so you can live more fully. This helps you see that you are on an adventurous journey with Me—where you make a difference, where your choices significantly impact the world.

> *The Spirit Himself bears witness with our spirit that we are children of God.* —ROMANS 8:16 NKJV

> *This God is our God for ever and ever; he will be our guide even to the end.* —PSALM 48:14

Also read:
JOHN 10:7–10 NKJV

Before You Turn Out the Light

Did you live abundantly today? Look ahead to tomorrow, knowing who you are and Whose you are.

May 2
MORNING

Living in dependence on Me is the way to enjoy abundant life. You are learning to appreciate tough times because they amplify your awareness of My Presence. Tasks that you used to dread are becoming rich opportunities to enjoy My closeness. When you feel tired, you remember that I am your Strength; you take pleasure in leaning on Me. I am pleased by your tendency to turn to Me more and more frequently, especially when you are alone.

When you are with other people, you often lose sight of My Presence. Your fear of displeasing people puts you in bondage to them, and they become your primary focus. When you realize this has happened, whisper My Name; this tiny act of trust brings Me to the forefront of your consciousness, where I belong. As you bask in the blessing of My nearness, My life can flow through you to others. This is abundant life!

PSALM 18:1–2; PROVERBS 29:25;
JOHN 10:10 NKJV

May 2
EVENING

Be willing to keep climbing this high mountain with Me. This journey is training you to see from a heavenly perspective that transcends your circumstances. The higher up the mountain you climb, the steeper and more challenging your path becomes—but the greater your adventure as well.

The Lord God is my Strength, my personal bravery, and my invincible army; He makes my feet like hinds' feet and will make me to walk [not to stand still in terror, but to walk] and make [spiritual] progress upon my high places [of trouble, suffering, or responsibility]! —Habakkuk 3:19 amp

Our citizenship is in heaven. And we eagerly await a Savior from there, the Lord Jesus Christ, who, by the power that enables him to bring everything under his control, will transform our lowly bodies so that they will be like his glorious body. —Philippians 3:20–21

Also read:
Matthew 17:1–2 nkjv

Before You Turn Out the Light

While you pause to enjoy the view, be unafraid: I will only take you higher.

May 3
MORNING

You cannot serve two masters. If I am truly your Master, you will desire to please Me above all others. If pleasing people is your goal, you will be enslaved to them. People can be harsh taskmasters when you give them this power over you.

If I am the Master of your life, I will also be your *First Love*. Your serving Me is rooted and grounded in My vast, unconditional Love for you. The lower you bow down before Me, the higher I lift you up into intimate relationship with Me. *The Joy of living in My Presence* outshines all other pleasures. I want you to reflect My joyous Light by living in increasing intimacy with Me.

MATTHEW 6:24; REVELATION 2:4;
EPHESIANS 3:16–17; PSALM 16:11

May 3
EVENING

I OFTEN WITHHOLD SUCCESS until people are weak enough to handle it. So when trials of many kinds come your way, receive those things as gifts from Me, believing that I know what I am doing and My way is perfect. *After you have suffered a little while, I Myself will make you what you ought to be, ground you securely, and strengthen you.*

> *Consider it pure joy, my brothers, whenever you face trials of many kinds, because you know that the testing of your faith develops perseverance.* —JAMES 1:2–3

> *And after you have suffered a little while, the God of all grace [Who imparts all blessing and favor], Who has called you to His [own] eternal glory in Christ Jesus, will Himself complete and make you what you ought to be, establish and ground you securely, and strengthen, and settle you.* —1 PETER 5:10 AMP

Also read:
2 SAMUEL 22:31

Before You Turn Out the Light

Try to reframe how you perceive adversity and failure. They are among the ways I prepare you to share in My eternal Glory.

May 4
MORNING

MEET ME IN MORNING STILLNESS, while the earth is fresh with the dew of My Presence. *Worship Me in the beauty of holiness.* Sing love songs to My holy Name. As you give yourself to Me, My Spirit swells within you till you are flooded with divine Presence.

The world's way of pursuing riches is grasping and hoarding. You attain *My* riches by letting go and giving. The more you give yourself to Me and My ways, the more I fill you with *inexpressible, heavenly Joy.*

PSALM 29:2 NKJV; PSALM 9:10;
1 PETER 1:8

May 4
EVENING

YOU KNOW THAT YOU FALL SHORT of My holy standard every single day; nonetheless, in *My* sight you are gloriously righteous. Your *redemption, the forgiveness of sins*, was accomplished *through My blood*—poured out freely because I love you. *How wide and long and high and deep* is this vast ocean of Love I have for you.

> *I pray that out of his glorious riches he may strengthen you with power through his Spirit in your inner being, so that Christ may dwell in your hearts through faith. And I pray that you, being rooted and established in love, may have power, together with all the saints, to grasp how wide and long and high and deep is the love of Christ, and to know this love that surpasses knowledge—that you may be filled to the measure of all the fullness of God.* —EPHESIANS 3:16–19

Also read:
EPHESIANS 1:7 NKJV; EPHESIANS 1:4

Before You Turn Out the Light

Try to absorb these words of blessing: You are holy and blameless in My sight.

May 5
MORNING

Come to Me for all that you need. Come into My Presence with thanksgiving, for thankfulness opens the door to My treasures. When you are thankful, you affirm the central truth that I am Good. *I am Light, in whom there is no darkness at all.* The assurance that I am entirely Good meets your basic need for security. Your life is not subject to the whims of a sin-stained deity.

Relax in the knowledge that the One who controls your life is totally trustworthy. Come to Me with confident expectation. There is nothing you need that I cannot provide.

PSALM 95:2; 1 JOHN 1:5; PSALM 19:7;
HEBREWS 4:16 ESV

May 5
EVENING

DON'T WAIT until you're already discouraged to bring Me your concerns. Let the Light of My Face shine upon you as we discuss these matters. Eventually, this heavenly Light will break through the fog in your mind, enabling you to see things from My perspective.

> *You have made known to me the paths of life; you will fill me with joy in your presence.* —ACTS 2:28

> *He put a new song in my mouth, a hymn of praise to our God. Many will see and fear and put their trust in the LORD.* —PSALM 40:3

Also read:
2 CORINTHIANS 9:15; NUMBERS 6:25

Before You Turn Out the Light

Whether or not I change your circumstances,
expect Me to put a new song in your heart.

May 6
MORNING

Do not search for security in the world you inhabit. You tend to make mental checklists of things you need to do in order to gain control of your life. If only you could check everything off your list, you could relax and be at peace. But the more you work to accomplish that goal, the more things crop up on your list. The harder you try, the more frustrated you become.

There is a better way to find security in this life. Instead of scrutinizing your checklist, focus your attention on My Presence with you. This continual contact with Me will keep you in My Peace. Moreover, I will help you sort out what is important and what is not, what needs to be done now and what does not. *Fix your eyes not on what is seen* (your circumstances), *but on what is unseen* (My Presence).

HEBREWS 3:1; ISAIAH 26:3 NKJV;
2 CORINTHIANS 4:18

May 6
EVENING

Hope keeps your soul—the eternal part of you—safe and secure in the midst of life's storms. To be effective, your hope must be solidly in Me, the Savior-God who died to pay the penalty for your sins. When your hope is connected to Me, you share in My vibrant, eternal Life.

> *We [who are holding on to the hope of God's salvation promises] have this hope as an anchor for the soul, firm and secure. It enters the inner sanctuary behind the curtain, where Jesus, who went before us, has entered on our behalf. He has become a high priest forever, in the order of Melchizedek.* —Hebrews 6:19–20

> *Praise be to the God and Father of our Lord Jesus Christ! In his great mercy he has given us new birth into a living hope through the resurrection of Jesus Christ from the dead.* —1 Peter 1:3

Also read:
Hebrews 10:23 NKJV

Before You Turn Out the Light

Make sure you've connected your hope to
Me, not just for now but for eternity.

May 7
MORNING

If you learn to trust Me—really trust Me—with your whole being, then nothing can separate you from My Peace. Everything you endure can be put to good use by allowing it to train you in trusting Me. This is how you foil the works of evil, growing in grace through the very adversity that was meant to harm you. Joseph was a prime example of this divine reversal, declaring to his brothers: *"You meant evil against me, but God meant it for good."*

Do not fear what this day, or any day, may bring your way. Concentrate on trusting Me and on doing what needs to be done. Relax in My sovereignty, remembering that I go before you, as well as with you, into each day. *Fear no evil*, for I can bring good out of every situation you will ever encounter.

Isaiah 26:4; Genesis 50:20 nasb;

Psalm 23:4

May 7
EVENING

THE ART OF LIVING RESPONSIVELY rests upon a foundation of trust—in My absolute goodness, My infinite wisdom, My loving Presence. To build on this trust-foundation, you need to be perceptive, seeing things from My perspective as well as yours. The times when you do succeed in living responsively will be the best in your life: You will feel fully alive and richly connected with Me.

> *"Are not two sparrows sold for a penny? Yet not one of them will fall to the ground apart from the will of your Father. And even the very hairs of your head are all numbered. So don't be afraid; you are worth more than many sparrows."* —MATTHEW 10:29–31

> *But I trust in your unfailing love; my heart rejoices in your salvation.* —PSALM 13:5

Also read:

HEBREWS 1:3

Before You Turn Out the Light

Search for what I am doing in the big picture, not just what I did in the details of your day.

May 8
MORNING

Do not long for the absence of problems in your life. That is an unrealistic goal since *in this world you will have trouble*. You have an eternity of problem-free living reserved for you in heaven. Rejoice in that inheritance, which no one can take away from you, but do not seek your heaven on earth.

Begin each day anticipating problems, asking Me to equip you for whatever difficulties you will encounter. The best equipping is My living Presence, *My hand that never lets go of yours*. Discuss everything with Me. Take a lighthearted view of trouble, seeing it as a challenge that you and I together can handle. Remember that I am on your side, and *I have overcome the world*.

JOHN 16:33; ISAIAH 41:13; PHILIPPIANS 4:13

May 8
EVENING

Rejoice that I am your God forevermore—today, tomorrow, and throughout all eternity. I am also your Guide. You can draw near Me at any time simply by whispering My Name.

Within your temple, O God, we meditate on your unfailing love. Like your name, O God, your praise reaches to the ends of the earth; your right hand is filled with righteousness. . . . For this God is our God for ever and ever; he will be our guide even to the end. —Psalm 48:9–10, 14

Also read:
Genesis 28:16; Philippians 4:6–7 nkjv

Before You Turn Out the Light

Meditate on the wondrous assurance that I am your God and your Guide, even to the end.

May 9
MORNING

DON'T BE SO HARD ON YOURSELF. I can bring good even out of your mistakes. Your finite mind tends to look backward, longing to undo decisions you have come to regret. This is a waste of time and energy, leading only to frustration. Instead of floundering in the past, release your mistakes to Me. Look to Me in trust, anticipating that My infinite creativity can weave both good choices and bad into a lovely design.

Because you are human, you will continue to make mistakes. Thinking that you should live an error-free life is symptomatic of pride. Your failures can be a source of blessing, humbling you and giving you empathy for other people in their weaknesses. Best of all, failure highlights your dependence on Me. I am able to bring beauty out of the morass of your mistakes. Trust Me, and watch to see what I will do.

ROMANS 8:28; PROVERBS 11:2;

MICAH 7:7

May 9
EVENIN G

YOUR SENSE OF RESPONSIBILITY to make judgments about everything is both hurtful and distorted. This attitude easily deteriorates into criticizing and complaining, and though you may not realize it, much of this negativity is ultimately directed at Me—the One who is sovereign over all things. Thankful words are the best replacements for your criticisms and complaints.

Humble yourselves, therefore, under God's mighty hand, that he may lift you up in due time. Cast all your anxiety on him because he cares for you. —1 PETER 5:6–7

"Do not judge, or you too will be judged." —MATTHEW 7:1

Also read:
PSALM 29:11

Before You Turn Out the Light

Change your thought patterns: Replace every negative with a positive by choosing to trust and thank Me.

May 10
MORNING

DO NOT RESIST OR RUN from the difficulties in your life. These problems are not random mistakes; they are hand-tailored blessings designed for your benefit and growth. Embrace all the circumstances that I allow in your life, trusting Me to bring good out of them. View problems as opportunities to rely more fully on Me.

When you start to feel stressed, let those feelings alert you to your need for Me. Thus, your needs become doorways to deep dependence on Me and increasing intimacy between us. Although self-sufficiency is acclaimed in the world, reliance on Me produces abundant living in My kingdom. Thank Me for the difficulties in your life since they provide protection from the idolatry of self-reliance.

JOHN 15:5; 2 CORINTHIANS 1:8–9;
EPHESIANS 5:20

May 10
EVENING

WHEN YOU ARE GOING THROUGH a dark time—a hard time—it's easy to project that darkness into the future. Because I am Sovereign God, I am able to *turn your darkness into Light.* Continue walking worshipfully with Me—a walk of faith.

> *You are my lamp, O Lord; the Lord turns my darkness into light.* —2 Samuel 22:29

> *We walk by faith, not by sight.* —2 Corinthians 5:7 NKJV

Also read:
Isaiah 61:1; Proverbs 4:18

Before You Turn Out the Light

Through eyes of faith, look ahead to brighter times. The first gleam of dawn is on the path before you.

May 11
MORNING

Thank Me for your problems. As soon as your mind gets snagged on a difficulty, bring it to Me with thanksgiving. Then ask Me to show you My way to handle the situation. The very act of thanking Me releases your mind from its negative focus. As you turn your attention to Me, the problem fades in significance and loses its power to trip you up. Together we can deal with the situation, either facing it head-on or putting it aside for later consideration.

Most of the situations that entangle your mind are not today's concerns; you have borrowed them from tomorrow. In this case, I lift the problem out of today and deposit it in the future, where it is veiled from your eyes. In its place I give you My Peace, which flows freely from My Presence.

Philippians 4:6; Psalm 25:4–5;
John 14:27

May 11
EVENING

Y̲OU ARE UTTERLY DEPENDENT ON ME for everything, including your next breath. When you thank Me during a difficult day, you are assuming the proper stance for a child of God. If you persevere in this thankfulness, resisting the temptation to grumble, you can find Joy and Peace in the midst of your struggles.

Give thanks in all circumstances, for this is God's will for you in Christ Jesus. —1 Thessalonians 5:18

Therefore, since we are receiving a kingdom that cannot be shaken, let us be thankful, and so worship God acceptably with reverance and awe. —Hebrews 12:28

Also read:
Acts 3:15; James 1:17

Before You Turn Out the Light

If you are struggling to be thankful, pause right now to remember who I am: the Author of your life and faith.

May 12
MORNING

Learn to relate to others through My Love rather than yours. Your human love is ever so limited, full of flaws and manipulation. My loving Presence, which always enfolds you, is available to bless others as well as you. Instead of trying harder to help people through your own paltry supplies, become aware of My unlimited supply, which is accessible to you continually. Let My Love envelop your outreach to other people.

Many of My precious children have fallen prey to burnout. A better description of their condition might be "drainout." Countless interactions with needy people have drained them, without their conscious awareness. You are among these weary ones, who are like wounded soldiers needing R & R. Take time to rest in the Love-Light of My Presence. I will gradually restore to you the energy that you have lost over the years. *Come to Me, all you who are weary and burdened, and you will find rest for your souls.*

PSALM 36:5; EXODUS 33:14;
MATTHEW 11:28–29

May 12
EVENING

Your relationship with Me is so saturated in grace that the two are forever inseparable. I want you to rest in the perfection of your salvation. My glorious grace makes you holy and blameless in My sight, so nothing you do or fail to do can ever separate you from My Love.

For by grace you have been saved through faith. —Ephesians 2:8 nkjv

For I am convinced that neither death nor life, neither angels nor demons, neither the present nor the future, nor any powers, neither height nor depth, nor anything else in all creation, will be able to separate us from the love of God that is in Christ Jesus our Lord. —Romans 8:38–39

Also read:
Isaiah 61:10; Ephesians 1:4–6

Before You Turn Out the Light

As you reflect on the events of today, call this truth to mind: It is impossible for you to become un-graced!

May 13
MORNING

Thank Me in the midst of the crucible. When things seem all wrong, look for growth opportunities. Especially look for areas where you need to let go, leaving your cares in My able hands. Do you trust Me to orchestrate your life events as I choose, or are you still trying to make things go according to your will? If you keep trying to carry out your intentions while I am leading you in another direction, you deify your desires.

Be on the lookout for what I am doing in your life. Worship Me by living close to Me, *thanking Me in all circumstances.*

1 Peter 5:6–7; Psalm 62:8;
1 Thessalonians 5:18

May 13
EVENING

YOU CAN *CONSIDER* something a joyful opportunity even when you are feeling quite joyless. You may need to ponder your circumstances at length before you can view them in a positive light, but as you look at your circumstances from My perspective, you come to understand that these multiple problems are *testing your faith*. As you cling to Me moment by moment, I enable you to persevere.

> *Consider it pure joy . . . whenever you face trials of many kinds, because you know that the testing of your faith develops perseverance.* —JAMES 1:2–3

> *No discipline seems pleasant at the time, but painful. Later on, however, it produces a harvest of righteousness and peace for those who have been trained by it.* —HEBREWS 12:11

Also read:
MATTHEW 19:26 NKJV

Before You Turn Out the Light

This is an opportunity to trump your roller-coaster feelings with faith in Me. Make the most of it.

May 14
MORNING

I AM A MIGHTY GOD. *Nothing is too difficult for Me.* I have chosen to use weak ones like you to accomplish My purposes. Your weakness is designed to open you up to My Power. Therefore, do not fear your limitations or measure the day's demands against your strength. What I require of you is to stay connected to Me, living in trusting dependence on My limitless resources. When you face unexpected demands, there is no need to panic. Remember that *I am with you.* Talk with Me, and listen while I talk you through each challenging situation.

I am not a careless God. When I allow difficulties to come into your life, I equip you fully to handle them. Relax in My Presence, trusting in My Strength.

LUKE 1:37; DEUTERONOMY 31:8;
2 CORINTHIANS 12:9

May 14
EVENT

YOUR TIME AND ENERGY permit you to do only a small percentage of the many possibilities that are beckoning you. The more you bring your thoughts and plans to Me—seeking My guidance—the more effectively I can show you the way forward. Since *all things hold together in Me*, your life holds together better when there is more of Me in it!

> *By [Christ] all things were created: things in heaven and on earth, visible and invisible, whether thrones or powers or rulers or authorities; all things were created by him and for him. He is before all things, and in him all things hold together.* —COLOSSIANS 1:16–17

> *Let the morning bring me word of your unfailing love, for I have put my trust in you. Show me the way I should go, for to you I lift up my soul.* —PSALM 143:8

Also read:
PSALM 32:8

Before You Turn Out the Light

Stay in communication with Me as you prepare for tomorrow. I will show you what is most important.

May 15
MORNING

SPENDING TIME alone with Me is essential for your well-being. It is not a luxury or an option; it is a necessity. Therefore, do not feel guilty about taking time to be with Me. Remember that Satan is *the accuser of believers.* He delights in heaping guilt feelings upon you, especially when you are enjoying My Presence. When you feel Satan's arrows of accusation, you are probably on the right track. Use your *shield of faith* to protect yourself from him. Talk with Me about what you are experiencing, and ask Me to show you the way forward. *Resist the devil, and he will flee from you. Come near to Me, and I will come near to you.*

REVELATION 12:10; EPHESIANS 6:16;
JAMES 4:7–8

May 15
EVENING

Do NOT FEEL GUILTY about taking time to seek My Face; you are simply responding to the tugs of divinity within you. My Love and forgiveness satisfy soul-hunger as nothing else can, so it is good that you yearn for more than this world can provide. I delight in your seeking heart.

Look to the LORD and his strength; seek his face always. —PSALM 105:4

Why spend money on what is not bread, and your labor on what does not satisfy? Listen, listen to me, and eat what is good, and your soul will delight in the richest of fare. —ISAIAH 55:2

Also read:
2 CORINTHIANS 4:4

Before You Turn Out the Light

Keep coming to Me with your emptiness and longings. I am the One who satisfies.

May 16
MORNING

I AM YOUR LORD! Seek Me as Friend and Lover of your soul, but remember that I am also King of kings—sovereign over all. You can make some plans as you gaze into the day that stretches out before you. But you need to hold those plans tentatively, anticipating that I may have other ideas. The most important thing to determine is what to do right now. Instead of scanning the horizon of your life, looking for things that need to be done, concentrate on the task before you and the One who never leaves your side. Let everything else fade into the background. This will unclutter your mind, allowing Me to occupy more and more of your consciousness.

Trust Me to show you what to do when you have finished what you are doing now. I will guide you step by step as you bend your will to Mine. Thus you stay close to Me on the *path of Peace*.

REVELATION 17:14; PROVERBS 19:21;
LUKE 1:79

May 16
EVENING

I AM GOD YOUR SAVIOR. I guide you according to *My truth*, and I teach you important lessons as you follow the path I've prepared for you. Your difficulties can even be blessings when they draw you into deeper dependence on Me.

Guide me in your truth and teach me, for you are God my Savior, and my hope is in you all day long. —PSALM 25:5

Count it all joy, my brothers, when you meet trials of various kinds. —JAMES 1:2 ESV

Also read:
PSALM 16:8–9, 11 NKJV

Before You Turn Out the Light

Hand your difficulties and trials to
Me, your God and Savior.

May 17
MORNING

As you sit quietly in My Presence, remember that I am a God of abundance. I will never run out of resources; My capacity to bless you is unlimited. You live in a world of supply and demand, where necessary things are often scarce. Even if you personally have enough, you see poverty in the world around you. It is impossible for you to comprehend the lavishness of My provisions: the fullness of My *glorious riches*.

Through spending time in My Presence, you gain glimpses of My overflowing vastness. These glimpses are tiny foretastes of what you will experience eternally in heaven. Even now you have access to as much of Me as you have faith to receive. Rejoice in My abundance—*living by faith, not by sight*.

PHILIPPIANS 4:19; PHILIPPIANS 3:20–21;
2 CORINTHIANS 5:7

May 17
EVENING

REJOICE THAT *MY SONG IS WITH YOU* throughout the night as I lovingly watch over you. A tender intimacy with Me can develop when you *remember Me on your bed—meditating on Me in the night watches.* Whether you are waking or sleeping, I am always present with you, for I am indeed *the God of your life*!

> *By day the LORD directs his love, at night his song is with me—a prayer to the God of my life.* —PSALM 42:8

> *When I remember You on my bed, I meditate on You in the night watches. Because You have been my help, therefore in the shadow of Your wings I will rejoice. My soul follows close behind You; Your right hand upholds me.* —PSALM 63:6–8 NKJV

Also read:
1 PETER 5:8–9

Before You Turn Out the Light

Pause to remember Me and My glorious works in your life.

May 18
MORNING

Come to Me with your plans held in abeyance. *Worship Me in spirit and in truth,* allowing My Glory to permeate your entire being. Trust Me enough to let Me guide you through this day, accomplishing My purposes in My timing. Subordinate your myriad plans to My Master Plan. I am sovereign over every aspect of your life!

The challenge continually before you is to trust Me and search for My way through each day. Do not blindly follow your habitual route, or you will miss what I have prepared for you. *As the heavens are higher than the earth, so are My ways higher than your ways and My thoughts than your thoughts.*

John 4:24; Isaiah 50:4;
Isaiah 55:8–9 NKJV

May 18
EVENTING

WORRY IS LARGELY A MATTER OF THINKING about things at the wrong time—for example, when you're lying in bed. I want you to discipline your mind to minimize worry and maximize worship. This will require much ongoing effort, but you'll find that it's a path to freedom.

> *Then Jesus said to his disciples: "Therefore I tell you, do not worry about your life, what you will eat; or about your body, what you will wear. Life is more than food, and the body more than clothes. Consider the ravens: They do not sow or reap, they have no storeroom or barn; yet God feeds them. And how much more valuable you are than birds! Who of you by worrying can add a single hour to his life? Since you cannot do this very little thing, why do you worry about the rest?"* —LUKE 12:22–26

> *Worship Him who made heaven and earth, the sea and springs of water.* —REVELATION 14:7 NKJV

Before You Turn Out the Light

Are you troubled by worry-thoughts? Tell yourself, "Not now!" and direct your thinking toward Me.

May 19
MORNING

I WANT YOU TO KNOW how safe and secure you are in My Presence. That is a fact, totally independent of your feelings. You are on your way to heaven; nothing can prevent you from reaching that destination. There you will see Me face to Face, and your Joy will be off the charts by any earthly standards. Even now, you are never separated from Me, though you must see Me through eyes of faith. I will walk with you till the end of time and onward into eternity.

Although My Presence is a guaranteed promise, that does not necessarily change your feelings. When you forget I am with you, you may experience loneliness or fear. It is through awareness of My Presence that Peace displaces negative feelings. Practice the discipline of walking consciously with Me through each day.

JOHN 10:28–29; 1 CORINTHIANS 13:12;
PSALM 29:11

May 19
EVENING

LET ME HELP YOU break free from fear of other people's disapproval: First, replace your fear of displeasing people with eagerness to please Me—the Lord of the universe. Second, develop deeper trust in Me. *My glorious riches* never run short, nor does My Love for you.

So we make it our goal to please him, whether we are at home in the body or away from it. —2 CORINTHIANS 5:9

And my God will meet all your needs according to his glorious riches in Christ Jesus. —PHILIPPIANS 4:19

Also read:
PROVERBS 29:25; PSALM 102:27

Before You Turn Out the Light

Make pleasing Me your highest priority—
and My favor will rest on you.

May 20
MORNING

WHEN YOUR SINS WEIGH HEAVILY upon you, come to Me. Confess your wrongdoing, which I know all about before you say a word. Stay in the Light of My Presence, receiving forgiveness, cleansing, and healing. Remember that I have clothed *you in My righteousness*, so nothing can separate you from Me. Whenever you stumble or fall, I am there to help you up.

Man's tendency is to hide from his sin, seeking refuge in the darkness. There he indulges in self-pity, denial, self-righteousness, blaming, and hatred. But *I am the Light of the world*, and My illumination decimates the darkness. Come close to Me and let My Light envelop you, driving out darkness and permeating you with Peace.

1 JOHN 1:7; ISAIAH 61:10;
JOHN 8:12

May 20

EVENING

There are hurting parts of you that I desire to heal; however, some of them have been with you so long that you consider them part of your identity. Only repeatedly exposing them to My healing Presence will bring you long-term freedom. When that happens, you will be released to experience Joy in much fuller measure.

> *Therefore, there is now no condemnation for those who are in Christ Jesus.* —Romans 8:1

> *The Lord has done great things for us, and we are filled with joy.* —Psalm 126:3

> *Also read:*
> Psalm 118:5

Before You Turn Out the Light

Let Me share the Joy of your healing and multiply it many times over.

May 21
MORNING

I, THE CREATOR OF THE UNIVERSE, am with you and for you. What more could you need? When you feel some lack, it is because you are not connecting with Me at a deep level. I offer abundant Life; your part is to trust Me, refusing to worry about anything.

It is not so much adverse events that make you anxious as it is your thoughts about those events. Your mind engages in efforts to take control of a situation, to bring about the result you desire. Your thoughts close in on the problem like ravenous wolves. Determined to make things go your way, you forget that I am in charge of your life. The only remedy is to switch your focus from the problem to My Presence. Stop all your striving, and watch to see what I will do. *I am the Lord!*

ROMANS 8:31–32; MICAH 7:7;

1 CORINTHIANS 12:3

May 21
EVENING

YOU ARE ACCUSTOMED TO WORRY-THOUGHTS roaming freely in your brain, so you must train yourself to bring all your cares into My Presence. Remember that you are never alone in your struggles: I am always aware of you and your circumstances. I can help you because *I have all authority in heaven and on earth.*

> *Let [God] have all your worries and cares, for he is always thinking about you and watching everything that concerns you.* —1 PETER 5:7 TLB

> *Jesus came and spoke to [the disciples], saying, "All authority has been given to Me in heaven and on earth."* —MATTHEW 28:18 NKJV

Also read:
MATTHEW 18:1–4

Before You Turn Out the Light

If your mind and heart have wandered today, give yourself grace—and return to Me now.

May 22
MORNING

WHEN THINGS DON'T GO AS YOU would like, accept the situation immediately. If you indulge in feelings of regret, they can easily spill over the line into resentment. Remember that I am sovereign over your circumstances, and *humble yourself under My mighty hand*. Rejoice in what I am doing in your life, even though it is beyond your understanding.

I am the Way, the Truth, and the Life. In Me you have everything you need, both for this life and for the life yet to come. Don't let the impact of the world shatter your thinking or draw you away from focusing on Me. The ultimate challenge is to keep fixing your eyes on Me, no matter what is going on around you. When I am central in your thinking, you are able to view circumstances from My perspective.

1 PETER 5:5–6; JOHN 14:6

May 22
EVENING

YOU NEED TO ACCEPT NOT ONLY YOURSELF but also the choices you have made. Fantasizing about having done things differently is a time-wasting trap. Take time to talk with Me and relax in My Presence—your perfectionist tendencies will dissolve as you soak in My transforming grace.

As a father has compassion on his children, so the Lord has compassion on those who fear him; for he knows how we are formed, he remembers that we are dust. —PSALM 103:13–14

In him we have redemption through his blood, the forgiveness of sins, in accordance with the riches of God's grace that he lavished on us with all wisdom and understanding. —EPHESIANS 1:7–8

Also read:
PSALM 119:76

Before You Turn Out the Light

Keep living close to Me. My infinite wisdom enables Me to weave even your errors into an intricate work that is good.

May 23
MORNING

APPROACH EACH NEW DAY with desire to find Me. Before you get out of bed, I have already been working to prepare the path that will get you through this day. There are hidden treasures strategically placed along the way. Some of the treasures are trials, designed to shake you free from earth-shackles. Others are blessings that reveal My Presence: sunshine, flowers, birds, friendships, answered prayer. I have not abandoned this sin-wracked world; I am still richly present in it.

Search for deep treasure as you go through this day. You will find Me all along the way.

PROVERBS 16:9 AMP; COLOSSIANS 2:2–3; ISAIAH 33:6

May 23
EVENING

I AM TENDERLY PRESENT WITH YOU each step of your journey. As you stay close to Me, I show you the way forward. Little by little, *I turn your darkness into Light.*

The LORD is my shepherd, I shall not be in want. . . . Even though I walk through the valley of the shadow of death, I will fear no evil, for you are with me; your rod and your staff, they comfort me. —PSALM 23:1, 4

You, O LORD, keep my lamp burning; my God turns my darkness into light. —PSALM 18:28

Also read:
JOHN 21:19 NKJV

Before You Turn Out the Light

Follow Me obediently through the dark
valleys and the confusion.

May 24
MORNING

BRING ME YOUR MIND for rest and renewal. Let Me infuse My Presence into your thoughts. As your mind stops racing, your body relaxes and you regain awareness of Me. This awareness is vital to your spiritual well-being; it is your lifeline, spiritually speaking.

There are actually more than four dimensions in this world where you live. In addition to the three dimensions of space and the one of time, there is the dimension of openness to My Presence. This dimension transcends the others, giving you glimpses of heaven while you still reside on earth. This was part of My original design for mankind. Adam and Eve used to walk with Me in the garden, before their expulsion from Eden. I want you to walk with Me in the garden of your heart, where I have taken up permanent residence.

GENESIS 3:8; PSALM 89:15;
PROVERBS 4:23

May 24
EVENING

THE PROMISE OF MY PRESENCE is for all time: No matter where you go or what circumstances you encounter, I *will* be with you. This is the basis of your courage and confidence. Though fear and discouragement may sometimes slink into your heart, this is not their rightful home; your heart is *My* dwelling place.

> *The LORD himself goes before you and will be with you; he will never leave you nor forsake you. Do not be afraid; do not be discouraged.* —DEUTERONOMY 31:8

> *I pray that out of his glorious riches he may strengthen you with power through his Spirit in your inner being, so that Christ may dwell in your hearts through faith.* —EPHESIANS 3:16–17

Also read:
1 JOHN 4:18 NASB

Before You Turn Out the Light

Ask My Spirit to cast out all fear, and let
My perfect Love renew your hope.

May 25
MORNING

THE WORLD IS TOO MUCH WITH YOU, My child. Your mind leaps from problem to problem to problem, tangling your thoughts in anxious knots. When you think like that, you leave Me out of your worldview and your mind becomes darkened. Though I yearn to help, I will not violate your freedom. I stand silently in the background of your mind, waiting for you to remember that I am with you.

When you turn from your problems to My Presence, your load is immediately lighter. Circumstances may not have changed, but we carry your burdens together. Your compulsion to "fix" everything gives way to deep, satisfying connection with Me. Together we can handle whatever this day brings.

ISAIAH 41:10; ZEPHANIAH 3:17;
PSALM 34:19

May 25

EVENING

Unless you deal with it properly, anxiety can be toxic—both to you and to others. When you *cast your anxiety on Me*, I remove it so far away that it cannot harm anyone. In fact, I delight in doing this very thing because I *care for you* so compassionately.

Cast all your anxiety on Him because
He cares for you. —1 Peter 5:7

Shout for joy, O heavens; rejoice, O earth; burst into song,
O mountains! For the Lord comforts his people and will
have compassion on his afflicted ones. —Isaiah 49:13

Also read:
Romans 8:9; Galatians 5:22–23 nkjv

Before You Turn Out the Light

Simply releasing your anxiety is not sufficient.
Treat it like a grenade, heaving it as hard as you can
away from yourself and toward My sure hands.

May 26
MORNING

In a world of unrelenting changes, I am the One who never changes. *I am the Alpha and the Omega, the First and the Last, the Beginning and the End.* Find in Me the stability for which you have yearned.

I created a beautifully ordered world: one that reflects My perfection. Now, however, the world is under the bondage of sin and evil. Every person on the planet faces gaping jaws of uncertainty. The only antidote to this poisonous threat is drawing closer to Me. In My Presence you can face uncertainty with perfect Peace.

> REVELATION 22:13; ROMANS 5:12;
> JOHN 16:33 AMP

May 26
EVENING

MAKE ME YOUR PRIMARY FOCUS. *Since I am the same yesterday, today, and forever,* I can be the fixed point that helps you stay on course as you make your way through this ever-changing world. As you keep redirecting your thoughts to Me, I show you the way forward—and *I give you My Peace.*

> *I lift up my eyes to the hills—where does my help come from? My help comes from the LORD, the Maker of heaven and earth. He will not let your foot slip—he who watches over you will not slumber.* —PSALM 121:1–3

> *Jesus Christ is the same yesterday, today, and forever.* —HEBREWS 13:8 NKJV

Also read:
JOHN 14:27 NKJV

Before You Turn Out the Light

Even now, fend off the distractions that are threatening to crowd Me out so that I can cover you in My Peace.

May 27
MORNING

Seek My Face at the beginning of your day. This practice enables you to "put Me on" and "wear Me" throughout the day. Most people put on clothes soon after arising from bed. Similarly, the sooner you "put Me on" by communicating with Me, the better prepared you are for whatever comes your way.

To "wear Me" is essentially to have My mind: to think My thoughts. Ask the Holy Spirit to control your thinking; be transformed by this renewal within you. Thus you are well-equipped to face whatever people and situations I bring your way. Clothing your mind in Me is your best preparation for each day. This discipline brings Joy and Peace to you and those around you.

PSALM 27:8 NKJV; ROMANS 13:14;
1 CORINTHIANS 2:16; COLOSSIANS 3:12

May 27
EVENING

THERE IS GREAT POWER IN MY NAME: Simply whispering "Jesus" can turn a hard day into a good one. When you pray My Name, you are actually calling upon My very Being. As you look to Me, *My Face shines upon you* in radiant approval—helping you feel secure.

> *Salvation is found in no one else, for there is no other name under heaven given to men by which we must be saved.* —ACTS 4:12

> *The Lord make His face to shine upon and enlighten you and be gracious (kind, merciful, and giving favor) to you; the Lord lift up His [approving] countenance upon you and give you peace (tranquility of heart and life continually).* —NUMBERS 6:25–26 AMP

Also read:
JAMES 4:8; ACTS 2:21

Before You Turn Out the Light

Did you remember to call on My Name today? Will you in this moment? I joyfully respond every time you do.

May 28
MORNING

LET ME ANOINT YOU with My Presence. *I am King of kings and Lord of lords, dwelling in unapproachable Light. When you draw near to Me, I respond by coming closer to you.* As My Presence envelops you, you may feel overwhelmed by My Power and Glory. This is a form of worship: sensing your smallness in comparison to My Greatness.

Man has tended to make himself the measure of all things. But man's measure is too tiny to comprehend My majestic vastness. That is why most people do not see Me at all, even though *they live and move and have their being in Me.*

Enjoy the radiant beauty of My Presence. Declare My glorious Being to the world!

1 TIMOTHY 6:15–16; JAMES 4:8;
ACTS 17:28; PSALM 145:3–6

May 28
EVENING

This world is increasingly dark, but the Light of My Presence is as bright as ever. In fact, My Glory shines more vividly against the dark backdrop of evil. When Christlike goodness collides with worldly vileness, be on the lookout for miracles!

> *Blessed are those who have learned to acclaim you, who walk in the light of your presence, O Lord. They rejoice in your name all day long; they exult in your righteousness.* —Psalm 89:15–16

> *Therefore God exalted him to the highest place and gave him the name that is above every name, that at the name of Jesus every knee should bow, in heaven and on earth and under the earth, and every tongue confess that Jesus Christ is Lord, to the glory of God the Father.* —Philippians 2:9–11

Also read:
Isaiah 61:10 nkjv

Before You Turn Out the Light

Use My Name as a prayer, a praise, a protection. It never loses its power.

May 29
MORNING

I AM WITH YOU, watching over you constantly. I am Immanuel (*God with you*); My Presence enfolds you in radiant Love. Nothing, including the brightest blessings and the darkest trials, can separate you from Me. Some of My children find Me more readily during dark times, when difficulties force them to depend on Me. Others feel closer to Me when their lives are filled with good things. They respond with thanksgiving and praise, thus opening wide the door to My Presence.

I know precisely what you need to draw nearer to Me. Go through each day looking for what I have prepared for you. Accept every event as My hand-tailored provision for your needs. When you view your life this way, the most reasonable response is to be thankful. Do not reject any of My gifts; find Me in every situation.

MATTHEW 1:23; PSALM 34:5;
COLOSSIANS 2:6–7

May 29
EVENING

REMIND YOURSELF FREQUENTLY that I live inside you and I am mighty! Let your awareness of My indwelling Presence drive out discouragement and fill you *with great Joy*. As My Life flows into yours, you are strengthened with divine might.

> *[The Lord] said to me, My grace (My favor and lovingkindness and mercy) is enough for you [sufficient against any danger and enables you to bear the trouble manfully]; for My strength and power are made perfect (fulfilled and completed) and show themselves most effective in [your] weakness. Therefore, I will all the more gladly glory in my weaknesses and infirmities, that the strength and power of Christ (the Messiah) may rest (yes, may pitch a tent over and dwell) upon me!* —2 CORINTHIANS 12:9 AMP

Also read:
ZEPHANIAH 3:17 NKJV; JUDE V. 24

Before You Turn Out the Light

Ponder what it means to have My Power
dwelling inside you—and be glad!

May 30
MORNING

TIME WITH ME cannot be rushed. When you are in a hurry, your mind flitters back and forth between Me and the tasks ahead of you. Push back the demands pressing in on you; create a safe space around you, a haven in which you can rest with Me. I also desire this time of focused attention, and I use it to bless you, strengthening and equipping you for the day ahead. Thus, spending time with Me is a wise investment.

Bring Me the sacrifice of your precious time. This creates sacred space around you—space permeated with My Presence and My Peace.

PSALM 119:27; 2 CHRONICLES 16:9;
HEBREWS 13:15 NKJV

May 30
EVENING

No matter how passionately in love a bride and groom may be, their vows last only until one of them dies. My commitment to you, however, is absolutely unlimited. When you asked Me to be your Savior, I wed you for eternity. *Neither death nor life, nor anything else in all creation can separate you from My Love!*

> *For I am convinced that neither death nor life, neither angels nor demons, neither the present nor the future, nor any powers, neither height nor depth, nor anything else in all creation, will be able to separate us from the love of God that is in Christ Jesus our Lord.* —ROMANS 8:38–39

Also read:
1 KINGS 19:12; HABAKKUK 3:17–19

Before You Turn Out the Light

Find your joy and assurance in My unwavering commitment to you.

May 31
MORNING

The Peace that I give you transcends your intellect. When most of your mental energy goes into efforts to figure things out, you are unable to receive this glorious gift. I look into your mind and see thoughts spinning round and round: going nowhere, accomplishing nothing. All the while, My Peace hovers over you, searching for a place to land.

Be still in My Presence, inviting Me to control your thoughts. Let My Light soak into your mind and heart until you are aglow with My very Being. This is the most effective way to receive My Peace.

2 Thessalonians 3:16; Zechariah 2:13; Job 22:21

May 31
EVENING

The more you manipulate and maneuver for control, the more anxious you become. Rather than striving for peace of mind through these means, abandon yourself to Me—My hand is the only thing you can grasp without damaging your soul. Let Me help you open your hands and receive all that I have for you.

> *"Therefore whoever humbles himself as this little child is the greatest in the kingdom of heaven."* —Matthew 18:4 NKJV

> *"For I am the Lord, your God, who takes hold of your right hand and says to you, Do not fear; I will help you."* —Isaiah 41:13

Also read:
1 Timothy 2:8; John 20:19

Before You Turn Out the Light

To receive My Peace, unclench your tightened fist,
and grasp My hand in childlike dependence.

June

"For I am the LORD, your God, who takes hold of your right hand and says to you, Do not fear; I will help you."

ISAIAH 41:13

June 1
MORNING

I AM INVOLVED in each moment of your life. I have carefully mapped out every inch of your journey through this day, even though much of it may feel haphazard. Because the world is in a fallen condition, things always seem to be unraveling around the edges. Expect to find trouble in this day. At the same time, trust that *My way is perfect*, even in the midst of such messy imperfection.

Stay conscious of Me as you go through this day, remembering that I never leave your side. Let the Holy Spirit guide you step by step, protecting you from unnecessary trials and equipping you to get through whatever must be endured. As you trudge through the sludge of this fallen world, keep your mind in heavenly places with Me. Thus the Light of My Presence shines on you, giving you Peace and Joy that circumstances cannot touch.

PSALM 18:30; ISAIAH 41:13;
PSALM 36:9

June 1
EVENING

I KNOW THE PLANS I HAVE FOR YOU, plans to prosper you and not to harm you, plans to give you hope and a future. This promise provides a feast of encouragement. As you come to the table of My delights, be sure to bring your fork of trust and your spoon of thankfulness, and take plenty of time to enjoy Me.

> *"I know the plans I have for you," declares the LORD, "plans to prosper you and not to harm you, plans to give you hope and a future."* —JEREMIAH 29:11

> *"Why spend money on what is not bread, and your labor on what does not satisfy? Listen, listen to me, and eat what is good, and your soul will delight in the richest of fare."* —ISAIAH 55:2

Also read:

1 PETER 5:8 NASB; DEUTERONOMY 29:29 NKJV

Before You Turn Out the Light

Set aside time right now to feast on Me. In the present is where you can encounter Me.

June 2

MORNING

RELAX IN MY HEALING, holy Presence. *Be still* while I transform your heart and mind. *Let go* of cares and worries so that you can receive My Peace. *Cease striving, and know that I am God.*

Do not be like Pharisees who multiplied regulations, creating their own form of "godliness." They got so wrapped up in their own rules that they lost sight of Me. Even today, man-made rules about how to live the Christian life enslave many people. Their focus is on their performance, rather than on Me.

It is through knowing Me intimately that you become like Me. This requires spending time alone with Me. *Let go, relax, be still, and know that I am God.*

PSALM 46:10 NASB; MATTHEW 23:13;
1 JOHN 3:2

June 2
EVENING

As you commune with Me face to Face, you are free to express all your concerns. Some worries will evaporate as soon as you look at them in the strong Light of My Presence; other concerns remain, but you feel less anxious about them. Demonstrate your trust by pouring out your heart to Me.

> *"Then you will call upon Me and go and pray to Me, and I will listen to you."* —Jeremiah 29:12 NKJV

> *Find rest, O my soul, in God alone; my hope comes from him. He alone is my rock and my salvation; he is my fortress, I will not be shaken. My salvation and my honor depend on God; he is my mighty rock, my refuge. Trust in him at all times, O people; pour out your hearts to him, for God is our refuge.* —Psalm 62:5–8

Also read:
Psalm 56:3; Psalm 46:1

Before You Turn Out the Light

Affirm that in Me alone, your ever-present Helper, is deliverance from worry and fear.

June 3
MORNING

I WANT TO BE CENTRAL in your entire being. When your focus is firmly on Me, My Peace displaces fears and worries. They will encircle you, seeking entrance, so you must stay alert. Let trust and thankfulness stand guard, turning back fear before it can gain a foothold. *There is no fear in My Love*, which shines on you continually. Sit quietly in My Love-Light while I bless you with radiant Peace. Turn your whole being to trusting and loving Me.

2 THESSALONIANS 3:16; 1 JOHN 4:18;
NUMBERS 6:25–26 NKJV

June 3
EVENING

Putting Me first sounds so simple and straightforward, but the world, the flesh, and the devil war against your efforts to do this. *Delight yourself in Me* first and foremost. As you *walk in the Light* of My Presence, I open up the path before you—and *give you the desires of your heart.*

> *Delight yourself in the Lord and he will give you the desires of your heart.* —Psalm 37:4

> *If we walk in the light as He is in the light, we have fellowship with one another, and the blood of Jesus Christ His Son cleanses us from all sin.* —1 John 1:7 NKJV

Also read:
REVELATION 2:4 NKJV

Before You Turn Out the Light

Put Me first and let Me direct your steps.

June 4
MORNING

WELCOME CHALLENGING TIMES as opportunities to trust Me. You have Me beside you and My Spirit within you, so no set of circumstances is too much for you to handle. When the path before you is dotted with difficulties, beware of measuring your strength against those challenges. That calculation is certain to riddle you with anxiety. Without Me, you wouldn't make it past the first hurdle!

The way to walk through demanding days is to grip My hand tightly and stay in close communication with Me. Let your thoughts and spoken words be richly flavored with trust and thankfulness. Regardless of the day's problems, *I can keep you in perfect Peace* as you stay close to Me.

JAMES 1:2; PHILIPPIANS 4:13;

ISAIAH 26:3

June 4
EVENING

Though your circumstances may indeed be painful and difficult, they are not worthless. Come to Me with a courageous heart, hoping in Me, and I will bless you in many ways. Moreover, I will multiply your small act of bravery: *I will strengthen your heart.*

> *Be of good courage, and He shall strengthen your heart, all you who hope in the Lord.* —Psalm 31:24 NKJV

> *See, the Sovereign Lord comes with power, and his arm rules for him. See, his reward is with him, and his recompense accompanies him. He tends his flock like a shepherd: he gathers the lambs in his arms and carries them close to his heart; he gently leads those that have young.* —Isaiah 40:10–11

Also read:
REVELATION 21:8

Before You Turn Out the Light

Muster the courage to say *yes* to your life, trusting that I am in control of tomorrow and that I am with you now.

June 5
MORINING

REMEMBER THAT YOU LIVE IN a fallen world: an abnormal world tainted by sin. Much frustration and failure result from your seeking perfection in this life. There is nothing perfect in this world except Me. That is why closeness to Me satisfies deep yearnings and fills you with Joy.

I have planted longing for perfection in every human heart. This is a good desire, which I alone can fulfill. But most people seek this fulfillment in other people and earthly pleasures or achievements. Thus they create idols, before which they bow down. *I will have no other gods before Me!* Make Me the deepest desire of your heart. Let Me fulfill your yearning for perfection.

ROMANS 8:22; EXODUS 20:3;
PSALM 37:4

June 5
EVENT ~~~~ EVENING

Your heart contains many effects of the Fall. However, your unsatisfied yearnings can awaken you to the radiant perfection awaiting you in heaven. So let the frustration of living in a fallen world remind you that you originated in a perfect place (Eden) and you're on the way to an inexpressibly glorious place—heaven!

> *He lifted me out of the slimy pit, out of the mud and mire; he set my feet on a rock and gave me a firm place to stand. He put a new song in my mouth, a hymn of praise to our God. Many will see and fear and put their trust in the Lord.* —PSALM 40:2–3

> *But our citizenship is in heaven. And we eagerly await a Savior from there, the Lord Jesus Christ, who, by the power that enables him to bring everything under his control, will transform our lowly bodies so that they will be like his glorious body.* —PHILIPPIANS 3:20–21

Also read:

GENESIS 2:8

Before You Turn Out the Light

Search for Me first and foremost—I placed the longing for perfection in your heart so that you would.

June 6
MORNING

Seek My Face, and you will find fulfillment of your deepest longings. My world is filled with beautiful things; they are meant to be pointers to Me, reminders of My abiding Presence. The earth still declares My Glory to those who have eyes that see and ears that hear.

You had a darkened mind before you sought Me wholeheartedly. I chose to pour My Light into you so that you can be a beacon to others. There is no room for pride in this position. Your part is to reflect *My* Glory. I am the Lord!

PSALM 105:4; PSALM 19:1–2;
ISAIAH 60:2

June 6
EVENING

WHENEVER YOU ARE TEMPTED TO GRUMBLE, come to Me and talk it out. As you open up to Me, I will put My thoughts in your mind and My song in your heart. Your communion with Me will bless you in another way also: You will find in My Presence irrepressible Joy.

> *You have made known to me the paths of life; you will fill me with joy in your presence.* —ACTS 2:28

> *He put a new song in my mouth, a hymn of praise to our God. Many will see and fear and put their trust in the LORD.* —PSALM 40:3

Also read:
2 CORINTHIANS 9:15; NUMBERS 6:25

Before You Turn Out the Light

Don't wait until you're already discouraged to bring Me your concerns. Open up to Me as soon as you realize a need.

June 7
MORNING

I AM ALL AROUND YOU, like a cocoon of Light. My Presence with you is a promise, independent of your awareness of Me. Many things can block this awareness, but the major culprit is worry. My children tend to accept worry as an inescapable fact of life. However, worry is a form of unbelief; it is anathema to Me.

Who is in charge of your life? If it is you, then you have good reason to worry. But since I am in charge, worry is both unnecessary and counterproductive. When you start to feel anxious about something, relinquish the situation to Me. Back off a bit, redirecting your focus to Me. I will either take care of the problem Myself or show you how to handle it. In this world you will have problems, but you need not lose sight of Me.

LUKE 12:22–31; JOHN 16:33

June 7
EVENING

I AM TRAINING YOU TO DEPEND ON ME—*your Strength*. As you look to Me, *I make your feet like the feet of a deer*—I lighten your load so much that you hardly notice the jagged rocks beneath your feet or the steepness of your ascent. Before you know it, you are on the high places—with Me!

> *The Sovereign LORD is my strength; he makes my feet like the feet of a deer, he enables me to go on the heights.* —HABAKKUK 3:19

> *Though youths grow weary and tired, and vigorous young men stumble badly, yet those who wait for the LORD will gain new strength; they will mount up with wings like eagles, they will run and not get tired, they will walk and not become weary.* —ISAIAH 40:30–31 NASB

Also read:
PSALM 37:5 NKJV

Before You Turn Out the Light

Commit your way to Me. I enable you to go on the heights.

June 8
MORNING

I WANT YOU TO BE ALL MINE, filled with the Light of My Presence. I gave everything for you by living as a man, then dying for your sins and living again. Hold back nothing from Me. Bring your most secret thoughts into the Light of My Love. Anything you bring to Me I transform and cleanse from darkness. I know everything about you, far more than you know of yourself. But I restrain My yearning to "fix" you, waiting instead for you to come to Me for help. Imagine the divine restraint this requires, for *I have all Power in heaven and on earth.*

Seek My Face with a teachable spirit. Come into My Presence with thanksgiving, desiring to be transformed.

JOHN 12:46 NKJV; PSALM 90:8;
MATTHEW 28:18; PSALM 100:4

June 8
EVENING

BECAUSE YOUR MIND IS IN A FALLEN CONDITION, it *will* sometimes wander across the timeline into tomorrow's trouble. As soon as you realize you're worrying about tomorrow, take action: Simply leave those thoughts where they are (in the unreality of the future), and come quickly back to the present. I am always near.

> *"Therefore do not worry about tomorrow, for tomorrow will worry about itself. Each day has enough trouble of its own."* —MATTHEW 6:34

> *Therefore, holy brothers, who share in the heavenly calling, fix your thoughts on Jesus, the apostle and high priest whom we confess.* —HEBREWS 3:1

Also read:
EPHESIANS 2:4–5; PSALM 43:4

Before You Turn Out the Light

Forgo your worries about tomorrow. My Presence lovingly awaits your attention.

June 9
MORNING

*S*EEK TO LIVE IN MY LOVE, which *covers a multitude of sins*: both yours and others'. Wear My Love like a cloak of Light, covering you from head to toe. Have no fear, for *perfect Love decimates fear*. Look at other people through lenses of Love; see them from My perspective. This is how you walk in the Light, and it pleases Me.

I want My body of believers to be radiant with the Light of My Presence. How I grieve when pockets of darkness increasingly dim the Love-Light. Return to Me, your *First Love*! Gaze at Me in the splendor of holiness, and My Love will once again envelop you in Light.

1 PETER 4:8; 1 JOHN 4:18;
REVELATION 2:4

June 9
EVENING

When you trusted Me as Savior, I united Myself to you in eternal matrimony. Many things threaten to rip apart this holy bond—principalities and powers, controlling people, dire circumstances—but nothing can succeed, not even death. *My banner over you is Love.*

> *For I am persuaded that neither death nor life, nor angels nor principalities nor powers, nor things present nor things to come, nor height nor depth, nor any other created thing, shall be able to separate us from the love of God which is in Christ Jesus our Lord.* —Romans 8:38–39 nkjv

> *He has taken me to the banquet hall, and his banner over me is love.* —Song of Songs 2:4

Also read:
Psalm 145:18; Colossians 2:9

Before You Turn Out the Light

I am nearer than a whispered prayer. Reach out for Me.

June 10
MORNING

Rest in Me, My child. Give your mind a break from planning and trying to anticipate what will happen. *Pray continually*, asking My Spirit to take charge of the details of this day. Remember that you are on a journey with Me. When you try to peer into the future and plan for every possibility, you ignore your constant Companion, who sustains you moment by moment. As you gaze anxiously into the distance, you don't even feel the strong grip of My hand holding yours. How foolish you are, My child!

Remembrance of Me is a daily discipline. Never lose sight of My Presence with you. This will keep you resting in Me all day, every day.

1 Thessalonians 5:17; Psalm 139:9–10 nkjv; Psalm 62:5

June 10
EVENING

I WANT YOU TO LEARN TO RELAX more in My sovereignty, receiving each day as a good gift from Me—no matter what it contains. Accept the limitations of being a finite person, and keep turning toward Me. Awareness of My Face shining upon you can instill Joy into the most difficult day.

> *"Cease striving and know that I am God; I will be exalted among the nations, I will be exalted in the earth."* —PSALM 46:10 NASB

> *The LORD make His face shine upon you, and be gracious to you.* —NUMBERS 6:25 NKJV

Also read:
1 PETER 5:8 NASB; EPHESIANS 6:16

Before You Turn Out the Light

Relax in the truth of who you really are:
My beloved in whom I delight.

June 11
MORNING

Trust Me and don't be afraid, for I am your Strength and Song. Do not let fear dissipate your energy. Instead, invest your energy in trusting Me and singing My Song. The battle for control of your mind is fierce, and years of worry have made you vulnerable to the enemy. Therefore, you need to be vigilant in guarding your thoughts. Do not despise this weakness in yourself since I am using it to draw you closer to Me. Your constant need for Me creates an intimacy that is well worth all the effort. You are not alone in this struggle for your mind. My Spirit living within you is ever ready to help in this striving. Ask Him to *control your mind*; He will bless you with *Life and Peace*.

ISAIAH 12:2; ROMANS 8:9; ROMANS 8:6

June 11
EVENTING

ONE OF MY MOST CHALLENGING TASKS is renovating your mind, and My Spirit is always at work on this project: He prompts you gently and convicts you cleanly, showing you where you need to make changes and helping you develop new attitudes. Thus you grow not only closer to Me but also more like Me. This is a foretaste of what is to come when I am fully revealed: *You will be like Me, for you will see Me as I am.*

And do not be conformed to this world, but be transformed by the renewing of your mind. —ROMANS 12:2 NKJV

Beloved, now we are children of God; and it has not yet been revealed what we shall be, but we know that when He is revealed, we shall be like Him, for we shall see Him as He is. —1 JOHN 3:2 NKJV

Also read:
2 CORINTHIANS 3:17

Before You Turn Out the Light

The more you give up your worldly entanglements, the more you resemble Me. Diligently discern—and act on—what you need to change.

June 12
MORNING

LET ME HELP YOU get through this day. There are many possible paths to travel between your getting up in the morning and your lying down at night. Stay alert to the many choice-points along the way, being continually aware of My Presence. You will get through this day one way or the other. One way is to moan and groan, stumbling along with shuffling feet. This will get you to the end of the day eventually, but there is a better way. You can choose to walk with Me along the path of Peace, leaning on Me as much as you need. There will still be difficulties along the way, but you can face them confidently in My strength. Thank Me for each problem you encounter, and watch to see how I transform trials into blessings.

1 CORINTHIANS 10:10; LUKE 1:79;

2 SAMUEL 22:29–30

June 12
EVENING

The world abounds with negative things to think about, but remember: You can *choose* the subject of your thoughts. Cry out to Me and I will help you. Turn toward Me, letting My Light shine upon you.

> *This poor man cried out, and the L*ORD *heard him, and saved him out of all his troubles. The angel of the L*ORD *encamps all around those who fear Him, and delivers them.* —PSALM 34:6–7 NKJV

> *"I have told you these things, so that in me you may have peace. In this world you will have trouble. But take heart! I have overcome the world."* —JOHN 16:33

Also read:
HEBREWS 12:3 NKJV

Before You Turn Out the Light

Which negative things are shouting for your attention? Seek Me and My goodness instead.

June 13

MORNING

I AM CREATING something new in you: a bubbling spring of Joy that spills over into others' lives. Do not mistake this Joy for your own or try to take credit for it in any way. Instead, watch in delight as My Spirit flows through you to bless others. Let yourself become a reservoir of the Spirit's fruit.

Your part is to live close to Me, open to all that I am doing in you. Don't try to control the streaming of My Spirit through you. Just keep focusing on Me as we walk through this day together. Enjoy My Presence, which permeates you with *Love, Joy, and Peace.*

JOHN 3:8; PROVERBS 4:11–12;
GALATIANS 5:22

June 13
EVENING

The hope I offer is absolutely certain even though it refers to things not yet fully realized. It is utterly secure because I obtained it through My finished work on the cross. This hope is the foundation of the Joy and Peace you find in Me.

> *May the God of hope fill you with all joy and peace as you trust in him, so that you may overflow with hope by the power of the Holy Spirit.* —Romans 15:13

> *"In My Father's house are many mansions; if it were not so, I would have told you. I go to prepare a place for you. And if I go and prepare a place for you, I will come again and receive you to Myself; that where I am, there you may be also."* —John 14:2–3 NKJV

Also read:
Nehemiah 8:10 NKJV

Before You Turn Out the Light

Let me fill you with My Joy and Peace as
you await the hope of heaven.

June 14
MORNING

I HAVE LOVED YOU with an everlasting Love. Before time began, I knew you. For years you swam around in a sea of meaninglessness, searching for Love, hoping for hope. All that time I was pursuing you, aching to embrace you in My compassionate arms.

When time was right, I revealed Myself to you. I lifted you out of that sea of despair and set you down on a firm foundation. Sometimes you felt naked—exposed to the revealing Light of My Presence. I wrapped an ermine robe around you: *My robe of righteousness.* I sang you a Love song, whose beginning and end are veiled in eternity. I infused meaning into your mind and harmony into your heart. Join Me in singing My song. Together we will draw others *out of darkness into My marvelous Light.*

JEREMIAH 31:3; ISAIAH 61:10;
1 PETER 2:9 NKJV

June 14
EVENING

MY LOVE FOR YOU IS UNQUENCHABLE—it is even stronger than the bond between a mother and her baby. I want you to *really come to know—practically, through experience—My Love, which far surpasses mere knowledge.* Thus you can experience My Love in full measure.

> *[That you may really come] to know [practically, through experience for yourselves] the love of Christ, which far surpasses mere knowledge [without experience]; that you may be filled [through all your being] unto all the fullness of God [may have the richest measure of the divine Presence, and become a body wholly filled and flooded with God Himself]!* —EPHESIANS 3:19 AMP

Also read:
SONG OF SONGS 8:7 NKJV; HOSEA 2:19; ISAIAH 49:15–16

Before You Turn Out the Light

If you will reflect on the many times you've experienced My Love, you'll never have to wonder what I think of you.

June 15

MORNING

WHEN YOU APPROACH ME in stillness and in trust, you are strengthened. You need a buffer zone of silence around you in order to *focus on things that are unseen*. Since I am invisible, you must not let your senses dominate your thinking. The curse of this age is overstimulation of the senses, which blocks out awareness of the unseen world.

The tangible world still reflects My Glory to those who have eyes that see and ears that hear. Spending time alone with Me is the best way to develop seeing eyes and hearing ears. The goal is to be aware of unseen things even as you live out your life in the visible world.

2 CORINTHIANS 4:18; ISAIAH 6:3;
PSALM 119:18 NKJV; PSALM 130:5

June 15
EVENIN G

KNOWING ME IS SO MUCH MORE than an activity of the mind. Instead of running after other gods when you feel needy, concentrate on coming nearer to Me. No matter what is happening, trusting Me and drawing close to Me are excellent strategies for living well.

> *I pray that out of his glorious riches he may strengthen you with power through his Spirit in your inner being, so that Christ may dwell in your hearts through faith. And I pray that you, being rooted and established in love, may have power, together with all the saints, to grasp how wide and long and high and deep is the love of Christ, and to know this love that surpasses knowledge—that you may be filled to the measure of all the fullness of God.* —EPHESIANS 3:16–19

> *"Never will I leave you; never will I forsake you."* —HEBREWS 13:5

Also read:
PSALM 16:8

Before You Turn Out the Light

Are you feeling lonely? Continue to live and communicate as if I am with you—because I am!

June 16

MORNING

STAY ON THE HIGH ROAD WITH ME. Many voices clamor for your attention, trying to divert you to another path. But I have called you to walk ever so closely with Me, soaking in My Presence, living in My Peace. This is My unique design for you, planned before the world began.

I have called each of My children to a different path, distinctly designed for that one. Do not let anyone convince you that his path is the only right way. And be careful not to extol your path as superior to another's way. What I require of you is *to act justly, to love mercy, and to walk humbly with Me*—wherever I lead.

JOHN 14:27 NKJV; EPHESIANS 2:10;
MICAH 6:8

June 16
EVENING

MANY PEOPLE FEAR THE FUTURE, but ultimately yours is glorious—beyond anything you can imagine! If you persist in trusting Me no matter what, you can anticipate, via faith, the blessing that is ahead of you and start praising Me even in the dark. As you keep looking to Me, My heavenly Light shines more brightly in your heart.

> *"For I know the plans I have for you," declares the LORD, "plans to prosper you and not to harm you, plans to give you hope and a future."* —JEREMIAH 29:11

> *It is the God who commanded light to shine out of darkness, who has shone in our hearts to give the light of the knowledge of the glory of God in the face of Jesus Christ.* —2 CORINTHIANS 4:6 NKJV

Also read:
PSALM 42:5 NASB

Before You Turn Out the Light

Remind yourself how realistic it is to hope in Me,
for I have reserved a place in heaven for you.

June 17
MORNING

LEARN TO LAUGH at yourself more freely. Don't take yourself or your circumstances so seriously. Relax and know that I am *God with you*. When you desire My will above all else, life becomes much less threatening. Stop trying to monitor My responsibilities—things that are beyond your control. Find freedom by accepting the boundaries of your domain.

Laughter lightens your load and lifts your heart into heavenly places. Your laughter rises to heaven and blends with angelic melodies of praise. Just as parents delight in the laughter of their children, so I delight in hearing My children laugh. I rejoice when you trust Me enough to enjoy your life lightheartedly.

Do not miss the Joy of My Presence by carrying the weight of the world on your shoulders. Rather, *take My yoke upon you and learn from Me. My yoke is comfortable and pleasant; My burden is light and easily borne.*

PROVERBS 17:22; PROVERBS 31:25;
MATTHEW 1:23; MATTHEW 11:29–30 AMP

June 17
EVENING

I AM PLEASED when you ask My Spirit to think, live, and love through you. This is the collaborative way of living I had in mind when I created mankind. The more you collaborate with the Spirit, the freer you become—free to live exuberantly, to love extravagantly, to know Me in ever-increasing intimacy!

> *Do not conform any longer to the pattern of this world, but be transformed by the renewing of your mind. Then you will be able to test and approve what God's will is— his good, pleasing and perfect will.* —ROMANS 12:2

> *In the same way, the Spirit helps us in our weakness. We do not know what we ought to pray for, but the Spirit himself intercedes for us with groans that words cannot express. And he who searches our hearts knows the mind of the Spirit, because the Spirit intercedes for the saints in accordance with God's will.* —ROMANS 8:26–27

Also read:
ROMANS 8:6

Before You Turn Out the Light

Invite My Spirit to help you yield to My will and make you who I designed you to be.

June 18
MORNING

You are My beloved child. *I chose you before the foundation of the world*, to walk with Me along paths designed uniquely for you. Concentrate on keeping in step with Me instead of trying to anticipate My plans for you. If you trust that My plans are *to prosper you and not to harm you*, you can relax and enjoy the present moment.

Your hope and your future are rooted in heaven, where eternal ecstasy awaits you. Nothing can rob you of your iheritance of unimaginable riches and well-being. Sometimes I grant you glimpses of your glorious future, to encourage you and spur you on. But your main focus should be staying close to Me. I set the pace in keeping with your needs and My purposes.

EPHESIANS 1:4 NASB; PROVERBS 16:9;
JEREMIAH 29:11; EPHESIANS 1:13–14

June 18
EVENING

WHEN YOU OR OTHERS GAZE INTO THE FUTURE, making predictions, you are simply exercising your imaginations. I alone have access to what is "not yet." Recognizing the futility of future-gazing can help set you free to live more fully in the present.

Since no man knows the future, who can tell him what is to come? —ECCLESIASTES 8:7

"I am the Alpha and the Omega," says the Lord God, "who is, and who was, and who is to come, the Almighty." —REVELATION 1:8

Also read:
PSALM 32:10

Before You Turn Out the Light

Since I hold the future far beyond your reach, plant your mind in the present—and remain in My Presence.

June 19

MORNING

I AM THE FIRM FOUNDATION on which you can dance and sing and celebrate My Presence. This is My high and holy calling for you; receive it as a precious gift. *Glorifying and enjoying Me* is a higher priority than maintaining a tidy, structured life. Give up your striving to keep everything under control—an impossible task and a waste of precious energy.

My guidance for each of My children is unique. That's why listening to Me is so vital for your well-being. Let me prepare you for the day that awaits you and point you in the right direction. I am with you continually, so don't be intimidated by fear. Though it stalks you, it cannot harm you, as long as you cling to My hand. Keep your eyes on Me, enjoying Peace in My Presence.

PSALM 5:11; EPHESIANS 3:20–21;
JUDE VV. 24–25; JOSHUA 1:5

June 19
EVENING

I DELIGHT IN YOUR HEARTFELT DESIRE to "kick up your heels" in celebration of who I am. Those who walk in the Light of My Presence can rejoice in Me all day long, exulting in My righteousness. Glorify Me by living joyously in My energizing Light.

"I have brought you glory on earth by completing the work you gave me to do. And now, Father, glorify me in your presence with the glory I had with you before the world began." —JOHN 17:4–5

Blessed are those who have learned to acclaim you, who walk in the light of your presence, O LORD. They rejoice in your name all day long; they exult in your righteousness. —PSALM 89:15–16

Also read:
PSALM 139:1–2

Before You Turn Out the Light

Ponder how you can more consistently live in the Light of My Presence, celebrating your relationship with Me.

June 20
MORNING

I SPEAK TO YOU CONTINUALLY. My nature is to communicate, though not always in words. I fling glorious sunsets across the sky, day after day after day. I speak in the faces and voices of loved ones. I caress you with a gentle breeze that refreshes and delights you. I speak softly in the depths of your spirit, where I have taken up residence.

You can find Me in each moment, when you have eyes that see and ears that hear. Ask My Spirit to sharpen your spiritual eyesight and hearing. I rejoice each time you discover My Presence. Practice looking and listening for Me during quiet intervals. Gradually you will find Me in more and more of your moments. *You will seek Me and find Me, when you seek Me above all else.*

PSALM 8:1–4; PSALM 19:1–2;
1 CORINTHIANS 6:19; JEREMIAH 29:13

June 20
EVENIN G

IUNDERSTAND THAT MANY THOUGHTS come and go unbidden, but you can control your thinking more than you may realize. Train your mind to turn toward Me frequently. Remembrance of who I am can brighten even your darkest times, blessing you with Joy.

All this took place to fulfill what the Lord had said through the prophet: "The virgin will be with child and will give birth to a son and they will call him Immanuel" —which means "God with us." —MATTHEW 1:22–23

"I tell you the truth," Jesus answered, "before Abraham was born, I am!" —JOHN 8:58

Also read:
PHILIPPIANS 4:8

Before You Turn Out the Light

Take charge of your thoughts by reminding
yourself of My Presence in the present.

June 21

MORNING

WAIT PATIENTLY WITH ME while I bless you. Don't rush into My Presence with time-consciousness gnawing at your mind. I dwell in timelessness: *I am, I was, I will always be.* For you, time is a protection; you're a frail creature who can handle only twenty-four-hour segments of life. Time can also be a tyrant, ticking away relentlessly in your mind. Learn to master time, or it will be your master.

Though you are a time-bound creature, seek to meet Me in timelessness. As you focus on My Presence, the demands of time and tasks will diminish. *I will bless you and keep you, making My Face shine upon you graciously, giving you Peace.*

MICAH 7:7; REVELATION 1:8;
ECCLESIASTES 3:1; NUMBERS 6:24–26

June 21
EVENING

WAITING IN ITSELF IS NOT A VIRTUE; the important thing is *how* you wait—in a resigned, impatient way—or *in hope*, keeping your focus on Me. When your overarching hope is *for Me*, you have every reason to be confident. *I am your Help and your Shield.*

> *We wait in hope for the Lord; he is our*
> *help and our shield.* —Psalm 33:20

But I am like an olive tree flourishing in the house of God; I trust in God's unfailing love for ever and ever. —Psalm 52:8

Also read:
Matthew 28:18–20 NKJV

Before You Turn Out the Light

Put your hope fully in Me. I have shielded you from many hardships, and I will continue to protect you.

June 22

MORNING

THANK ME for the very things that are troubling you. You are on the brink of rebellion, precariously close to shaking your fist in My Face. You are tempted to indulge in just a little complaining about My treatment of you. But once you step over that line, torrents of rage and self-pity can sweep you away. The best protection against this indulgence is thanksgiving. It is impossible to thank Me and curse Me at the same time.

Thanking Me for trials will feel awkward and contrived at first. But if you persist, your thankful words, prayed in faith, will eventually make a difference in your heart. Thankfulness awakens you to My Presence, which overshadows all your problems.

PSALM 116:17 NKJV;
PHILIPPIANS 4:4–6; PSALM 100:2 NKJV

June 22

EVENING

No matter what hardships the world may throw at you, you have—in Me—everything you need to persevere. Despair is a deep pit, and sometimes you totter around its edges, precariously close to falling in. Your only hope at such times is to *fix your eyes on Me*: I am always nearby, eager to help you change your focus time after time.

We are hard pressed on every side, but not crushed; perplexed, but not in despair; persecuted, but not abandoned; struck down, but not destroyed. —2 Corinthians 4:8–9

Let us fix our eyes on Jesus, the author and perfecter of our faith, who for the joy set before him endured the cross, scorning its shame, and sat down at the right hand of the throne of God. —Hebrews 12:2

Also read:
1 Peter 2:25 nasb; John 10:28

Before You Turn Out the Light

To keep from falling into the pit, you must change your focus: from your circumstances to My Presence. Look for Me!

June 23
MORNING

Let My Love stream through you, washing away fear and distrust. A trusting response includes Me in your thoughts as you consider strategies to deal with a situation. My continual Presence is a promise, guaranteeing that you never have to face anything alone. My children teethe on the truth that I am always with them, yet they stumble around in a stupor, unaware of My loving Presence all around them. How that grieves Me!

When you walk through a day in trusting dependence on Me, My aching heart is soothed. Gently bring your attention back to Me whenever it wanders away. I look for persistence—rather than perfection—in your walk with Me.

PSALM 52:8; DEUTERONOMY 31:6;
EPHESIANS 4:30

June 23
EVENING

I CHALLENGE YOU to place your hope fully in *Me*. No matter what is happening in your life now, your story has an amazingly happy ending. Remember that I am with you continually, and I Myself *am* your Hope!

> *We wait in hope for the LORD; he is our help and our shield. In him our hearts rejoice, for we trust in his holy name. May your unfailing love rest upon us, O LORD, even as we put our hope in you.* —PSALM 33:20–22

> *Paul, an apostle of Jesus Christ, by the commandment of God our Savior and the Lord Jesus Christ, our hope.* —1 TIMOTHY 1:1 NKJV

Also read:

Titus 1:2

Before You Turn Out the Light

Take time to affirm your hope and trust in Me.

June 24
MORNING

HOLD MY HAND—AND TRUST. So long as you are conscious of My Presence with you, all is well. It is virtually impossible to stumble while walking in the Light with Me. I designed you to enjoy Me above all else. You find the deepest fulfillment of your heart in Me alone.

Fearful, anxious thoughts melt away in the Light of My Presence. When you turn away from Me, you are vulnerable to the darkness that is always at work in the world. Don't be surprised by how easily you sin when you forget to cling to My hand. In the world, dependency is seen as immaturity. But in My kingdom, dependence on Me is a prime measure of maturity.

ISAIAH 41:10; EPHESIANS 5:8 NKJV;
PSALM 62:5–6

June 24
EVENING

RECOGNIZING YOUR NEEDINESS is only half the battle. The other half is to believe that I can—and will—supply all you need. Wait expectantly in My Presence, ready to receive My Peace in full measure.

> *Now may the Lord of peace himself give you peace at all times and in every way. The Lord be with all of you.* —2 THESSALONIANS 3:16

> *My God shall supply all your need according to His riches in glory by Christ Jesus.* —PHILIPPIANS 4:19 NKJV

Also read:
JOHN 14:27

Before You Turn Out the Light

Acknowledge to Me not only your need but also your desire. Then wait on Me.

June 25
MORNING

OPEN YOUR HANDS and your heart to receive this day as a precious gift from Me. I begin each day with a sunrise, announcing My radiant Presence. By the time you rise from your bed, I have already prepared the way before you. I eagerly await your first conscious thought. I rejoice when you glance My way.

Bring Me the gift of thanksgiving, which opens your heart to rich communion with Me. Because I am God, from whom all blessings flow, thankfulness is the best way to draw near Me. Sing praise songs to Me; tell of My wondrous works. Remember that *I take great delight in you; I rejoice over you with singing.*

PSALM 118:24; PSALM 95:1–2;
ZEPHANIAH 3:17

June 25
EVENING

Your difficulties do not signify lack of faith or lack of blessing—they are means to help you stay on the path I have chosen for you. Though the way before you may be steep and rocky, it is nonetheless the path of Life. It is where you encounter My luminous Presence, radiating Peace that transcends your limitations.

> *Though the fig tree does not bud and there are no grapes on the vines, though the olive crop fails and the fields produce no food, though there are no sheep in the pen and no cattle in the stalls, yet I will rejoice in the LORD, I will be joyful in God my Savior. The sovereign LORD is my strength; he makes my feet like the feet of a deer, he enables me to go on the heights.* —HABAKKUK 3:17–19

> *And the peace of God, which transcends all understanding, will guard your hearts and your minds in Christ Jesus.* —PHILIPPIANS 4:7

Also read:
JUDE vv. 24–25

Before You Turn Out the Light

Have no doubt: I am blessing you according to your needs and My unique design for you.

June 26
MORNING

STAY CALMLY CONSCIOUS OF ME today, no matter what. Remember that I go before you as well as with you into the day. Nothing takes Me by surprise. I will not allow circumstances to overwhelm you so long as you look to Me. I will help you cope with whatever the moment presents. Collaborating with Me brings *blessings that far outweigh all your troubles*. Awareness of My Presence contains Joy that can endure all eventualities.

PSALM 23:1–4 NKJV; 2 CORINTHIANS 4:16–17;
PSALM 28:7

June 26

EVENING

I UNDERSTAND HOW VULNERABLE YOU ARE to things that impact your senses. Because of this human tendency, My Word exhorts you to be alert and prayerful—fixing your eyes on Me, bringing every thought captive to Me. Bring Me your restless heart, and wait while I speak Peace into its depths—stilling the troubled waters of your soul.

> *Then He arose and rebuked the wind, and said to the sea, "Peace, be still!" And the wind ceased, and there was a great calm.* —MARK 4:39 NKJV

> *We demolish arguments and every pretension that sets itself up against the knowledge of God, and we take captive every thought to make it obedient to Christ.* —2 CORINTHIANS 10:5

Also read:
EPHESIANS 6:18; HEBREWS 12:2

Before You Turn Out the Light

Find a quiet place, away from the noise of the world, where you can listen in My Presence and hear My voice.

June 27
MORNING

Rest with Me a while. You have journeyed up a steep, rugged path in recent days. The way ahead is shrouded in uncertainty. Look neither behind you nor before you. Instead, focus your attention on Me, your constant Companion. Trust that I will equip you fully for whatever awaits you on your journey.

I designed time to be a protection for you. You couldn't bear to see all your life at once. Though I am unlimited by time, it is in the present moment that I meet you. Refresh yourself in My company, breathing deep draughts of My Presence. The highest level of trust is to enjoy Me moment by moment. *I am with you, watching over you wherever you go.*

MATTHEW 11:28 NKJV; PSALM 143:8; GENESIS 28:15

June 27
EVENTING

Y<small>OUR CURRENT SITUATION</small> may feel like a gigantic mistake to you—something you should have been able to prevent. I urge you not to indulge in obsessing about what you could have done differently, for that is an exercise in unreality: The past cannot be different from what has actually occurred. I want to help you make a new beginning instead, starting right where you are.

We are assured and know that [God being a partner in their labor] all things work together and are [fitting into a plan] for good to and for those who love God and are called according to [His] design and purpose. —R<small>OMANS</small> 8:28 <small>AMP</small>

Also read:
D<small>EUTERONOMY</small> 29:29; L<small>UKE</small> 1:37

Before You Turn Out the Light

Now is the place to begin anew, remembering
that I supply all the resources you need.

June 28
MORNING

Taste and see that I am good. This command contains an invitation to experience My living Presence. It also contains a promise. The more you experience Me, the more convinced you become of My goodness. This knowledge is essential to your faith-walk. When adversities strike, the human instinct is to doubt My goodness. My ways are mysterious, even to those who know Me intimately. *As the heavens are higher than the earth, so are My ways and thoughts higher than your ways and thoughts.* Do not try to fathom My ways. Instead, spend time enjoying Me and experiencing My goodness.

PSALM 34:8; ISAIAH 55:8–9;
PSALM 100:5 NKJV

June 28
EVENING

I CREATED YOU with a great capacity to enjoy beauty and goodness. Your soul resonates with these blessings, drawing strength from them. Look the right way—toward blessings, toward Me—and the Joy of My Presence will shine upon you.

> *Finally, brethren, whatever things are true, whatever things are noble, whatever things are just, whatever things are pure, whatever things are lovely, whatever things are of good report, if there is any virtue and if there is anything praiseworthy—meditate on these things.* —PHILIPPIANS 4:8 NKJV

> *The LORD make His face shine upon you, and be gracious to you.* —NUMBERS 6:25 NKJV

Also read:
JOHN 10:27; PSALM 16:11 ESV

Before You Turn Out the Light

Turn your sights toward what is true, noble, lovely, and right—and be encouraged.

June 29

MORNING

As you get out of bed in the morning, be aware of My Presence with you. You may not be thinking clearly yet, but I am. Your early morning thoughts tend to be anxious ones until you get connected with Me. Invite Me into your thoughts by whispering My Name. Suddenly your day brightens and feels more user-friendly. You cannot dread a day that is vibrant with My Presence.

You gain confidence through knowing that I am with you—that you face nothing alone. Anxiety stems from asking the wrong question: "If such and such happens, can I handle it?" The true question is not whether you can cope with whatever happens, but whether you and I together can handle anything that occurs. It is this you-and-I-together factor that gives you confidence to face the day cheerfully.

PSALM 5:3; PSALM 63:1 NKJV;

PHILIPPIANS 4:13

June 29
EVENING

No matter what is going on in your life at this time, your hope in Me is secure. *Be constant in prayer*—especially when you are struggling. As you stay in communication with Me, I help you to *be steadfast and patient in suffering*.

> *Rejoice and exult in hope; be steadfast and patient in suffering and tribulation; be constant in prayer.* —Romans 12:12 AMP

> *"I give [My followers] eternal life, and they shall never perish; neither shall anyone snatch them out of My hand."* —John 10:28 NKJV

Also read:
Titus 2:11, 13; Romans 8:6

Before You Turn Out the Light

Your prayers need not be pretty or proper.
Just bring your petitions to Me.

June 30

MORNING

I AM THE TRUTH: the One who came to *set you free*. As the Holy Spirit controls your mind and actions more fully, you become free in Me. You are increasingly released to become the one I created you to be. This is a work that I do in you as you yield to My Spirit. I can do My best handiwork when you sit in the stillness of My Presence, focusing your entire being on Me.

Let My thoughts burst freely upon your consciousness, stimulating abundant Life. *I am the Way and the Truth and the Life.* As you follow Me, I lead you along paths of newness: ways you have never imagined. Don't worry about what is on the road up ahead. I want you to find your security in knowing Me, the One who died to *set you free*.

JOHN 8:32; PHILIPPIANS 2:13;
JOHN 14:6

June 30
EVENING

YOU CAN ASK MY SPIRIT to help you find freedom from condemning feelings. Feelings of condemnation drain you of energy, leaving you vulnerable. As My Spirit fills you with Life, you are empowered to live abundantly—to the full.

> *Therefore, there is now no condemnation for those who are in Christ Jesus, because through Christ Jesus the law of the Spirit of life set me free from the law of sin and death.* —ROMANS 8:1–2

> *"The thief comes only to steal and kill and destroy; I have come that they may have life, and have it to the full."* —JOHN 10:10

Also read:
PSALM 42:8; JOHN 8:44

Before You Turn Out the Light

Acknowledge with your heart that I do not condemn you. Then look to Me for My heavenly smile of approval.

July

*Therefore, there is now no condemnation
for those who are in Christ Jesus.*

ROMANS 8:1

July 1
MORNING

I AM LIFE AND LIGHT IN ABUNDANCE. As you spend time "soaking" in My Presence, you are energized and lightened. Through communing with Me, you transfer your heavy burdens to My strong shoulders. By gazing at Me, you gain My perspective on your life. This time alone with Me is essential for unscrambling your thoughts and smoothing out the day before you.

Be willing to fight for this precious time with Me. Opposition comes in many forms: your own desire to linger in bed; the evil one's determination to distract you from Me; the pressure of family, friends, and your own inner critic to spend your time more productively. As you grow in your desire to please Me above all else, you gain strength to resist these opponents. *Delight yourself in Me, for I am the deepest Desire of your heart.*

PSALM 48:9; DEUTERONOMY 33:12;
PSALM 37:4

July 1
EVENING

DURING THE WEE HOURS OF THE NIGHT, your thoughts are often distorted—even catastrophic. Although you may feel as if you're enveloped in darkness, remember that *darkness and light are alike to Me.* I am with you, and My Love for you never fails.

> *Even the darkness is not dark to You, and the night is as bright as the day. Darkness and light are alike to You.* —PSALM 139:12 NASB

> *Let the morning bring me word of your unfailing love, for I have put my trust in you. Show me the way I should go, for to you I lift up my soul.* —PSALM 143:8

Also read:
2 CORINTHIANS 5:7 NKJV; HEBREWS 12:2

Before You Turn Out the Light

Seek the Light of My Presence in this dark night. You need My Light supremely more than you need the light of day.

July 2
MORNING

Let Me show you My way for you this day. I guide you continually so you can relax and enjoy My Presence in the present. Living well is both a discipline and an art. Concentrate on staying close to Me, the divine Artist. Discipline your thoughts to trust Me as I work My ways in your life. Pray about everything; then leave outcomes up to Me. Do not fear My will, for through it I accomplish what is best for you. Take a deep breath and dive into the depths of absolute trust in Me. *Underneath are the everlasting arms!*

PSALM 5:2–3; ISAIAH 26:4 AMP;
DEUTERONOMY 33:27

July 2
EVENING

YOU TEND TO RELY HEAVILY on your thinking and planning, as if that is where your security lies. The essence of wisdom is to trust in Me more than in yourself or other people. I stand ready to *guide you with My counsel*, so bring all your concerns to Me.

> *Yet I am always with you; you hold me by my right hand. You guide me with your counsel, and afterward you will take me into glory. Whom have I in heaven but you? And earth has nothing I desire besides you. My flesh and my heart may fail, but God is the strength of my heart and my portion forever.* —PSALM 73:23–26

> *He who trusts in himself is a fool, but he who walks in wisdom is kept safe.* —PROVERBS 28:26

Also read:
PROVERBS 18:10 NKJV

Before You Turn Out the Light

Be guided by My wisdom rather than your own; I am the One who keeps you safe.

July 3
MORNING

My children make a pastime of judging one another—and themselves. But I am the only capable Judge, and I have acquitted you through My own blood. Your acquittal came at the price of My unparalleled sacrifice. That is why I am highly offended when I hear My children judge one another or indulge in self-hatred.

If you live close to Me and absorb My Word, the Holy Spirit will guide and correct you as needed. There is *no condemnation* for those who belong to Me.

> Luke 6:37; 2 Timothy 4:8;
> Titus 3:5; Romans 8:1

July 3
EVENING

Evaluating your worth on the basis of how you look, to yourself or to others, is always a trap—it's as if you are sifting sand, looking only at the grains of sand filtering through the sieve, ignoring the gold nuggets that remain. My approval of you is based entirely on My righteousness, which is yours for all eternity. When you look in a mirror, try to see yourself as you truly are—arrayed in perfect righteousness, adorned in glowing approval.

Satisfy us in the morning with your unfailing love, that we may sing for joy and be glad all our days. —Psalm 90:14

I delight greatly in the Lord; my soul rejoices in my God. For he has clothed me with garments of salvation and arrayed me in a robe of righteousness, as a bridegroom adorns his head like a priest, and as a bride adorns herself with her jewels. —Isaiah 61:10

Also read:
Psalm 21:6

Before You Turn Out the Light

Measure your worth by what is eternal: the "gold" of a well-nurtured soul that rests in My unfailing Love.

July 4
MORNING

When you worship Me *in spirit and truth*, you join with choirs of angels who are continually before My throne. Though you cannot hear their voices, your praise and thanksgiving are distinctly audible in heaven. Your petitions are also heard, but it is your gratitude that clears the way to My Heart. With the way between us wide open, My blessings fall upon you in rich abundance. The greatest blessing is nearness to Me—abundant Joy and Peace in My Presence. Practice praising and thanking Me continually throughout this day.

John 4:23–24; Colossians 3:16;
Psalm 100:4

July 4
EVENING

I ARRAYED YOU in a robe of perfect righteousness when I became your Savior—nothing and no one can strip you of that covering! You are chosen royalty, belonging to Me, that you may *proclaim My excellencies*. I am the One who *called you out of darkness into My marvelous Light*!

> *I delight greatly in the LORD; my soul rejoices in my God. For he has clothed me with garments of salvation and arrayed me in a robe of righteousness.* —ISAIAH 61:10

> *But you are a chosen race, a royal priesthood, a holy nation, a people for God's own possession, so that you may proclaim the excellencies of Him who has called you out of darkness into His marvelous light.* —1 PETER 2:9 NASB

Also read:
ROMANS 8:1–2 NASB

Before You Turn Out the Light

Celebrate the riches of your salvation, clothed in My royal garments, enjoying a guilt-free existence in Me.

July 5
MORMING

DRAW NEAR TO ME with a thankful heart, aware that your cup is overflowing with blessings. Gratitude enables you to perceive Me more clearly and to rejoice in our Love-relationship. *Nothing can separate you from My loving Presence!* That is the basis of your security. Whenever you start to feel anxious, remind yourself that your security rests in Me alone, and I am totally trustworthy.

You will never be in control of your life circumstances, but you can relax and trust in My control. Instead of striving for a predictable, safe lifestyle, seek to know Me in greater depth and breadth. I long to make your life a glorious adventure, but you must stop clinging to old ways. I am always doing something new within My beloved ones. Be on the lookout for all that I have prepared for you.

ROMANS 8:38–39; PSALM 56:3–4;
ISAIAH 43:19

July 5
EVENING

THE WORLD IN ITS FALLEN CONDITION is full of frustrations, but I still maintain that thanking Me is the best response. Seek to see things from My perspective, and you will discover treasures in your trials.

God saw all that he had made, and it was very good. And there was evening, and there was morning—the sixth day. —GENESIS 1:31

Forget the former things; do not dwell on the past. See, I am doing a new thing! Now it springs up; do you not perceive it? I am making a way in the desert and streams in the wasteland. —ISAIAH 43:18–19

Also read:
1 THESSALONIANS 5:18

Before You Turn Out the Light

Have you considered the possibility that I may be bringing good out of the very things that upset you? Release your concerns to me.

July 6
MORNING

I AM YOUR FATHER-GOD. Listen to Me! Learn what it means to be a child of the everlasting King. Your richest duty is devotion to Me. This duty is such a joyous privilege that it feels like a luxury. You tend to feel guilty about pushing back the boundaries of your life to make space for time alone with Me. The world is waiting to squeeze you into its mold and to crowd out time devoted to Me. The ways of the world have also warped your conscience, which punishes you for doing the very thing that pleases Me most: seeking My Face. Listen to Me above the clamor of voices trying to distract you. Ask My Spirit to control your mind, for He and I work in perfect harmony. Be still and attentive in My Presence. *You are on holy ground.*

ISAIAH 9:6; ZECHARIAH 9:9 NKJV;
ROMANS 8:15–16; EXODUS 3:5

July 6
EVENING

BEWARE OF DIVIDING UP YOUR LIFE into things you can do by yourself and things that require My help. The truth is, *everything* you do—even taking a breath—involves My assistance. Recognizing your utter dependence on Me builds a strong foundation on which you can do your work *heartily—from the soul*.

> *The Son is the radiance of God's glory and the exact representation of his being, sustaining all things by his powerful word. After he had provided purification for sins, he sat down at the right hand of the Majesty in heaven.* —HEBREWS 1:3

> *Whatever may be your task, work at it heartily (from the soul), as [something done] for the Lord and not for men.* —COLOSSIANS 3:23 AMP

Also read:
COLOSSIANS 1:10; JOSHUA 22:5

Before You Turn Out the Light

In your preparations for tomorrow, dedicate your efforts to Me . . . but also keep looking to Me for help.

July 7
MORNING

Trust Me in all your thoughts. I know that some thoughts are unconscious or semiconscious, and I do not hold you responsible for those. But you can direct conscious thoughts much more than you may realize. Practice thinking in certain ways—trusting Me, thanking Me—and those thoughts become more natural. Reject negative or sinful thoughts as soon as you become aware of them. Don't try to hide them from Me; confess them and leave them with Me. Go on your way lightheartedly. This method of controlling your thoughts will keep your mind in My Presence and your feet on the *path of Peace*.

PSALM 20:7; 1 JOHN 1:9;

LUKE 1:79

July 7
EVENING

Your thoughts are precious to Me because you are My treasure. I disarm evil thoughts and render them powerless. Then I help you think about things that are true, noble, right, pure, lovely, admirable—excellent and praiseworthy things. Ponder these things while resting in the Peace of My Presence.

Take the helmet of salvation and the sword of the Spirit, which is the word of God. —Ephesians 6:17

Finally, brothers, whatever is true, whatever is noble, whatever is right, whatever is pure, whatever is lovely, whatever is admirable—if anything is excellent or praiseworthy—think about such things. —Philippians 4:8

Also read:
Psalm 139:1–2

Before You Turn Out the Light

Remain alert a while longer, bringing your thoughts to Me.

July 8
MORNING

When you seek My Face, put aside thoughts of everything else. I am above all, as well as in all; your communion with Me transcends both time and circumstances. Be prepared to be blessed bountifully by My Presence, for I am a God of unlimited abundance. Open wide your heart and mind to receive more and more of Me. When your Joy in Me meets My Joy in you, there are fireworks of heavenly ecstasy. This is eternal life here and now: a tiny foretaste of what awaits you in the life to come. *Now you see only a poor reflection as in a mirror, but then you will see face to Face.*

PSALM 27:8 NKJV; JOHN 15:11;
1 CORINTHIANS 13:12

July 8
EVENING

Gaze at Me; glance at problems—this is the secret of living victoriously. I have called you to live *supernaturally*, and I have empowered you to do so. Ask My Spirit to help you fix your gaze on Me.

"I will pray the Father, and He will give you another Helper, that He may abide with you forever—the Spirit of truth, whom the world cannot receive, because it neither sees Him nor knows Him; but you know Him, for He dwells with you and will be in you." —John 14:16–17 nkjv

We fix our eyes not on what is seen, but on what is unseen. For what is seen is temporary, but what is unseen is eternal. —2 Corinthians 4:18

Also read:
Hebrews 12:2

Before You Turn Out the Light

Invite My Spirit to alert you when you are overly focused on your problems and to redirect your attention to Me.

July 9
MORNING

STOP WORRYING LONG ENOUGH to hear My voice. I speak softly to you, in the depths of your being. Your mind shuttles back and forth, hither and yon, weaving webs of anxious confusion. As My thoughts rise up within you, they become entangled in those sticky webs of worry. Thus, My voice is muffled, and you hear only white noise.

Ask My Spirit to quiet your mind so that you can think My thoughts. This ability is an awesome benefit of being My child, patterned after My own image. Do not be deafened by the noise of the world or that of your own thinking. Instead, *be transformed by the renewing of your mind*. Sit quietly in My Presence, letting My thoughts reprogram your thinking.

DEUTERONOMY 30:20; GENESIS 1:27;

ROMANS 12:2

July 9
EVENING

PEOPLE OFTEN CONSIDER THOUGHTS to be fleeting and worthless, but yours are so precious to Me that I read each one. My ability to read your every thought may be disconcerting to you; however, since secretiveness breeds loneliness, isn't it a relief that there is Someone from whom you cannot hide? Moreover, the fact that I care about every aspect of you—even all your thoughts—demonstrates how important you are to Me.

> *O Lord, you have searched me and you know me. You know when I sit and when I rise; you perceive my thoughts from afar.* —PSALM 139:1–2

Also read:
EPHESIANS 6:17; PHILIPPIANS 4:8

Before You Turn Out the Light

Get everything out in the open with Me. I know your every thought anyway.

July 10
MORNING

RELAX IN MY PEACEFUL PRESENCE. Do not bring performance pressures into our sacred space of communion. When you are with someone you trust completely, you feel free to be yourself. This is one of the joys of true friendship. Though I am *Lord of lords and King of kings*, I also desire to be your intimate Friend. When you are tense or pretentious in our relationship, I feel hurt. I know the worst about you, but I also see the best in you. I long for you to trust Me enough to be fully yourself with Me. When you are real with Me, I am able to bring out the best in you: the very gifts I have planted in your soul. Relax and enjoy our friendship.

2 THESSALONIANS 3:16 NKJV; REVELATION 17:14; JOHN 15:13–15

July 10
EVENING

WHEN YOU ARE FEELING UNGRATEFUL, you need to focus on *the goal of your faith: the salvation of your soul*. This glorious inheritance has been credited to your account ever since you trusted Me as your Savior-God. As you ponder the wonders of your salvation, you become free—free to receive Joy beyond description and full of Glory!

> *Though you have not seen him, you love him; and even though you do not see him now, you believe in him and are filled with an inexpressible and glorious joy, for you are receiving the goal of your faith, the salvation of your souls.* —1 PETER 1:8–9

> *I give them eternal life, and they shall never perish; no one can snatch them out of my hand.* —JOHN 10:28

Also read:
HEBREWS 4:12; PSALM 107:1

Before You Turn Out the Light

Be honest with Me. I know the attitudes of your heart already.

July 11
MORNING

Worship Me only. Idolatry has always been the downfall of My people. I make no secrets about being *a jealous God*. Current idols are more subtle than ancient ones because today's false gods are often outside the field of religion. People, possessions, status, and self-aggrandizement are some of the most popular deities today. Beware of bowing down before these things. False gods never satisfy; instead, they stir up lust for more and more.

When you seek Me instead of the world's idols, you experience My Joy and Peace. These intangibles slake the thirst of your soul, providing deep satisfaction. The glitter of the world is tinny and temporal. The Light of My Presence is brilliant and everlasting. Walk in the Light with Me. Thus you become a beacon through whom others are drawn to Me.

EXODUS 20:4–5; ISAIAH 55:12;

2 SAMUEL 22:29

July 11
EVENING

ULTIMATELY, YOU ARE ON A HIGHWAY TO HEAVEN. Though there are many ups and downs along the way, the overall gradient is upward. Do not expect easy conditions on such a high-reaching adventure, but do expect Me to support you all the way to heaven.

> *Therefore let everyone who is godly pray to you while you may be found; surely when the mighty waters rise, they will not reach him.* —PSALM 32:6

> *Then they returned . . . strengthening the disciples and encouraging them to remain true to the faith. "We must go through many hardships to enter the kingdom of God," they said.* —ACTS 14:21–22

Also read:
PROVERBS 3:5 AMP

Before You Turn Out the Light

Be confident in Me with all your heart and mind! I am preparing you to live face to Face with Me eternally.

July 12
MORNING

WHENEVER YOU FEEL DISTANT from Me, whisper My Name in loving trust. This simple prayer can restore your awareness of My Presence.

My Name is constantly abused in the world, where people use it as a curse word. This verbal assault reaches all the way to heaven; every word is heard and recorded. When you trustingly whisper My Name, My aching ears are soothed. The grating rancor of the world's blasphemies cannot compete with a trusting child's utterance: "Jesus." The power of My Name to bless both you and Me is beyond your understanding.

PROVERBS 18:10; ACTS 4:12; JOHN 16:24

July 12
EVENING

I called you to Myself in the most personal way: reaching down into the circumstances of your life, speaking into the intricacies of your heart and mind. Although I have vast numbers of followers, you are not a number to Me—I always speak to you *by name*. In fact, you are so precious to Me that *I have inscribed you on the palms of My hands*.

> *The Lord who created you, O Israel, says: Don't be afraid, for I have ransomed you; I have called you by name; you are mine.* —Isaiah 43:1 TLB

> *"See, I have inscribed you on the palms of My hands; your walls are continually before Me."* —Isaiah 49:16 NKJV

> *Also read:*
> Romans 8:38–39

Before You Turn Out the Light

Tell yourself the truth: I have called you personally;
I know you by name; you are My beloved.

July 13
MORNING

I WANT YOU TO EXPERIENCE the riches of your salvation: the Joy of being loved constantly and perfectly. You make a practice of judging yourself, based on how you look or behave or feel. If you like what you see in the mirror, you feel a bit more worthy of My Love. When things are going smoothly and your performance seems adequate, you find it easier to believe you are My beloved child. When you feel discouraged, you tend to look inward so you can correct whatever is wrong.

Instead of trying to "fix" yourself, *fix your gaze on Me, the Lover of your soul*. Rather than using your energy to judge yourself, redirect it to praising Me. Remember that I see you clothed in My righteousness, radiant in My perfect Love.

EPHESIANS 2:7–8; HEBREWS 3:1; PSALM 34:5

July 13
EVENING

I AM THE IDEAL INTERCESSOR FOR YOU because I understand you completely. Throughout my life on earth, I endured one temptation after the other; now *I live to make intercession for you*. Since I am infinite in all My ways, I am never too busy. I am always available to help you.

> *Therefore He is also able to save to the uttermost those who come to God through Him, since He always lives to make intercession for them.* —HEBREWS 7:25 NKJV

> *Then Jesus was led by the Spirit into the desert to be tempted by the devil. After fasting forty days and forty nights, he was hungry.* —MATTHEW 4:1–2

Also read:
JOHN 8:32; MARK 15:32

Before You Turn Out the Light

How can I pray for you today?

July 14
MORNING

KEEP WALKING with Me along the path I have chosen for you. Your desire to live close to Me is a delight to My heart. I could instantly grant you the spiritual riches you desire, but that is not My way for you. Together we will forge a pathway up the high mountain. The journey is arduous at times, and you are weak. Someday you will dance light-footed on the high peaks; but for now your walk is often plodding and heavy. All I require of you is to take the next step, clinging to My hand for strength and direction. Though the path is difficult and the scenery dull at the moment, there are sparkling surprises just around the bend. Stay on the path I have selected for you. It is truly the *path of Life*.

ISAIAH 40:31 NKJV; PSALM 37:23–24;
PSALM 16:11 NKJV

July 14
EVENING

WHEN PEOPLE BARE THEIR SOULS to you, you are indeed on holy ground: If you jump in with both feet—trying to rescue them—your muddy footprints pollute the terrain. To function effectively, ask the Holy Spirit to think through you, listen through you, love through you. He will sometimes give you words of wisdom to share, but your main role is to direct the person toward Me and My limitless resources.

"Do not come any closer," God said. "Take off your sandals, for the place where you are standing is holy ground." —EXODUS 3:5

Let the morning bring me word of your unfailing love, for I have put my trust in you. Show me the way I should go, for to you I lift up my soul. —PSALM 143:8

Also read:
PSALM 63:5

Before You Turn Out the Light

How inclined are you to play the hero? Keep in mind that your role is to listen and love; I handle the healing.

July 15
MORNING

Do not worry about tomorrow! This is not a suggestion but a command. I divided time into days and nights so that you would have manageable portions of life to handle. *My grace is sufficient for you*, but its sufficiency is for only one day at a time. When you worry about the future, you heap day upon day of troubles onto your flimsy frame. You stagger under this heavy load, which I never intended you to carry.

Throw off this oppressive burden with one quick thrust of trust. Anxious thoughts meander about and crisscross in your brain, but trusting Me brings you directly into My Presence. As you thus affirm your faith, shackles of worry fall off instantly. Enjoy My Presence continually by trusting Me at all times.

MATTHEW 6:34; 2 CORINTHIANS 12:9;
PSALM 62:8 NKJV

July 15
EVENING

When you're acutely aware of your insufficiency—rejoice! *You have been saved by grace, through faith.* You are exceedingly blessed because the kingdom of heaven is yours.

> *"Blessed are the poor in spirit, for theirs is the kingdom of heaven."* —Matthew 5:3 NKJV

> *For it is by grace you have been saved, through faith—and this not from yourselves, it is the gift of God.* —Ephesians 2:8

Also read:
2 Corinthians 9:15; Psalm 73:24 NKJV

Before You Turn Out the Light

Forgo feeling sorry for yourself, and instead say, "I am blessed and thankful—and on my way to Glory!"

July 16
MORNING

SELF-PITY IS A SLIMY, BOTTOMLESS PIT. Once you fall in, you tend to go deeper and deeper into the mire. As you slide down those slippery walls, you are well on your way to depression, and the darkness is profound.

Your only hope is to look up and see the Light of My Presence shining down on you. Though the Light looks dim from your perspective, deep in the pit, those rays of hope can reach you at any depth. While you focus on Me in trust, you rise ever so slowly out of the abyss of despair. Finally, you can reach up and grasp My hand. I will pull you out into the Light again. I will gently cleanse you, washing off the clinging mire. I will cover you with My righteousness and walk with you down the path of Life.

PSALM 40:2–3; PSALM 42:5 NASB;
PSALM 147:11

July 16
EVENING

KEEP YOUR EYES ON ME! I am with you, taking care of you in the best possible way. Don't let your past or present suffering contaminate your view of the future. I am the Lord of your future, and I have good things in store for you.

> *The LORD is good to those who wait for Him, to the soul who seeks Him.* —LAMENTATIONS 3:25 NKJV

> *"For I know the plans that I have for you," declares the LORD, "plans for welfare and not for calamity to give you a future and a hope."* —JEREMIAH 29:11 NASB

> *Also read:*
> ISAIAH 40:31 NKJV; ROMANS 8:28

Before You Turn Out the Light

Thank Me for this time of neediness. Depend totally on Me.

July 17
MORNING

*C*OME AWAY WITH *ME* for a while. The world, with its nonstop demands, can be put on hold. Most people put *Me* on hold, rationalizing that someday they will find time to focus on Me. But the longer people push Me into the background of their lives, the harder it is for them to find Me.

You live among people who glorify busyness; they have made time a tyrant that controls their lives. Even those who know Me as Savior tend to march to the tempo of the world. They have bought into the illusion that more is always better: more meetings, more programs, more activity.

I have called you to follow Me on a solitary path, making time alone with Me your highest priority and deepest Joy. It is a pathway largely unappreciated and often despised. However, *you have chosen the better thing, which will never be taken away from you*. Moreover, as you walk close to Me, I can bless others through you.

SONG OF SONGS 2:13; LUKE 10:41–42

July 17
EVENING

When you follow My divine guidelines, you can enjoy the Peace of My Presence. I am everywhere and I see everything, but My eyes are *especially* on those who are putting their hope in Me. This does not mean I shield them from all adversity; it means I bless them with My nearness in good times, in hard times—at all times.

> *The eyes of the Lord are on those who fear him, on those whose hope is in his unfailing love.* —Psalm 33:18

> *Now may the Lord of peace himself give you peace at all times and in every way. The Lord be with all of you.* —2 Thessalonians 3:16

Also read:
Romans 8:38–39 nkjv

Before You Turn Out the Light

Place your hope in My perfect Love.
My eyes are indeed on you!

July 18
MORNING

I AM NEARER than you think, richly present in all your moments. You are connected to Me by Love-bonds that nothing can sever. However, you may sometimes feel alone because your union with Me is invisible. Ask Me to open your eyes so that you can find Me everywhere. The more aware you are of My Presence, the safer you feel. This is not some sort of escape from reality; it is tuning in to *ultimate reality*. I am far more Real than the world you can see, hear, and touch. *Faith is the confirmation of things we do not see and the conviction of their reality, perceiving as real fact what is not revealed to the senses.*

PSALM 90:14; ACTS 17:27–28;
HEBREWS 11:1 AMP

July 18
EVENING

My PRESENCE IS ALWAYS WITH YOU, but I am very present in times of distress. As you look back over the years of your own life, you will see many instances of My meeting *your* needs in hard times. Since I am such a *well-proved Help*, you can trust Me to help you now!

> *God is our Refuge and Strength [mighty and impenetrable to temptation], a very present and well-proved help in trouble.* —PSALM 46:1 AMP

> *To him who is able to keep you from falling and to present you before his glorious presence without fault and with great joy—to the only God our Savior be glory, majesty, power and authority, through Jesus Christ our Lord, before all ages, now and forevermore!* —JUDE VV. 24–25

Also read:
JOSHUA 4:23

Before You Turn Out the Light

Remind yourself: "Jesus is here with me. In fact, He is *very present* with me in this hard situation." Then relax and draw strength from Me.

July 19
MORNING

Bring Me all your feelings, even the ones you wish you didn't have. Fear and anxiety still plague you. Feelings per se are not sinful, but they can be temptations to sin. Blazing missiles of fear fly at you day and night; these attacks from the evil one come at you relentlessly. Use your *shield of faith to extinguish those flaming arrows*. Affirm your trust in Me, regardless of how you feel. If you persist, your feelings will eventually fall in line with your faith.

Do not hide from your fear or pretend it isn't there. Anxiety that you hide in the recesses of your heart will give birth to fear of fear: a monstrous mutation. Bring your anxieties out into the Light of My Presence, where we can deal with them together. Concentrate on trusting Me, and fearfulness will gradually lose its foothold within you.

Ephesians 6:16; 1 John 1:5–7;
Isaiah 12:2

July 19
EVENING

INSTEAD OF TRYING TO PLEASE PEOPLE so they will give you what you want, trust in Me—the Supplier of all your needs. Because I remain the same forever, I am absolutely dependable. Trusting in people is risky; trusting in Me is wise. It keeps you safe.

Fear of man will prove to be a snare, but whoever trusts in the Lord is kept safe. —PROVERBS 29:25

But you remain the same, and your years will never end. —PSALM 102.27

Also read:
2 CORINTHIANS 5:9; PHILIPPIANS 4:19

Before You Turn Out the Light

Include Me in your thinking as you are making plans. Let your desire to please Me illuminate your thoughts and choices.

July 20
MORNING

SEEK MY FACE, and you will find all that you have longed for. The deepest yearnings of your heart are for intimacy with Me. I know because I designed you to desire Me. Do not feel guilty about taking time to be still in My Presence. You are simply responding to the tugs of divinity within you. I made you in My image, and I hid heaven in your heart. Your yearning for Me is a form of homesickness: longing for your true home in heaven.

Do not be afraid to be different from other people. The path I have called you to travel is exquisitely right for you. The more closely you follow My leading, the more fully I can develop your gifts. To follow Me wholeheartedly, you must relinquish your desire to please other people. However, your closeness to Me will bless others by enabling you to shine brightly in this dark world.

PSALM 42:1–2; PSALM 34:5;
PHILIPPIANS 2:15

July 20
EVENING

WHEN ONE OF MY BELOVED DRAWS NEAR TO ME in reverent awe, I open My heart and offer intimate friendship. From time to time, though, you overstep your bounds, forgetting who I am. When you remember My majestic Presence and return to Me repentantly, I rush to meet you and enfold you in My embrace.

> *Jesus said to them, "Most assuredly, I say to you, before Abraham was, I AM."* —JOHN 8:58 NKJV

> *So he got up and went to his father. But while he was still a long way off, his father saw him and was filled with compassion for him; he ran to his son, threw his arms around him and kissed him.* —LUKE 15:20

Also read:
1 TIMOTHY 6:14–15

Before You Turn Out the Light

Reach out for Me in reverence—and I will embrace you with Joy immeasurable.

July 21
MORNING

Rest in My Presence when you need refreshment. Resting is not necessarily idleness, as people often perceive it. When you relax in My company, you are demonstrating trust in Me. *Trust* is a rich word, laden with meaning and direction for your life. I want you to *lean on, trust, and be confident in Me*. When you lean on Me for support, I delight in your trusting confidence.

Many people turn away from Me when they are exhausted. They associate Me with duty and diligence, so they try to hide from My Presence when they need a break from work. How this saddens Me! As I spoke through My prophet Isaiah: *In returning to Me and resting in Me you shall be saved; in quietness and trust shall be your strength.*

PSALM 91:1; PROVERBS 3:5 AMP;

ISAIAH 30:15 AMP

July 21
EVENING

DON'T BE AFRAID TO BE HAPPY. This very moment is the right time to enjoy Me. Come boldly into My Presence, saying, "Jesus, I choose to enjoy You—here and now."

Happy are the people whose God is the Lord! —Psalm 144:15 nkjv

"Cease striving and know that I am God; I will be exalted among the nations, I will be exalted in the earth." —Psalm 46:10 nasb

Also read:
Psalm 46:1–3

Before You Turn Out the Light

You can let down and be happy in these closing moments of your day—all because you are Mine.

July 22
MORNING

FIND FREEDOM through seeking to please Me above all else. *You can have only one Master.* When you let others' expectations drive you, you scatter your energy to the winds. Your own desire to look good can also drain your energy. I am your Master, and I do not drive you to be what you are not. Your pretense displeases Me, especially when it is in My "service." Concentrate on staying close to Me at all times. It is impossible to be inauthentic while you are focusing on My Presence.

EPHESIANS 5:8–10; MATTHEW 23:8;
MATTHEW 6:1

July 22
EVENING

I CAME INTO YOUR LIFE TO *MAKE YOU FREE*. If you're involved in hurtful relationships, I will help you change them or break free; if you are trapped in addictions, I will help you take the first step toward freedom—honest confession of the truth. In every situation, *the truth will set you free*.

> *"You shall know the truth, and the truth shall make you free."* —JOHN 8:32 NKJV

> *There is therefore now no condemnation for those who are in Christ Jesus. For the law of the Spirit of life has set you free in Christ Jesus from the law of sin and death.* —ROMANS 8:1–2 ESV

> *Also read:*
> PSALM 31:19–20; MALACHI 4:2

Before You Turn Out the Light

Pursue freedom in the truth of who I am
and what I have done for you.

July 23
MORNING

I AM THE LIGHT OF THE WORLD. Men crawl through their lives cursing the darkness, but all the while I am shining brightly. I desire each of My followers to be a Light-bearer. The Holy Spirit who lives in you can shine from your face, making Me visible to people around you. Ask My Spirit to live through you as you wend your way through this day. Hold My hand in joyful trust, for I never leave your side. The Light of My Presence is shining upon you. Brighten up the world by reflecting who I AM.

JOHN 8:12; MATTHEW 5:14–16;
2 CORINTHIANS 3:18; EXODUS 3:14

July 23
EVENING

MANY PEOPLE ATTACH THEMSELVES to hurtful people or harmful things because they yearn to escape their aloneness. But you are *never* alone, for you are Mine. I chose you *before the creation of the world*, and I personally brought you out of that darkness into My Light.

> *You are a chosen generation, a royal priesthood, a holy nation, His own special people, that you may proclaim the praises of Him who called you out of darkness into His marvelous light.* —1 PETER 2:9 NKJV

> *Praise be to the God and Father of our Lord Jesus Christ, who has blessed us in the heavenly realms with every spiritual blessing in Christ. For he chose us in him before the creation of the world to be holy and blameless in his sight.* —EPHESIANS 1:3–4

Also read:
PSALM 37:4

Before You Turn Out the Light

I called you out of aloneness and into My Light so that you might proclaim My praises. How will you do this tomorrow?

July 24
MORNING

THANKFULNESS OPENS THE DOOR to My Presence. Though I am always with you, I have gone to great measures to preserve your freedom of choice. I have placed a door between you and Me, and I have empowered you to open or close that door. There are many ways to open it, but a grateful attitude is one of the most effective.

Thankfulness is built on a substructure of trust. When thankful words stick in your throat, you need to check up on your foundation of trust. When thankfulness flows freely from your heart and lips, let your gratitude draw you closer to Me. I want you to learn the art of *giving thanks in all circumstances.* See how many times you can thank Me daily; this will awaken your awareness to a multitude of blessings. It will also cushion the impact of trials when they come against you. Practice My Presence by practicing the discipline of thankfulness.

PSALM 100:4; PSALM 31:14;
1 THESSALONIANS 5:18

July 24
EVENING

I AM NOT ONLY THE GIVER OF TRUE PEACE; I Myself am your Peace. It is every bit as available to you as I am. Rejoice as you explore with Me the immense proportions of My gift: Peace at all times and in every way!

For God was pleased to have all his fullness dwell in him, and through him to reconcile to himself all things, whether things on earth or things in heaven, by making peace through his blood, shed on the cross. —COLOSSIANS 1:19–20

Now may the Lord of peace himself give you peace at all times and in every way. The Lord be with all of you. —2 THESSALONIANS 3:16

Also read:
EPHESIANS 2:14; 1 PETER 5:7

Before You Turn Out the Light

Even when you are feeling anxious, thank Me for the gift of My Peace.

July 25
MORNING

As you listen to birds calling to one another, hear also My Love-call to you. I speak to you continually: through sights, sounds, thoughts, impressions, scriptures. There is no limit to the variety of ways I can communicate with you. Your part is to be attentive to My messages, in whatever form they come. When you set out to find Me in a day, you discover that the world is vibrantly alive with My Presence. You can find Me not only in beauty and birdcalls, but also in tragedy and faces filled with grief. I can take the deepest sorrow and *weave it into a pattern for good.*

Search for Me and My messages as you go through this day. *You will seek Me and find Me when you seek Me with your whole being.*

JOHN 10:27; ROMANS 8:28 AMP;
JEREMIAH 29:13

July 25
EVENING

It's easier to tone down your thinking when your body is still for a time since mind and body are so intricately connected. Ponder the wonder of My Presence with you. Refresh yourself in My promises: I will counsel you and watch over you . . . I will supply every need of yours according to My riches in Glory. Peace I leave with you. My Peace I give you.

Jesus came and stood among them and said, "Peace be with you!" —John 20:26

"Peace I leave with you; my peace I give you. I do not give to you as the world gives. Do not let your hearts be troubled and do not be afraid." —John 14:27

Also read:
Psalm 32:8; Philippians 4:19 nasb

Before You Turn Out the Light

When your mind becomes quiet enough, listen for
My resurrection blessing: "Peace be with you."

July 26
MORNING

RELAX AND LET ME LEAD YOU through this day. I have everything under control: *My* control. You tend to peer anxiously into the day that is before you, trying to figure out what to do and when. Meanwhile, the phone or the doorbell rings, and you have to reshuffle your plans. All that planning ties you up in knots and distracts you from Me. Attentiveness to Me is not only for your quiet time, but for all your time. As you look to Me, I show you what to do *now* and *next*.

Vast quantities of time and energy are wasted in obsessive planning. When you let *Me* direct your steps, you are set free to enjoy Me and to find what I have prepared for you this day.

PSALM 32:8; PSALM 119:35;
PSALM 143:8

July 26
EVENING

As you walk with Me along your life-path, let the hope of heaven shine brightly on you, lighting up your perspective dramatically. Every moment you are getting closer to your heavenly home. As you look to Me in faith—trusting in My finished work on the cross—the Light of heaven's hope shines upon you and brightens the path just before you.

> *"Come to me, all you who are weary and burdened, and I will give you rest."* —Matthew 11:28

> *The Lord will rescue me from every evil deed and bring me safely into his heavenly kingdom. To him be the glory forever and ever.* —2 Timothy 4:18 ESV

Also read:
Romans 8:24–25 NKJV; Psalm 89:15

Before You Turn Out the Light

View Me as your constant Companion, eager to help you take the next step on your earthly journey.

July 27
MORNING

Hope is a golden cord connecting you to heaven. This cord helps you hold your head up high, even when multiple trials are buffeting you. I never leave your side, and I never let go of your hand. But without the cord of hope, your head may slump and your feet may shuffle as you journey uphill with Me. Hope lifts your perspective from your weary feet to the glorious view you can see from the high road. You are reminded that the road we're traveling together is ultimately a highway to heaven. When you consider this radiant destination, the roughness or smoothness of the road ahead becomes much less significant. I am training you to hold in your heart a dual focus: My continual Presence and the hope of heaven.

Romans 12:12; 1 Thessalonians 5:8;
Hebrews 6:18–19

July 27
EVENING

SOMETIMES YOU LIMP THROUGH A DAY feeling empty and alone, but I say to you at such times, *"You do not have because you do not ask."* Since I am the Creator and Sustainer of the universe, nothing can thwart My promises. As you marvel at how great, glorious, and trustworthy I am, your praises will fill you with hope—and with rich awareness of My Presence.

> *Why are you in despair, O my soul? And why have you become disturbed within me? Hope in God, for I shall again praise Him for the help of His presence.* —PSALM 42:5 NASB

> *You lust and do not have. You murder and covet and cannot obtain. You fight and war. Yet you do not have because you do not ask.* —JAMES 4:2 NKJV

Also read:
MATTHEW 28:19–20

Before You Turn Out the Light

Do not hesitate to ask for My help. I am with you always.

July 28
MORNING

Let My Love seep into the inner recesses of your being. Do not close off any part of yourself from Me. I know you inside and out, so do not try to present a "cleaned-up" self to Me. Wounds that you shut away from the Light of My Love will fester and become wormy. Secret sins that you "hide" from Me can split off and develop lives of their own, controlling you without your realizing it.

Open yourself fully to My transforming Presence. Let My brilliant Love-Light search out and destroy hidden fears. This process requires time alone with Me, as My Love soaks into your innermost being. Enjoy *My perfect Love, which expels every trace of fear.*

PSALM 139:1–4, 23–24;
1 JOHN 4:18 AMP

July 28
EVENING

JOYFULLY RECEIVE THE FORGIVENESS I bought for you with My own blood. As you *walk in the Light* with Me, there is a continual cleansing work going on within you. This purifying work of My blood helps you stay close to Me and to others who walk in My Light.

If we confess our sins, He is faithful and just to forgive us our sins and to cleanse us from all unrighteousness. —1 JOHN 1:9 NKJV

If we walk in the light, as he is in the light, we have fellowship with one another, and the blood of Jesus, his Son, purifies us from all sin. —1 JOHN 1:7

Also read:
ISAIAH 61:10; PSALM 89:15–16

Before You Turn Out the Light

Once you have confessed your sins to Me,
receive My forgiveness without fear.

July 29
MORNING

Come to Me continually. I am meant to be the Center of your consciousness, the *Anchor of your soul*. Your mind will wander from Me, but the question is how far you allow it to wander. An anchor on a short rope lets a boat drift only slightly before the taut line tugs the boat back toward the center. Similarly, as you drift away from Me, My Spirit within you gives a tug, prompting you to return to Me. As you become increasingly attuned to My Presence, the length of rope on your soul's Anchor is shortened. You wander only a short distance before feeling that inner tug—telling you to return to your true Center in Me.

Hebrews 6:19; 1 John 2:28;
Matthew 22:37

July 29
EVENING

WHEN YOU ARE WORKING on a challenging project, you tend to seek My Face and My help frequently. This pleases Me—and it enhances the work you are doing. I encourage you to live more and more of your life in this way. This prayer-privilege is not a chore; it's a joyous lifeline!

> *"My sheep listen to my voice; I know them, and they follow me. I give them eternal life, and they shall never perish; no one can snatch them out of my hand."* —JOHN 10:27–28

> *Pray in the Spirit on all occasions with all kinds of prayers and requests. With this in mind, be alert and always keep on praying for all the saints.* —EPHESIANS 6:18

Also read:
PSALM 105:3 ESV; MARK 9:7–8 ESV

Before You Turn Out the Light

Plan to work in rhythm with Me tomorrow
even more than you did today.

July 30
MORNING

Worship Me in the beauty of holiness. I created beauty to declare the existence of My holy Being. A magnificent rose, a hauntingly glorious sunset, oceanic splendor—all these things were meant to proclaim My Presence in the world. Most people rush past these proclamations without giving them a second thought. Some people use beauty, especially feminine loveliness, to sell their products.

How precious are My children who are awed by nature's beauty; this opens them up to My holy Presence. Even before you knew Me personally, you responded to My creation with wonder. This is a gift, and it carries responsibility with it. Declare My glorious Being to the world. *The whole earth is full of My radiant beauty—My Glory!*

PSALM 29:2 NKJV; 1 SAMUEL 2:2;
ISAIAH 6:3

July 30
EVENING

I WANT YOU TO ENJOY the wonder of My loving Presence with you always, but do not lose sight of My holiness. Your awareness that I am holy God can bless and protect you. When you realize you have sinned, turn quickly from the offensive way and turn back toward Me; I will receive you warmly—with *no condemnation*.

So David said to Nathan, "I have sinned against the LORD." And Nathan said to David, "The LORD also has put away your sin; you shall not die." —2 SAMUEL 12:13 NKJV

There is now no condemnation for those who are in Christ Jesus. —ROMANS 8:1

Also read:
REVELATION 4:8 NKJV; ACTS 13:22

Before You Turn Out the Light

I am holy, the Lord God Almighty. Repent and separate yourself from sin.

July 31
MORNING

Trust Me in the depths of your being. It is there that I live in constant communion with you. When you feel flustered and frazzled on the outside, do not get upset with yourself. You are only human, and the swirl of events going on all around you will sometimes feel overwhelming. Rather than scolding yourself for your humanness, remind yourself that I am both with you and within you.

I am with you at all times, encouraging and supportive rather than condemning. I know that deep within you, where I live, My Peace is your continual experience. Slow down your pace of living for a time. Quiet your mind in My Presence. Then you will be able to hear Me bestowing the resurrection blessing: *Peace be with you.*

COLOSSIANS 1:27; MATTHEW 28:20;

JOHN 20:19

July 31
EVENING

I BLESS YOU AND KEEP YOU; *I make My Face shine upon you; I turn My Face toward you and give you Peace.* I want you to meditate on this blessing, for it expresses well the overflow of My heart toward you. Those who come to Me find not only My approval but also *rest for their souls*.

> *"The LORD bless you and keep you; the LORD make his face shine upon you and be gracious to you; the LORD turn his face toward you and give you peace."* —NUMBERS 6:24–26

> *"Come to me, all you who are weary and burdened, and I will give you rest. Take my yoke upon you and learn from me, for I am gentle and humble in heart, and you will find rest for your souls. For my yoke is easy and my burden is light."* —MATTHEW 11:28–30

Also read:
PSALM 34:8 NKJV; JOHN 6:40

Before You Turn Out the Light

Come—believing—for My goodness and Life!

August

"Whoever believes in me, as the Scripture has said, streams of living water will flow from within him."

JOHN 7:38

August 1
MORNING

*N*OTHING CAN SEPARATE YOU *from My Love.* Let this divine assurance trickle through your mind and into your heart and soul. Whenever you start to feel fearful or anxious, repeat this unconditional promise: "Nothing can separate me from Your Love, Jesus."

Most of mankind's misery stems from feeling unloved. In the midst of adverse circumstances, people tend to feel that love has been withdrawn and they have been forsaken. This feeling of abandonment is often worse than the adversity itself. Be assured that I never abandon any of My children, not even temporarily. *I will never leave you or forsake you!* My Presence watches over you continually. *I have engraved you on the palms of My hands.*

ROMANS 8:38–39; JOSHUA 1:5;
ISAIAH 49:15–16

August 1
EVENING

THE ONLY THINGS THAT SEEM ENDLESS are your problems and your pain. But I am *here*—tenderly present—ready to help you get safely through. At such times it can help to remember that I have clothed you in *garments of salvation*; because you wear My *robe of righteousness*, you are on your way to heaven!

I will greatly rejoice in the Lord, my soul shall be joyful in my God; for He has clothed me with the garments of salvation, He has covered me with the robe of righteousness, as a bridegroom decks himself with ornaments, and as a bride adorns herself with her jewels. —Isaiah 61:10 NKJV

"For God so loved the world, that he gave his only Son, that whoever believes in him should not perish but have eternal life." —John 3:16 ESV

Also read:
Lamentations 3:22–23 NRSV

Before You Turn Out the Light

Nothing you will face tomorrow can compare with My snatching you from the jaws of hell and granting you eternal life. Thank Me for this mercy-gift.

August 2
MORNING

BRING ME THE SACRIFICE OF YOUR TIME: a most precious commodity. In this action-addicted world, few of My children take time to sit quietly in My Presence. But for those who do, blessings flow like *streams of living water*. I, the One from whom all blessings flow, am also blessed by our time together. This is a deep mystery; do not try to fathom it. Instead, glorify Me by delighting in Me. Enjoy Me now and forever!

PSALM 21:6; JOHN 7:37–38;
PSALM 103:11; PSALM 34:3

August 2
EVENING

THERE ARE INDEED MANY MEASURES OF SUCCESS in the world, and most of them are meaningless. To avoid confusion, you need a rule of thumb: Seek to please Me. The more you commune with Me as you go through a day, the more you walk in My ways.

Jesus replied: "'Love the Lord your God with all your heart and with all your soul and with all your mind.' This is the first and greatest commandment." —MATTHEW 22:37–38

This is what the Lord says: "Stand at the crossroads and look; ask for the ancient paths, ask where the good way is, and walk in it, and you will find rest for your souls." —JEREMIAH 6:16

Also read:
PSALM 90:8; PSALM 63:5 NKJV

Before You Turn Out the Light

Stay in touch with Me as tomorrow approaches so the Light of My Presence can illumine your path.

August 3
MORNING

Watch your words diligently. Words have such great power to bless or to wound. When you speak carelessly or negatively, you damage others as well as yourself. This ability to verbalize is an awesome privilege, granted only to those I created in My image. You need help in wielding this mighty power responsibly.

Though the world applauds quick-witted retorts, My instructions about communication are quite different: *Be quick to listen, slow to speak, and slow to become angry.* Ask My Spirit to help you whenever you speak. I have trained you to pray—"Help me, Holy Spirit"—before answering the phone, and you have seen the benefits of this discipline. Simply apply the same discipline to communicating with people around you. If they are silent, pray before speaking to them. If they are talking, pray before responding. These are split-second prayers, but they put you in touch with My Presence. In this way, your speaking comes under the control of My Spirit. As positive speech patterns replace your negative ones, the increase in your Joy will amaze you.

Proverbs 12:18; James 1:19;
Ephesians 4:29

August 3
EVENING

HUMAN MINDS, though capable of brilliance, tend to be undisciplined and rebellious. To counteract this weakness, I have provided help in the Person of the Holy Spirit. He offers Life and Peace to those who yield themselves to Him.

> *Those who live according to the sinful nature have their minds set on what that nature desires; but those who live in accordance with the Spirit have their minds set on what the Spirit desires. The mind of sinful man is death, but the mind controlled by the Spirit is life and peace.* —ROMANS 8:5–6

> *And we know that in all things God works for the good of those who love him, who have been called according to his purpose.* —ROMANS 8:28

Also read:
PSALM 118:24

Before You Turn Out the Light

Enabled by My Spirit, replace your anxious, accusing thoughts with My Peace and My Truth.

August 4

MORNING

Hold My hand, and walk joyously with Me through this day. Together we will savor the pleasures and endure the difficulties it brings. Be on the lookout for everything I have prepared for you: stunning scenery, bracing winds of adventure, cozy nooks for resting when you are weary, and much more. I am your Guide, as well as your constant Companion. I know every step of the journey ahead of you, all the way to heaven.

You don't have to choose between staying close to Me and staying on course. Since *I am the Way*, staying close to Me is staying on course. As you focus your thoughts on Me, I will guide you carefully along today's journey. Don't worry about what is around the next bend. Just concentrate on enjoying My Presence and staying in step with Me.

PHILIPPIANS 4:13 NKJV; ISAIAH 58:11;
JOHN 14:6; COLOSSIANS 4:2

August 4
EVENING

WHEN YOU GET SO FOCUSED ON YOUR PLANS that you hardly see anything else, you are unavailable to Me. If you start feeling frustrated or distant from Me, take time to seek My Face—the magnetic attraction of My Love will empower you to resist the pull of your planning path. This frees you to respond to My initiatives, joining in the things I have already set in motion.

In his heart a man plans his course, but the LORD determines his steps. —PROVERBS 16:9

For we are God's [own] handiwork (His workmanship), recreated in Christ Jesus, [born anew] that we may do those good works which God predestined (planned beforehand) for us [taking paths which He prepared ahead of time], that we should walk in them [living the good life which He prearranged and made ready for us to live]. —EPHESIANS 2:10 AMP

Also read:
NAHUM 1:7

Before You Turn Out the Light

Do you trust in your plans more than in Me? Make yourself available for sacred use, ready to do My will.

August 5
MORNING

SIT QUIETLY IN MY PRESENCE while I bless you. Make your mind like a still pool of water, ready to receive whatever thoughts I drop into it. Rest in My sufficiency as you consider the challenges this day presents. Do not wear yourself out by worrying about whether you can cope with the pressures. Keep looking to Me and communicating with Me as we walk through this day together.

Take time to rest by the wayside, for I am not in a hurry. A leisurely pace accomplishes more than hurried striving. When you rush, you forget who you are and Whose you are. Remember that you are royalty in My kingdom.

PSALM 37:7; ROMANS 8:16–17;
1 PETER 2:9

August 5
EVENING

MY CHOSEN have consistently forgotten Me and the great works I've done on their behalf. To help in your endeavor to remember, view yourself first and foremost as My beloved, since that is your ultimate identity, and fill your mind with Bible verses that convince you of My perfect Love for you. Pour out your heart to Me, for I am your Refuge.

> *Then Moses stretched out his hand over the sea, and all that night the LORD drove the sea back with a strong east wind and turned it into dry land. The waters were divided, and the Israelites went through the sea on dry ground, with a wall of water on their right and on their left.* —EXODUS 14:21–22

> *Trust in him at all times, O people; pour out your hearts to him, for God is our refuge.* —PSALM 62:8

Also read:
MATTHEW 11:28

Before You Turn Out the Light

Endeavor to remember all that I have done for you—and to ask for My help in remembering.

August 6
MORNING

When things seem to be going all wrong, stop and affirm your trust in Me. Calmly bring these matters to Me, and leave them in My capable hands. Then, simply do the next thing. Stay in touch with Me through thankful, trusting prayers, resting in My sovereign control. Rejoice in Me—exult in the God of your salvation! As you trust in Me, *I make your feet like the feet of a deer. I enable you to walk and make progress upon your high places of trouble, suffering, or responsibility.*

JOB 13:15 NKJV; PSALM 18:33;
HABAKKUK 3:17–19 AMP

August 6
EVENING

EVEN THOUGH YOU INHABIT a world full of trouble, I assure you that I am completely, 100 percent good! *I am light, and in Me there is no darkness at all.* Turn to Me in tough times, and you will find Me faithful.

> *This is the message which we have heard from Him and declare to you, that God is light and in Him is no darkness at all.* —1 JOHN 1:5 NKJV

> *When I am afraid, I put my trust in you.* —PSALM 56:3 ESV

Also read:
NAHUM 1:7; MATTHEW 28:19–20

Before You Turn Out the Light

Hide yourself in Me wherever you feel the darkness encroaching.

August 7
MORNING

UNDERSTANDING WILL NEVER BRING YOU PEACE. That's why I have instructed you to *trust in Me, not in your understanding*. Human beings have a voracious appetite for trying to figure things out in order to gain a sense of mastery over their lives. But the world presents you with an endless series of problems. As soon as you master one set, another pops up to challenge you. The relief you had anticipated is short-lived. Soon your mind is gearing up again: searching for understanding (mastery) instead of seeking Me (your Master).

The wisest of all men, Solomon, could never think his way through to Peace. His vast understanding resulted in feelings of futility rather than in fulfillment. Finally, he lost his way and succumbed to the will of his wives by worshiping idols.

My Peace is not an elusive goal, hidden at the center of some complicated maze. Actually, you are always enveloped in Peace, which is inherent in My Presence. As you look to Me, you gain awareness of this precious Peace.

PROVERBS 3:5–6; ROMANS 5:1;
2 THESSALONIANS 3:16

August 7
EVENING

YOU NEED ME CONTINUALLY—not only for daily bread and blessings, but also for the myriad decisions you must make each day. The more consistently you rely on Me, the better your life will be. Not only will I meet all your needs through My glorious riches; I will also delight you with the Joy of My Presence.

And my God shall supply all your needs according to His riches in glory by Christ Jesus. —PHILIPPIANS 4:19 NKJV

Then will I go to the altar of God, to God, my joy and my delight. —PSALM 43:4

Also read:
MATTHEW 7:13–14

Before You Turn Out the Light

Have gratitude for all the ways I keep you intimately connected to Me, including your joyful dependence on Me.

August 8
MORNING

I SPEAK TO YOU from deepest heaven. You hear Me in the depths of your being. *Deep calls unto deep.* You are blessed to hear Me so directly. Never take this privilege for granted. The best response is a heart overflowing with gratitude. I am training you to cultivate a thankful mind-set. This is like *building your house on a firm rock, where life's storms cannot shake you.* As you learn these lessons, you are to teach them to others. I will open up the way before you, one step at a time.

PSALM 42:7–8 NKJV; PSALM 95:1–2;
MATTHEW 7:24–25

August 8
EVENING

When you rejoice in Me during times of sadness, a marvelous thing happens: Your words of hope and trust in Me lift you above your circumstances. This sets your feet on an upward path of gratitude—where your Joy increases step by step. This *sacrifice of praise* is most pleasing to Me!

> *Why are you in despair, O my soul? And why have you become disturbed within me? Hope in God, for I shall again praise Him for the help of His presence.* —Psalm 42:5 nasb

> *You guide me with your counsel, and afterward you will receive me to glory.* —Psalm 73:24 esv

Also read:
2 Corinthians 6:4, 10; Hebrews 13:15

Before You Turn Out the Light

Have confidence in Me as your Savior-God!
Praise Me regardless of your feelings.

August 9
MORNING

WEAR MY ROBE OF RIGHTEOUSNESS with ease. I custom-made it for you, to cover you from head to toe. The price I paid for this covering was astronomical—My own blood. You could never purchase such a royal garment, no matter how hard you worked. Sometimes you forget that My righteousness is a gift, and you feel ill at ease in your regal robe. I weep when I see you squirming under the velvety fabric, as if it were made of scratchy sackcloth.

I want you to trust Me enough to realize your privileged position in My kingdom. Relax in the luxuriant folds of your magnificent robe. Keep your eyes on Me as you practice walking in this garment of salvation. When your behavior is unfitting for one in My kingdom, do not try to throw off your royal robe. Instead, throw off the unrighteous behavior. Then you will be able to feel at ease in this glorious garment, enjoying the gift I fashioned for you before the foundation of the world.

ISAIAH 61:10; 2 CORINTHIANS 5:21;
EPHESIANS 4:22–24

August 9
EVENING

Since you joined My royal family, I have brought much Light into your life. However, this is only *like the first gleam of dawn* compared with *the full Light of day* that awaits all who walk on *the path of the righteous*. When you reach your heavenly home, your new, imperishable eyes will be able to perceive the full Light of My Glory. *In righteousness you will see My Face*—and *be satisfied*.

> *The path of the righteous is like the first gleam of dawn, shining ever brighter till the full light of day.* —Proverbs 4:18

> *As for me, I will see Your face in righteousness; I shall be satisfied when I awake in Your likeness.* —Psalm 17:15 nkjv

Also read:
Malachi 4:2; Acts 9:8–9

Before You Turn Out the Light

Request My help to keep your feet on the path of righteousness—tonight, tomorrow . . . all the way to heaven.

August 10
MORNING

Relax in My healing, holy Presence. Allow Me to transform you through this time alone with Me. As your thoughts center more and more on Me, trust displaces fear and worry. Your mind is somewhat like a seesaw. As your trust in Me goes up, fear and worry automatically go down. Time spent with Me not only increases your trust; it also helps you discern what is important and what is not.

Energy and time are precious, limited entities. Therefore, you need to use them wisely, focusing on what is truly important. As you walk close to Me, saturating your mind with Scripture, I will show you how to spend your time and energy. *My Word is a lamp to your feet; My Presence is a Light for your path.*

Romans 12:2 nkjv; Psalm 52:8;
Ephesians 5:15–16 nkjv; Psalm 119:105

August 10
EVENING

MANY OF THE HARD THINGS you have experienced were, unknown to you, My skillful operations on your heart. Marvel at the wonder of being *a new creation, grafted into Me—the Messiah*. You are forever set free from the condemning *law of sin and death*.

> *"I will give you a new heart and put a new spirit within you; I will take the heart of stone out of your flesh and give you a heart of flesh."* —Ezekiel 36:26 NKJV

> *Therefore if any person is [ingrafted] in Christ (the Messiah) he is a new creation (a new creature altogether); the old [previous moral and spiritual condition] has passed away.* —2 Corinthians 5:17 AMP

Also read:
Romans 8:1–2; Hebrews 1:2

Before You Turn Out the Light

Trust Me to do what you cannot do: remove the little stones that mar the beauty of your heart.

August 11
MORNING

Come to Me. Come to Me. Come to Me. This is My continual invitation to you, proclaimed in holy whispers. When your heart and mind are quiet, you can hear Me inviting you to draw near. Coming close to Me requires no great effort on your part; it is more like ceasing to resist the magnetic pull of My Love. Open yourself to My loving Presence so that I may fill you with My fullness. I want you to experience *how wide and long and high and deep is My Love for you so that you can know My Love that surpasses knowledge.* This vast ocean of Love cannot be measured or explained, but it can be experienced.

REVELATION 22:17; JOHN 6:37;
EPHESIANS 3:16–19

August 11
EVENING

When One of my own calls out to Me, I never fail to respond. I may not provide instant relief, as if I were just a genie, but I go to work immediately, setting in motion the conditions you need. When you have settled down enough to see clearly, I invite you to come near Me, where you can find completeness.

Perseverance must finish its work so that you may be mature and complete, not lacking anything. —James 1:4

Submit yourselves, then, to God. Resist the devil, and he will flee from you. Come near to God and he will come near to you. —James 4:7–8

Also read:
Psalm 145:19; 2 Corinthians 4:6–7

Before You Turn Out the Light

Center your attention on Me while I work in your circumstances and make you complete.

August 12

MORNING

Come to Me when you are weak and weary. Rest snugly in My everlasting arms. I do not despise your weakness, My child. Actually, it draws Me closer to you because weakness stirs up My compassion—My yearning to help. Accept yourself in your weariness, knowing that I understand how difficult your journey has been.

Do not compare yourself with others who seem to skip along their life-paths with ease. Their journeys have been different from yours, and I have gifted them with abundant energy. I have gifted you with fragility, providing opportunities for your spirit to blossom in My Presence. Accept this gift as a sacred treasure: delicate, yet glowing with brilliant Light. Rather than struggling to disguise or deny your weakness, allow Me to bless you richly through it.

ISAIAH 42:3; ISAIAH 54:10;
ROMANS 8:26

August 12
EVENING

My lovingkindness is an eternal gift, so come to Me when you are feeling weak and vulnerable. Remember that you are redeemed royalty, purchased with My own blood. Hold still while I *crown you with lovingkindness and tender mercies.*

Bless the Lord, O my soul; and all that is within me, bless His holy name! Bless the Lord, O my soul, and forget not all His benefits: who forgives all your iniquities, who heals all your diseases, who redeems your life from destruction, who crowns you with lovingkindness and tender mercies. —Psalm 103:1–4 NKJV

The Lord has appeared of old to me, saying: "Yes, I have loved you with an everlasting love; therefore with lovingkindness I have drawn you." —Jeremiah 31:3 NKJV

Also read:
Psalm 62:8

Before You Turn Out the Light

Acknowledge your weakness and your need. I have infinite reservoirs of blessing for you.

August 13
MORNING

LEARN TO ENJOY LIFE MORE. Relax, remembering that I am *God with you*. I crafted you with enormous capacity to know Me and enjoy My Presence. When My people wear sour faces and walk through their lives with resigned rigidity, I am displeased. When you walk through a day with childlike delight, savoring every blessing, you proclaim your trust in Me, your ever-present Shepherd. The more you focus on My Presence with you, the more fully you can enjoy life. Glorify Me through your pleasure in Me. Thus you proclaim My Presence to the watching world.

MATTHEW 1:23; JOHN 10:10–11;
JUDE VV. 24–25

August 13
EVENTING

YOU HAVE EVERY REASON TO BE CHEERFUL because *I have overcome the world*. A joyful heart will improve your health—spiritually, emotionally, and physically. Take time to praise Me for all that I am—the One from whom all blessings flow.

> *A cheerful heart is good medicine, but a crushed spirit dries up the bones.* —PROVERBS 17:22

> *"I have told you these things, so that in Me you may have [perfect] peace and confidence. In the world you have tribulation and trials and distress and frustration; but be of good cheer [take courage; be confident, certain, undaunted]! For I have overcome the world. [I have deprived it of power to harm you and have conquered it for you.]"* —JOHN 16:33 AMP

Also read:
ROMANS 8:39

Before You Turn Out the Light

Fill your mind with thankful thoughts
till your heart overflows with Joy.

August 14
MORNING

I AM YOURS FOR ALL ETERNITY. *I am the Alpha and the Omega: the One who is and was and is to come.* The world you inhabit is a place of constant changes—more than your mind can absorb without going into shock. Even the body you inhabit is changing relentlessly in spite of modern science's attempts to prolong youth and life indefinitely. *I, however, am the same yesterday and today and forever.*

Because I never change, your relationship with Me provides a rock-solid foundation for your life. I will never leave your side. When you move on from this life to the next, My Presence beside you will shine brighter with each step. You have nothing to fear because I am with you for all time and throughout eternity.

REVELATION 1:8; HEBREWS 13:8;
PSALM 102:25–27; PSALM 48:14

August 14
EVENING

I AM THE FIRM FOUNDATION on which you can dance and sing praises and continually celebrate My Presence—just as you long to. When you praise Me, your Joy increases, as does your awareness of My holy Presence. Your body may or may not be mightily engaged in this endeavor, but *I see into your heart*. That is where the ultimate celebration of My Presence takes place.

> *David, wearing a linen ephod, danced before the Lord with all his might.* —2 SAMUEL 6:14

> *But the Lord said to Samuel, "Do not look at his appearance or at his physical stature, because I have refused him. For the Lord does not see as man sees; for man looks at the outward appearance, but the Lord looks at the heart."* —1 SAMUEL 16:7 NKJV

Also read:
DEUTERONOMY 33:27; PSALM 16:11

Before You Turn Out the Light

Go ahead: Dance, sing, pray, and delight in My Presence, just as you long to. I give you every reason to live exuberantly.

August 15
MORNING

I AM THE GOD OF ALL TIME and all that is. Seek Me not only in morning quietness but consistently throughout the day. Do not let unexpected problems distract you from My Presence. Instead, talk with Me about everything, and watch confidently to see what I will do.

Adversity need not interrupt your communion with Me. When things go "wrong," you tend to react as if you're being punished. Instead of this negative response, try to view difficulties as blessings in disguise. *Make Me your Refuge by pouring out your heart to Me, trusting in Me at all times.*

PSALM 105:3 NKJV; PSALM 55:17;
PSALM 32:6; PSALM 62:8

August 15
EVENING

I*T'S GOOD THAT YOU CLING TO MY *hope-cord* as a lifeline when you're struggling with various problems. However, your tendency to be problem-focused robs you of much Joy. As you cling to hope, looking to Me for help, you can be joyful and patient in the midst of affliction.

There is surely a future hope for you, and your hope will not be cut off. —PROVERBS 23:18

We have this hope as an anchor for the soul, firm and secure. It enters the inner sanctuary behind the curtain, where Jesus, who went before us, has entered on our behalf. —HEBREWS 6:19–20

Also read:
1 THESSALONIANS 5:8; ROMANS 12:12

Before You Turn Out the Light

Make the effort to focus more on My Presence than on your difficulties. It is worth it.

August 16
MORNING

MEET ME in early morning splendor. I eagerly await you here. In the stillness of this holy time with Me, I *renew your strength* and saturate you with Peace. While others turn over for extra sleep or anxiously tune in to the latest news, you commune with the Creator of the universe. I have awakened in your heart strong desire to know Me. This longing originated in Me, though it now burns brightly in you.

When you seek My Face in response to My Love-call, both of us are blessed. This is a deep mystery, designed more for your enjoyment than for your understanding. I am not a dour God who discourages pleasure. I delight in your enjoyment of *everything that is true, noble, right, pure, lovely, admirable. Think on these things*, and My Light in you will shine brighter day by day.

ISAIAH 40:31; PSALM 27:4;
PHILIPPIANS 4:8

August 16
EVENING

Nothing is wasted when it is shared with Me. I can bring *beauty out of the ashes* of lost dreams; I can glean Joy out of sorrow, Peace out of adversity. This divine alchemy will become a reality in your experience as you learn how to share more and more of your life with Me.

> *"Peace I leave with you; my peace I give to you. I do not give to you as the world gives. Do not let your hearts be troubled and do not be afraid."* —John 14:27

Also read:
Isaiah 61:1, 3; Matthew 19:26

Before You Turn Out the Light

Do you believe I am able to make you whole?
Present your brokenness to Me.

August 17
MORNING

Find Me in the midst of the maelstrom. Sometimes events whirl around you so quickly that they become a blur. Whisper My Name in recognition that I am still with you. Without skipping a beat in the activities that occupy you, you find strength and Peace through praying My Name. Later, when the happenings have run their course, you can talk with Me more fully.

Accept each day just as it comes to you. Do not waste your time and energy wishing for a different set of circumstances. Instead, trust Me enough to yield to My design and purposes. Remember that nothing can separate you from My loving Presence; *you are Mine.*

PHILIPPIANS 2:9–11; PSALM 29:11;
ISAIAH 43:1

August 17
EVENING

REMEMBER THAT I AM THE POTTER and you are the clay. When you accept My ways with you trustingly—without rebelling or running away—you find freedom through My Spirit. Even more wondrously, I empower you to reflect Me to others with ever-increasing Glory!

> *"I have told you these things, so that in me you may have peace. In this world you will have trouble. But take heart! I have overcome the world."* —JOHN 16:33

> *Now the Lord is the Spirit, and where the Spirit of the Lord is, there is freedom. And we, who with unveiled faces all reflect the Lord's glory, are being transformed into his likeness with ever-increasing glory, which comes from the Lord, who is the Spirit.* —2 CORINTHIANS 3:17–18

Also read:

ISAIAH 64:8

Before You Turn Out the Light

I am shaping you into My likeness with each passing day. Remain malleable in My skillful hands.

August 18
MORNING

Expect to encounter adversity in your life, remembering that you live in a deeply fallen world. Stop trying to find a way that circumvents difficulties. The main problem with an easy life is that it masks your need for Me. When you became a Christian, I infused My very Life into you, empowering you to live on a supernatural plane by depending on Me.

Anticipate coming face to face with impossibilities: situations totally beyond your ability to handle. This awareness of your inadequacy is not something you should try to evade. It is precisely where I want you—the best place to encounter Me in *My Glory and Power*. When you see armies of problems marching toward you, cry out to Me! Allow Me to fight for you. Watch Me working on your behalf, as you *rest in the shadow of My Almighty Presence*.

JOB 5:7; REVELATION 19:1;
PSALM 91:1

August 18
EVENING

*S*INCE I AM THE LIVING WORD, affirming your trust in My promises is an excellent way to draw near Me. As you bask in the beauty of My Presence, you may find yourself wanting to praise Me. Do not restrain that holy impulse; while you are worshiping Me, new hope will grow within you.

In the beginning was the Word, and the Word was with God, and the Word was God. —JOHN 1:1

Why are you in despair, O my soul? And why have you become disturbed within me? Hope in God, for I shall again praise Him for the help of His presence. —PSALM 42:5 NASB

Also read:
MARK 10:27; ACTS 17:28

Before You Turn Out the Light

Don't hold back! Give voice to your praise and to your trust in the things I have promised.

August 19

MORNING

I CONTINUALLY CALL YOU to closeness with Me. I know the depth and breadth of your need for Me. I can read the emptiness of your thoughts when they wander away from Me. I offer rest for your soul, as well as refreshment for your mind and body. As you increasingly find fulfillment in Me, other pleasures become less important. Knowing Me intimately is like having a private wellspring of Joy within you. This spring flows freely from My throne of grace, so your Joy is independent of circumstances.

Waiting in My Presence keeps you connected to Me, aware of all that I offer you. If you feel any deficiency, you need to refocus your attention on Me. This is how you trust Me in the moments of your life.

PSALM 131:2; PSALM 21:6; PSALM 37:7;
JEREMIAH 17:7 NKJV

August 19
EVENING

*W*ALK AS A CHILD OF LIGHT, for My radiance is all around you and also within you; it transforms you inside and out. Remember that *you were once darkness* until My Spirit quickened you to Life, empowering you to live in My holy Presence. Dwell on this blessed remembrance until gratitude wells up within you.

> *For you were once darkness, but now you are light in the Lord. Walk as children of light.* —EPHESIANS 5:8 NKJV

> *Planted in the house of the LORD, they will flourish in the courts of our God.* —PSALM 92:13 NASB

Also read:
EPHESIANS 1:4–6; NUMBERS 6:25 NKJV

Before You Turn Out the Light

I urge you to live so near Me that you flourish in My transforming Light. Brainstorm some ideas to help you thrive.

August 20

MORNING

I AM A GOD WHO HEALS. I heal broken bodies, broken minds, broken hearts, broken lives, and broken relationships. My very Presence has immense healing powers. You cannot live close to Me without experiencing some degree of healing. However, it is also true that *you have not because you ask not.* You receive the healing that flows naturally from My Presence, whether you seek it or not. But there is more—much more—available to those who ask.

The first step in receiving healing is to live ever so close to Me. The benefits of this practice are too numerous to list. As you grow more and more intimate with Me, I reveal My will to you more directly. When the time is right, I prompt you to ask for healing of some brokenness in you or in another person. The healing may be instantaneous, or it may be a process. That is up to Me. Your part is to trust Me fully and to thank Me for the restoration that has begun.

I rarely heal all the brokenness in a person's life. Even My servant Paul was told, *"My grace is sufficient for you,"* when he sought healing for the *thorn in his flesh.* Nonetheless, much healing is available to those whose lives are intimately interwoven with Mine. *Ask, and you will receive.*

JAMES 4:2 KJV; 2 CORINTHIANS 12:7–9; MATTHEW 7:7

August 20
EVENING

I AM WITH YOU, within you, all around you—continually at work in your life. Dare to ask great things of Me, remembering who I am. Pondering My limitless ability to help you will strengthen your faith and encourage you to pray boldly.

> *Now to Him who is able to do exceedingly abundantly above all that we ask or think, according to the power that works in us . . .* —EPHESIANS 3:20 NKJV

> *"For everyone who asks and keeps on asking receives; and he who seeks and keeps on seeking finds; and to him who knocks and keeps on knocking, the door shall be opened."* —LUKE 11:10 AMP

JEREMIAH 30:17; LUKE 18:2, 7

Before You Turn Out the Light

Dare to pray boldly because of who I am.

August 21
MORNING

Wait with Me for a while. I have much to tell you. You are walking along the path I have chosen for you. It is both a privileged and a perilous way: experiencing My glorious Presence and heralding that reality to others. Sometimes you feel presumptuous to be carrying out such an assignment.

Do not worry about what other people think of you. The work I am doing in you is hidden at first. But eventually blossoms will burst forth, and abundant fruit will be born. Stay on the path of Life with Me. Trust Me wholeheartedly, letting My Spirit fill you with Joy and Peace.

> Isaiah 30:18; 1 Kings 8:23;
> Galatians 5:22–23

August 21
EVENING

I AM AS NEAR AS A WHISPERED PRAYER, listening attentively even to your softest utterance. This sort of closeness, with hushed words of love, is always available to you in your relationship with Me. *I am near to all who call on Me*, even if your call is the faintest whisper.

The LORD is near to all who call on him, to all who call on him in truth. —PSALM 145:18

The LORD said, "Go out and stand on the mountain in the presence of the LORD, for the LORD is about to pass by." Then a great and powerful wind tore the mountains apart and shattered the rocks before the LORD, but the LORD was not in the wind. After the wind there was an earthquake, but the LORD was not in the earthquake. After the earthquake came a fire, but the LORD was not in the fire. And after the fire came a gentle whisper. —1 KINGS 19:11–12

Also read:
JOHN 14:6 NKJV; JOSHUA 1:5

Before You Turn Out the Light

Do you want to feel closer to Me? Whisper your words to Me tonight rather than praying them silently.

August 22
MORNING

Trust Me, and don't be afraid. I want you to view trials as exercises designed to develop your trust-muscles. You live in the midst of fierce spiritual battles, and fear is one of Satan's favorite weapons. When you start to feel afraid, affirm your trust in Me. Speak out loud, if circumstances permit. *Resist the devil in My Name, and he will slink away from you.* Refresh yourself in My holy Presence. Speak or sing praises to Me, and My Face will shine radiantly upon you.

Remember that there is *no condemnation for those who belong to Me.* You have been judged NOT GUILTY for all eternity. *Trust Me, and don't be afraid; for I am your Strength, Song, and Salvation.*

JAMES 4:7; ROMANS 8:1–2;

ISAIAH 12:2

August 22

EVENING

You have a perfectly loving, infinitely strong Father, so bring your fears freely to Him. Open your heart to receive vast quantities of His Love. The more of this Love you hold in your heart, the less room there is for fear.

For you did not receive the spirit of bondage again to fear, but you received the Spirit of adoption by whom we cry out, "Abba, Father." —Romans 8:15 nkjv

There is no fear in love. But perfect love drives out fear, because fear has to do with punishment. —1 John 4:18

Also read:
2 Corinthians 3:17; John 15:9

Before You Turn Out the Light

Allow your Father in heaven to hold you close to His heart, where you know you are safe.

August 23
MORNING

ENTRUST YOUR LOVED ONES TO ME; release them into My protective care. They are much safer with Me than in your clinging hands. If you let a loved one become an idol in your heart, you endanger that one—as well as yourself. Joseph and his father, Jacob, suffered terribly because *Jacob loved Joseph more than any of his other sons* and treated him with special favor. So Joseph's brothers hated him and plotted against him. Ultimately, I used that situation for good, but both father and son had to endure years of suffering and separation from one another.

I detest idolatry, even in the form of parental love, so beware of making a beloved child your idol. When you release loved ones to Me, you are free to cling to My hand. As you entrust others into My care, I am free to shower blessings on them. *My Presence will go with them wherever they go, and I will give them rest*. This same Presence stays with you as you relax and place your trust in Me. Watch to see what I will do.

GENESIS 37:3–4; EPHESIANS 3:20;
EXODUS 33:14

August 23
EVENING

ONE OF THE BEST WAYS to draw upon My strength is to sing praises to Me. When you praise Me in the midst of a hard day, both you and I are blessed. I come near, and I hide you *in the secret place of My Presence*.

You are my hiding place; you will protect me from trouble and surround me with songs of deliverance. —PSALM 32:7

You shall hide them in the secret place of Your presence from the plots of man; You shall keep them secretly in a pavilion from the strife of tongues. —PSALM 31:20 NKJV

Also read:
PSALM 143:9; PSALM 22:3 AMP

Before You Turn Out the Light

Break free of your problems by worshiping Me
in songs, in shouts, even in whispers.

August 24
MORNING

I AM ALL AROUND YOU, hovering over you even as you seek My Face. I am nearer than you dare believe, closer than the air you breathe. If My children could only recognize My Presence, they would never feel lonely again. *I know every thought before you think it, every word before you speak it.* My Presence impinges on your innermost being. Can you see the absurdity of trying to hide anything from Me? You can easily deceive other people, and even yourself, but I read you like an open, large-print book.

Deep within themselves, most people have some awareness of My imminent Presence. Many people run from Me and vehemently deny My existence because My closeness terrifies them. But My own children have nothing to fear, for I have cleansed them by My blood and clothed them in My righteousness. Be blessed by My intimate nearness. Since I live in you, let Me also live through you, shining My Light into the darkness.

PSALM 139:1–4; EPHESIANS 2:13;
2 CORINTHIANS 5:21

August 24
EVENING

When your circumstances are stressful, it is easy for you to become irritable, but I want you to demonstrate gentleness. This is possible to the extent that you find Joy in Me. Since I am *the same yesterday, today, and forever*, there is *always* much for you to rejoice about.

> *Rejoice in the Lord always. I will say it again:*
> *Rejoice! Let your gentleness be evident to all.*
> *The Lord is near.* —Philippians 4:4–5

> *Jesus Christ is the same yesterday, today,*
> *and forever.* —Hebrews 13:8 NKJV

Also read:
Galatians 5:22–23 esv; Psalm 107:43

Before You Turn Out the Light

Be joyful in the knowledge that I am near and I never change.

August 25
MORNING

I am the eternal I am; I always have been, and I always will be. In My Presence you experience Love and Light, Peace and Joy. I am intimately involved in all your moments, and I am training you to be aware of Me at all times. Your assignment is to collaborate with Me in this training process.

I have taken up residence within you; I am central in your innermost being. Your mind goes off in tangents from its holy Center, time after time. Do not be alarmed by your inability to remain focused on Me. Simply bring your thoughts gently back to Me each time they wander. The quickest way to redirect your mind to me is to whisper My Name.

Exodus 3:14; 1 Corinthians 3:16;
Psalm 25:14–15

August 25
EVENING

YOUR MIND IS A SPIRITUAL BATTLEFIELD—that's why I urge you to stay alert! The evil one is *the father of lies*; his deceptions can worm their way into your mind if you let down your guard. When you ask for protection, always pray in My Name, because I defeated the devil utterly on the cross!

> *Be self-controlled and alert. Your enemy the devil prowls around like a roaring lion looking for someone to devour.* —1 PETER 5:8

> *"He [the devil] was a murderer from the beginning, not holding to the truth, for there is no truth in him. When he lies, he speaks his native language, for he is a liar and the father of lies."* —JOHN 8:44

Also read:
ROMANS 8:6

Before You Turn Out the Light

Begin your time with Me this evening with a prayer for protection.

August 26
MORNING

Trust Me in the midst of a messy day. Your inner calm—your Peace in My Presence—need not be shaken by what is going on around you. Though you live in this temporal world, your innermost being is rooted and grounded in eternity. When you start to feel stressed, detach yourself from the disturbances around you. Instead of desperately striving to maintain order and control in your little world, relax and remember that circumstances cannot touch My Peace.

Seek My Face, and I will share My mind with you, opening your eyes to see things from My perspective. *Do not let your heart be troubled, and do not be afraid.* The Peace I give is sufficient for you.

JOHN 16:33; PSALM 105:4;
JOHN 14:27

August 26
EVENING

The apostle Paul had endured tremendous affliction: He had been imprisoned, beaten, and stoned; he had been shipwrecked three times; he had often been hungry, thirsty, and cold. Yet he considered his massive troubles *a weightless trifle* because he was comparing them with *eternal Glory*. I am training you to view your problems this way too—from an eternal perspective.

Our light and momentary troubles are achieving for us an eternal glory that far outweighs them all. —2 Corinthians 4:17

Also read:

2 Corinthians 11:24–27 NKJV

Before You Turn Out the Light

Evaluate how well you are handling the adversity in your life. I don't waste anything, including your suffering.

August 27
MORNING

SPEND TIME WITH ME for the pure pleasure of being in My company. I can brighten up the dullest of gray days; I can add sparkle to the routines of daily life. You have to repeat so many tasks day after day. This monotony can dull your thinking until your mind slips into neutral. A mind that is unfocused is vulnerable to the world, the flesh, and the devil, all of which exert a downward pull on your thoughts. As your thinking processes deteriorate, you become increasingly confused and directionless. The best remedy is to refocus your mind and heart on Me, your constant Companion.

Even the most confusing day opens up before you as you go step by step with Me. My Presence goes with you wherever you go, providing *Light for your path*.

PSALM 43:4; PSALM 63:7–8;
PSALM 119:105

August 27
EVENING

WHILE YOU LABOR through your earthly afflictions, keep your eyes on the promised reward: boundless Joy in heaven! Even now you can enjoy growing awareness of Me. No matter what is happening, there is *fullness of Joy* to be found in My Presence.

> *"Therefore you now have sorrow; but I will see you again and your heart will rejoice, and your joy no one will take from you."* —JOHN 16:22 NKJV

> *"A woman giving birth to a child has pain because her time has come; but when her baby is born she forgets the anguish because of her joy that a child is born into the world."* —JOHN 16:21

Also read:
PSALM 16:11 NKJV

Before You Turn Out the Light

In your sadness, trust Me enough to anticipate feeling joyful again. This takes the sting out of every temporary sorrow.

August 28
MORNING

Grow strong in the Light of My Presence. As My Face shines upon you, you receive nutrients that enhance your growth in grace. I designed you to commune with Me face to Face, and this interaction strengthens your soul. Such communion provides a tiny glimpse of what awaits you in heaven, where all barriers between you and My Glory will be removed. This meditative time with Me blesses you doubly: You experience My Presence here and now, and you are refreshed by the hope of heaven, where you will know Me in ecstatic Joy.

PSALM 4:6–8; REVELATION 21:23;
2 PETER 3:13

August 28
EVENING

THE CHOICE TO BE BOLD rests on your confidence that I am with you and *for* you. Remember that I am a God of surprises: I am not limited by the way things are or by the paltry possibilities you can see. *With Me all things are possible!*

> *Have I not commanded you? Be strong and courageous. Do not be terrified; do not be discouraged, for the L*ORD *your God will be with you wherever you go.* —JOSHUA 1:9

> *Jesus looked at them and said to them, "With men this is impossible, but with God all things are possible."* —MATTHEW 19:26 NKJV

Also read:
LAMENTATIONS 3:25–26 NKJV

Before You Turn Out the Light

I will increase your strength and your courage when you look to Me. Refuse to grow discouraged.

August 29

MORNING

Demonstrate your trust in Me by sitting quietly in My Presence. Put aside all that is waiting to be done, and refuse to worry about anything. This sacred time together strengthens you and prepares you to face whatever the day will bring. By waiting with Me before you begin the day's activities, you proclaim the reality of My living Presence. This act of faith—waiting before working—is noted in the spirit world, where your demonstration of trust weakens *principalities and powers of darkness*.

The most effective way to resist evil is to draw near Me. When you need to take action, I will guide you clearly through My Spirit and My Word. The world is so complex and overstimulating that you can easily lose your sense of direction. Doing countless unnecessary activities will dissipate your energy. When you spend time with Me, I restore your sense of direction. As you look to Me for guidance, I enable you to do less but accomplish more.

Luke 12:22–25; Ephesians 6:12 nkjv; Proverbs 16:3

August 29

EVENING

I DESIGNED YOU TO BE FILLED with heavenly contents: My Love, Joy, and Peace. I am eager to pour out My abundance upon and within you, but this takes time—focused time with Me. Come to Me and linger in My Presence. As you wait with Me, My very Life streams into you, filling you up with heavenly substance.

> *But the fruit of the Spirit is love, joy, peace, patience.* —GALATIANS 5:22

> *"In the same way, let your light shine before men, that they may see your good deeds and praise your Father in heaven."* —MATTHEW 5:16

Also read:
2 CORINTHIANS 4:7 AMP; COLOSSIANS 1:27

Before You Turn Out the Light

Do not rush these moments with Me—I am filling you with everything you need.

August 30
MORINING

There is no place so desolate that you cannot find Me there. When Hagar fled from her mistress, Sarah, into the wilderness, she thought she was utterly alone and forsaken. But Hagar encountered Me in that desolate place. There she addressed Me as *the Living One who sees me*. Through that encounter with My Presence, she gained courage to return to her mistress.

No set of circumstances could ever isolate you from My loving Presence. Not only do I see you always; I see you as a redeemed saint, gloriously radiant in My righteousness. That is why *I take great delight in you and rejoice over you with singing*!

Genesis 16:13–14 amp; Psalm 139:7–10;
Zephaniah 3:17

August 30
EVENING

Although I am never the author of evil, I am fully able to use bad things for good. This does not remove your suffering, but it does redeem it—infusing it with meaning. So if you are in a storm of difficulties, I say to you, *"Take courage. It is I."*

> *Jesus immediately said to them: "Take courage! It is I. Don't be afraid."* —Matthew 14:27

> *"You will seek Me and find Me, when you search for Me with all your heart."* —Jeremiah 29:13 NKJV

Also read:
1 Kings 19:12; Isaiah 9:6 NKJV

Before You Turn Out the Light

Are you hearing My voice? Listen for Me above the storm.

August 31
MORNING

GROW STRONG IN YOUR WEAKNESS. Some of My children I've gifted with abundant strength and stamina. Others, like you, have received the humble gift of frailty. Your fragility is not a punishment, nor does it indicate lack of faith. On the contrary, weak ones like you must live by faith, depending on Me to get you through the day. I am developing your ability to trust Me, to lean on Me rather than on your understanding. Your natural preference is to plan out your day, knowing what will happen when. My preference is for you to depend on Me continually, trusting Me to guide you and strengthen you as needed. This is how you grow strong in your weakness.

JAMES 4:13–15; PROVERBS 3:5 AMP;
ISAIAH 40:28–31

August 31
EVENING

MANY OF THE FUTURE THINGS you anxiously anticipate will not actually reach you. My promise is for things you face in the present, and it is sufficient. So when you are feeling the strain of an uphill journey, tell yourself the truth: *"I have strength for all things through Christ who empowers me!"*

> *I have strength for all things in Christ Who empowers me [I am ready for anything and equal to anything through Him Who infuses inner strength into me; I am self-sufficient in Christ's sufficiency].* —PHILIPPIANS 4:13 AMP

> *The LORD is my strength and my shield; my heart trusts in him, and I am helped. My heart leaps for joy and I will give thanks to him in song.* —PSALM 28:7

Also read:
JOHN 15:4 NKJV

Before You Turn Out the Light

Count on Me to provide strength—just when you need it—for everything that touches your life.

September

"I am the light of the world. Whoever follows me will never walk in darkness, but will have the light of life."

JOHN 8:12

September 1
MORNING

Seek Me with your whole being. I desire to be found by you, and I orchestrate the events of your life with that purpose in mind. When things go well and you are blessed, you can feel Me smiling on you. When you encounter rough patches along your life-journey, trust that My Light is still shining upon you. My reasons for allowing these adversities may be shrouded in mystery, but My continual Presence with you is an absolute promise. Seek Me in good times; seek Me in hard times. You will find Me watching over you all the time.

DEUTERONOMY 4:29; HEBREWS 10:23;
PSALM 145:20; PSALM 121:7–8

September 1
EVENIN G

When Sorrow becomes your travel companion, embrace her as a blessing from Me. If you receive her into your heart, she will bring new depth and richness to your soul. She can teach you more about Me—a Man of sorrows, familiar with suffering—and also give you hope based on the promise of My Presence.

He was despised and rejected by men, a man of sorrows, and familiar with suffering. Like one from whom men hide their faces he was despised, and we esteemed him not. —Isaiah 53:3

Why are you in despair, O my soul? And why have you become disturbed within me? Hope in God, for I shall again praise Him for the help of His presence. —Psalm 42:5 nasb

Also read:
2 Corinthians 6:10

Before You Turn Out the Light

Praise Me for the help of My Presence.

September 2
MORNING

Living in dependence on Me is a glorious adventure. Most people scurry around busily, trying to accomplish things through their own strength and ability. Some succeed enormously; others fail miserably. But both groups miss what life is meant to be: living and working in collaboration with Me.

When you depend on Me continually, your whole perspective changes. You see miracles happening all around, while others see only natural occurrences and "coincidences." You begin each day with joyful expectation, watching to see what I will do. You accept weakness as a gift from Me, knowing that *My Power plugs in most readily to consecrated weakness.* You keep your plans tentative, knowing that My plans are far superior. *You consciously live, move, and have your being in Me,* desiring that I live in you. I in you and you in Me. This is the intimate adventure I offer you.

2 Corinthians 12:9–10; Acts 17:28;
Colossians 2:6–7; John 14:20

September 2
EVENING

In the Psalms, David wrote about the beauty of days lived with Me always before him and beside him. Whatever you do, do it for Me—with Me, through Me, in Me. Even menial tasks glow with the Joy of My Presence when you do them for Me.

I have set the Lord always before me. Because he is at my right hand, I will not be shaken. —Psalm 16:8

And whatever you do, do it heartily, as to the Lord and not to men, knowing that from the Lord you will receive the reward of the inheritance; for you serve the Lord Christ. —Colossians 3:23–24 NKJV

Also read:
Romans 8:38–39

Before You Turn Out the Light

Set Me ever before you, and I will pour into your efforts with vibrant Life.

September 3
MORNING

Let the dew of My Presence refresh your mind and heart. So many, many things vie for your attention in this complex world of instant communication. The world has changed enormously since I first gave the command to *be still, and know that I am God*. However, this timeless truth is essential for the well-being of your soul. As dew refreshes grass and flowers during the stillness of the night, so My Presence revitalizes you as you sit quietly with Me.

A refreshed, revitalized mind is able to sort out what is important and what is not. In its natural condition, your mind easily gets stuck on trivial matters. Like the spinning wheels of a car trapped in mud, the cogs of your brain spin impotently when you focus on a trivial thing. As soon as you start communicating with Me about the matter, your thoughts gain traction, and you can move on to more important things. Communicate with Me continually, and I will put My thoughts into your mind.

Psalm 46:10; Luke 10:39–42;
1 Corinthians 14:33 nkjv

September 3
EVENING

THERE IS NOTHING WRONG with seeking solutions, but problem-solving can turn into an addiction, your mind spinning with so many plans and possibilities that you become confused and exhausted. To protect yourself from this mental exhaustion, you need to remind yourself that *I am with you always*, taking care of you. Choose to *be joyful in Me, your Savior*, for I am indeed enough!

> *"[Go and make disciples,] teaching them to obey everything I have commanded you. And surely I am with you always, to the very end of the age."* —MATTHEW 28:20

> *Though the fig tree does not bud and there are no grapes on the vines, though the olive crop fails and the fields produce no food, though there are no sheep in the pen and no cattle in the stalls, yet I will rejoice in the LORD, I will be joyful in God my Savior.* —HABAKKUK 3:17–18

Also read:
MATTHEW 1:21–23 NKJV

Before You Turn Out the Light

Rejoice in Me and My sufficiency in this moment. My Spirit will help you.

September 4
MORNING

IN CLOSENESS TO ME, you are safe. In the intimacy of My Presence, you are energized. No matter where you are in the world, you know you belong when you sense My nearness. Ever since the Fall, man has experienced a gaping emptiness that only My Presence can fill. I designed you for close communication with your Creator. How I enjoyed walking in the garden with Adam and Eve before the evil one deceived them!

When you commune with Me in the garden of your heart, both you and I are blessed. This is My way of living in the world—through you! Together we will push back the darkness, for *I am the Light of the world.*

PSALM 32:7; ROMANS 1:6;
GENESIS 3:8–9; JOHN 8:12

September 4
EVENING

I AM YOUR SHEPHERD, tenderly leading you step by step through your life. I want you to realize how precious you are to Me—how much I delight in you. I long for you to reciprocate by delighting in Me.

Delight yourself in the LORD and he will give you the desires of your heart. —PSALM 37:4

Let us then approach the throne of grace with confidence, so that we may receive mercy and find grace to help us in our time of need. —HEBREWS 4:16

Also read:
1 TIMOTHY 6:15–16; REVELATION 1:14–16

Before You Turn Out the Light

Approach Me with anticipation. Our communion together will bless us both.

September 5
MORNING

I AM YOUR BEST FRIEND, as well as your King. Walk hand in hand with Me through your life. Together we will face whatever each day brings: pleasures, hardships, adventures, disappointments. Nothing is wasted when it is shared with Me. *I can bring beauty out of the ashes* of lost dreams. I can glean Joy out of sorrow, Peace out of adversity. Only a Friend who is also the King of kings could accomplish this divine alchemy. There is no other like Me!

The friendship I offer you is practical and down-to-earth, yet it is saturated with heavenly Glory. Living in My Presence means living in two realms simultaneously: the visible world and unseen, eternal reality. I have equipped you to stay conscious of Me while walking along dusty, earthbound paths.

JOHN 15:13–15; ISAIAH 61:3;
2 CORINTHIANS 6:10

September 5
EVENING

When conditions that are troubling you get worse instead of better, it's easy to feel as if I am letting you down—as if I really don't care about what you're going through. Though there are many things you don't understand, you can rest in My unfailing Love. This Love is independent of all circumstances, and it will never be taken away from you.

> *Humble yourselves under the mighty hand of God, that He may exalt you in due time, casting all your care upon Him, for He cares for you.* —1 Peter 5:6–7 nkjv

> *And [the Lord] said, "My Presence will go with you, and I will give you rest."* —Exodus 33:14 nkjv

Also read:
Psalm 46:10 nasb; Micah 7:7

Before You Turn Out the Light

Hand Me your anxiety, and fall back into
My strong arms with a sigh of trust.

September 6
MORNING

Do everything in dependence on Me. The desire to act independently—apart from Me—springs from the root of pride. Self-sufficiency is subtle, insinuating its way into your thoughts and actions without your realizing it. But *apart from Me, you can do nothing*: that is, nothing of eternal value. My deepest desire for you is that you learn to depend on Me in every situation. I move heaven and earth to accomplish this purpose, but you must collaborate with Me in this training. Teaching you would be simple if I negated your free will or overwhelmed you with My Power. However, I love you too much to withdraw the godlike privilege I bestowed on you as My image-bearer. Use your freedom wisely by relying on Me constantly. Thus you enjoy My Presence and My Peace.

John 15:5; Ephesians 6:10;
Genesis 1:26–27

September 6
EVENING

MANY PEOPLE VIEW DEPENDENCE as a despicable condition, so they strive to be as self-sufficient as possible. I designed you to need Me continually—and to delight in that neediness. *Delight yourself in Me* more and more; this increases your Joy and glorifies Me.

> *The Lord, He is the One who goes before you. He will be with you, He will not leave you nor forsake you; do not fear nor be dismayed.* —Deuteronomy 31:8 NKJV

> *With my whole heart I have sought You; oh, let me not wander from Your commandments! Your word I have hidden in my heart, that I might not sin against You. Blessed are You, O Lord! Teach me Your statutes.* —Psalm 119:10–12 NKJV

Also read:
1 Thessalonians 5:16–17; Psalm 37:4

Before You Turn Out the Light

There is always Joy to be found in Me. Speak to Me in this hour, knowing that I hear and I care.

September 7
MORNING

ENJOY THE WARMTH OF MY PRESENCE shining upon you. Feel your face tingle as you bask in My Love-Light. I delight in you more than you can imagine. I approve of you continuously, for I see you cloaked in My Light, *arrayed in My righteousness. There is no condemnation for those who are clothed in Me!* That is why I abhor the use of guilt as a means of motivation among Christians.

Some pastors try to whip their people into action with guilt-inducing sermons. This procedure can drive many people to work harder, but the end does not justify the means. Guilt-evoking messages can undermine the very foundation of grace in a believer's heart. A pastor may feel successful when his people are doing more, but I look at their hearts. I grieve when I see grace eroding, with weeds of anxious works creeping in. I want you to relax in the assurance of My perfect Love. *The law of My Spirit of Life has set you free from the law of sin and death.*

ISAIAH 61:10; ROMANS 8:1–2

September 7
EVENING

Instead of shaking the bushes—trying to make things happen—wait to see what I am doing. I am at work in many areas of your life long before you can discern results. When the time is right, you will see the results of My handiwork. You may even get a glimpse of My Glory!

> *Then Jesus said, "Did I not tell you that if you believed, you would see the glory of God?"* —John 11:40

> *We live by faith, not by sight.* —2 Corinthians 5:7

Also read:
Psalm 38:15 ; Revelation 21:23

Before You Turn Out the Light

Content yourself with a quiet, simple life that accepts each moment as a gift from Me.

September 8

MORNING

Accept each day exactly as it comes to you. By that, I mean not only the circumstances of your day but also the condition of your body. Your assignment is to trust Me absolutely, resting in My sovereignty and faithfulness.

On some days, your circumstances and your physical condition feel out of balance: The demands on you seem far greater than your strength. Days like that present a choice between two alternatives—giving up or relying on Me. Even if you wrongly choose the first alternative, I will not reject you. You can turn to Me at any point, and I will help you crawl out of the mire of discouragement. I will infuse My strength into you moment by moment, giving you all that you need for this day. Trust Me by relying on My empowering Presence.

PSALM 42:5; 2 CORINTHIANS 13:4;

JEREMIAH 31:25

September 8
EVENING

I WANT YOU TO KNOW *the hope to which I have called you—the riches of My glorious inheritance.* When present circumstances are weighing you down, grasp onto hope for dear life! It will help you not only to survive but to thrive—to live joyously.

> *[May God] give you the Spirit of wisdom and of revelation in the knowledge of him, having the eyes of your hearts enlightened, that you may know what is the hope to which he has called you, what are the riches of his glorious inheritance in the saints.* —EPHESIANS 1:17–18 ESV

> *There is surely a future hope for you, and your hope will not be cut off.* —PROVERBS 23:18

Also read:
ROMANS 12:12

Before You Turn Out the Light

Review the riches that are yours as described in My Word. We are co-heirs of all these blessings!

September 9
MORNING

Walk with Me along paths of trust. The most direct route between point A and point B on your life-journey is the path of unwavering trust in Me. When your faith falters, you choose a trail that meanders and takes you well out of your way. You will get to point B eventually, but you will have lost precious time and energy. As soon as you realize you have wandered from your trust-path, look to Me and whisper, "I trust You, Jesus." This affirmation will help you get back on track.

The farther you roam along paths of unbelief, the harder it is to remember that I am with you. Anxious thoughts branch off in all directions, taking you farther and farther from awareness of My Presence. You need to voice your trust in Me frequently. This simple act of faith will keep you walking along straight paths with Me. *Trust in Me with all your heart, and I will make your paths straight.*

ISAIAH 26:4; PSALM 9:10;
PSALM 25:4–5; PROVERBS 3:5–6

September 9
EVENING

Each of My followers has a unique relationship with Me, composed of all your communication with Me, your love for Me, your receptivity and responsiveness to Me. Sometimes when you are seeking My Face, the reality of My glorious Being outshines your current circumstances and lifts you above them. You feel free, and your spirit soars with Me. You rejoice in Me and are strengthened by that divine Joy. Thus you enjoy glimpses of heaven while continuing to dwell on earth.

Now faith is being sure of what we hope for and certain of what we do not see. —Hebrews 11:1

Then Jesus said, "Did I not tell you that if you believed, you would see the glory of God?" —John 11:40

Also read:
Ephesians 2:6; Nehemiah 8:10

Before You Turn Out the Light

Believe this: Though I am invisible, I am both Real and really with you. This is foundational to knowing Me.

September 10
MORNING

I AM ALWAYS AVAILABLE TO YOU. Once you have trusted Me as your Savior, I never distance Myself from you. Sometimes you may *feel* distant from Me. Recognize that as feeling; do not confuse it with reality. The Bible is full of My promises to be with you always. As I assured Jacob, when he was journeying away from home into unknown places, *I am with you and will watch over you wherever you go.* My last recorded promise to My followers was: *Surely I am with you always, to the very end of the age.* Let these assurances of My continual Presence fill you with Joy and Peace. No matter what you may lose in this life, you can never lose your relationship with Me.

ISAIAH 54:10; GENESIS 28:15;
MATTHEW 28:19–20

September 10
EVENING

The way to find Joy in adversity is to encounter *Me*. You can pray, "Jesus, help me find You in the midst of this mess!" As you *remain in Me*, I enable you to see things from My perspective.

> *Oh, the depth of the riches of the wisdom and knowledge of God! How unsearchable his judgments, and his paths beyond tracing out!* —ROMANS 11:33

> *"Remain in me, and I will remain in you. No branch can bear fruit by itself; it must remain in the vine. Neither can you bear fruit unless you remain in me."* —JOHN 15:4

Also read:
JAMES 1:2–3 NKJV

Before You Turn Out the Light

Unplug from your problems as you prepare to sleep, and plug in to My Presence.

September 11
MORNING

REJOICE IN ME ALWAYS! No matter what is going on, you can rejoice in your Love-relationship with Me. This is *the secret of being content in all circumstances*. So many people dream of the day when they will finally be happy: when they are out of debt, when their children are out of trouble, when they have more leisure time, and so on. While they daydream, their moments are trickling into the ground like precious balm spilling wastefully from overturned bottles.

Fantasizing about future happiness will never bring fulfillment because fantasy is unreality. Even though I am invisible, I am far more Real than the world you see around you. My reality is eternal and unchanging. Bring your moments to Me, and I will fill them with vibrant Joy. *Now* is the time to rejoice in My Presence!

PHILIPPIANS 4:4, 12;
PSALM 102:27; 1 PETER 1:8

September 11

EVENING

Living to please Me is a wise investment—not only for rewards in heaven but also for daily pleasure on earth. I am meant to be the Center of your existence, the Sun around which you orbit. Awareness of My amazing Love will help you enjoy the radiant pleasures of My Presence.

And without faith it is impossible to please God, because anyone who comes to him must believe that he exists and that he rewards those who earnestly seek him. —HEBREWS 11:6

We . . . do not cease to pray for you, and ask . . . that you may walk worthy of the Lord, fully pleasing Him, being fruitful in every good work and increasing in the knowledge of God. —COLOSSIANS 1:9–10 NKJV

Also read:

2 CORINTHIANS 10:5

Before You Turn Out the Light

Place Me at the center of your existence. Journal it; pray it; picture it in your mind.

September 12
MORNING

RECEIVE MY PEACE. It is My continual gift to you. The best way to receive this gift is to sit quietly in My Presence, trusting Me in every area of your life. *Quietness and trust* accomplish far more than you can imagine: not only in you, but also on earth and in heaven. When you trust Me in a given area, you release that problem or person into My care.

Spending time alone with Me can be a difficult discipline because it goes against the activity addiction of this age. You may appear to be doing nothing, but actually you are participating in battles going on within spiritual realms. You are waging war—not with *the weapons of the world*, but with heavenly weapons, which *have divine power to demolish strongholds*. Living close to Me is a sure defense against evil.

JOHN 14:27; ISAIAH 30:15;
2 CORINTHIANS 10:4

September 12
EVENING

WHEN YOU REALIZE that your deepest desire is for Me, you are well on the way to finding satisfaction. As you go along this path of Life, you will encounter companions I have chosen for you—Joy and Peace. Though they are intangible, their company is quite beneficial: They can relieve the thirst of your soul.

As the deer pants for streams of water, so my soul pants for you, O God. My soul thirsts for God, for the living God. When can I go and meet with God? —PSALM 42:1–2

Let the peace of Christ rule in your hearts, since as members of one body you were called to peace. —COLOSSIANS 3:15

Also read:
PSALM 143:6; PSALM 16:11

Before You Turn Out the Light

Walk with Joy and Peace into this night—
and on into tomorrow. These companions
will enhance your awareness of Me.

September 13
MORNING

Come to Me and rest. Give your mind a break from its habitual judging. You form judgments about this situation, that situation, this person, that person, yourself, even the weather—as if judging were your main function in life. But I created you first and foremost to *know Me* and to live in rich communication with Me. When you become preoccupied with passing judgment, you usurp My role.

Relate to Me as creature to Creator, sheep to Shepherd, subject to King, clay to Potter. Allow Me to have My way in your life. Rather than evaluating My ways with you, accept them thankfully. The intimacy I offer you is not an invitation to act as if you were My equal. Worship Me as *King of kings* while walking hand in hand with Me down the path of Life.

Matthew 7:1; John 17:3; Romans 9:20–21;
1 Timothy 6:15

September 13
EVENING

IN MY PRESENCE YOU HAVE INFINITE APPROVAL. You often judge yourself on the basis of what you see in the mirror even though you know how fickle and shallow that ever-changing image is. Try to see yourself as you truly are—arrayed in perfect righteousness, adorned in glowing approval.

Surely you have granted him eternal blessings and made him glad with the joy of your presence. —PSALM 21:6

I delight greatly in the LORD; my soul rejoices in my God. For he has clothed me with garments of salvation and arrayed me in a robe of righteousness, as a bridegroom adorns his head like a priest, and as a bride adorns herself with her jewels. —ISAIAH 61:10

Also read:
PSALM 90:14

Before You Turn Out the Light

Are you finding gladness in My Presence? Look into My eyes and see for yourself: I love you, and I have made you lovely.

September 14
MORNING

WORSHIP ME by living close to Me. This was My original design for man, into whom *I breathed My very breath of Life*. This is My desire for you: that you stay near Me as you walk along your life-path. Each day is an important part of that journey. Although you may feel as if you are going nowhere in this world, your spiritual journey is another matter altogether, taking you along steep, treacherous paths of adventure. That is why *walking in the Light of My Presence* is essential to keep you from stumbling. By staying close to Me, you present yourself as a *living sacrifice*. Even the most routine part of your day can be *a spiritual act of worship, holy and pleasing to Me*.

GENESIS 2:7; PSALM 89:15; ROMANS 12:1–2

September 14

EVENING

GENUINE WORSHIP requires that you know Me as I truly am. You cannot comprehend Me perfectly or completely, but you *can* strive to know Me accurately as I am revealed in the Bible. By deepening your understanding of Me, you are transformed and I am glorified—in beautiful worship.

> *Give unto the L*ORD *the glory due to His name; worship the L*ORD *in the beauty of holiness.* —PSALM 29:2 NKJV

> *Now we see but a poor reflection as in a mirror; then we shall see face to face. Now I know in part; then I shall know fully, even as I am fully known.* —1 CORINTHIANS 13:12

Also read:
ISAIAH 6:3 NKJV

Before You Turn Out the Light

How does your world reflect My Glory? Consider this, and worship Me in the beauty of My holiness.

September 15
MORNING

Rest in Me, My child. This time devoted to Me is meant to be peaceful, not stressful. You don't have to perform in order to receive My Love. I have boundless, unconditional Love for you. How it grieves Me to see My children working for Love: trying harder and harder, yet never feeling good enough to be loved.

Be careful that your devotion to Me does not become another form of works. I want you to come into My Presence joyfully and confidently. You have nothing to fear, for you wear My own righteousness. Gaze into My eyes, and you will see no condemnation, only Love and delight in the one I see. Be blessed as *My Face shines radiantly upon you, giving you Peace.*

JOHN 15:13; 2 CORINTHIANS 5:21 NKJV;
ZEPHANIAH 3:17; NUMBERS 6:25–26

September 15
EVENING

BRING YOUR FEELINGS OF FAILURE into the Light of My Presence, where we can examine them together. In My brilliant Light, the feelings shrivel and shrink because they are based on lies. Let the Light of My unfailing Love shine upon you, dispelling the darkness, lifting you closer and closer to Me.

How priceless is your unfailing love! Both high and low among men find refuge in the shadow of your wings. They feast on the abundance of your house; you give them drink from your river of delights. For with you is the fountain of life; in your light we see light. —PSALM 36:7–9

But thanks be to God! He gives us the victory through our Lord Jesus Christ. —1 CORINTHIANS 15:57

Also read:
PSALM 6:4

Before You Turn Out the Light

For as long as you need, sit here with Me and soak in My Love.

September 16

MORNING

I DESIGNED YOU to live in union with Me. This union does not negate who you are; it actually makes you more fully yourself. When you try to live independently of Me, you experience emptiness and dissatisfaction. You may *gain the whole world* and yet lose everything that really counts.

Find fulfillment through living close to Me, yielding to My purposes for you. Though I may lead you along paths that feel alien to you, trust that I know what I am doing. If you follow Me wholeheartedly, you will discover facets of yourself that were previously hidden. I know you intimately—far better than you know yourself. In union with Me, you are complete. In closeness to Me, you are transformed more and more into the one I designed you to be.

MARK 8:36; PSALM 139:13–16;
2 CORINTHIANS 3:17–18

September 16

EVENING

I REFUSE TO DWELL IN PEOPLE who think they are already "good enough" without Me. I have called such hypocrites *whitewashed tombs: beautiful on the outside* but putrid on the inside. As you ponder the miraculous truth that *I live in you*, let your heart overflow with Joy. I am not a short-term tenant, indwelling you only as long as your behavior pleases Me. I have come to stay—permanently.

> *I have been crucified with Christ and I no longer live, but Christ lives in me. The life I live in the body, I live by faith in the Son of God, who loved me and gave himself for me.* —GALATIANS 2:20

> *"Woe to you, teachers of the law and Pharisees, you hypocrites! You are like whitewashed tombs, which look beautiful on the outside but on the inside are full of dead men's bones and everything unclean."* —MATTHEW 23:27

Also read:
EPHESIANS 2:10 NKJV; JOHN 10:10 NASB

Before You Turn Out the Light

Yield to My ongoing renewal work within you, and you will become more of the masterpiece I designed you to be.

September 17
MORNING

You will not find My Peace by engaging in excessive planning, attempting to control what will happen to you in the future. That is a commonly practiced form of unbelief. When your mind spins with multiple plans, Peace may sometimes seem to be within your grasp; yet it always eludes you. Just when you think you have prepared for all possibilities, something unexpected pops up and throws things into confusion.

I did not design the human mind to figure out the future. That is beyond your capability. I crafted your mind for continual communication with Me. Bring Me all your needs, your hopes and fears. Commit everything into My care. Turn from the path of planning to the path of Peace.

1 Peter 5:6–7; Proverbs 16:9;
Psalm 37:5 nkjv

September 17
EVENING

THE FUTURE IS ONE OF THOSE *SECRET THINGS* beyond your domain. Release it to Me, the rightful Owner. Refuse to worry about the future, and you will find your resources for today quite sufficient. Remember that I am part of those resources and *nothing is impossible with* Me!

> *The secret things belong to the LORD our God, but the things revealed belong to us and to our children forever, that we may follow all the words of this law.* —DEUTERONOMY 29:29

> *"For nothing is impossible with God."* —LUKE 1:37

Also read:
ROMANS 8:28 AMP

Before You Turn Out the Light

Concentrate on *now*—and leave every *next* to Me.

September 18
MORNING

SEEK TO PLEASE ME above all else. Let that goal be your focal point as you go through this day. Such a mind-set will protect you from scattering your energy to the winds. The free will I bestowed on you comes with awesome responsibility. Each day presents you with choice after choice. Many of these decisions you ignore and thus make by default. Without a focal point to guide you, you can easily lose your way. That's why it is so important to stay in communication with Me, living in thankful awareness of My Presence.

You inhabit a fallen, disjointed world, where things are constantly unraveling around the edges. Only a vibrant relationship with Me can keep you from coming unraveled too.

MATTHEW 6:33; JOHN 8:29;
COLOSSIANS 3:23–24

September 18
EVENING

YOU ARE BEING RENEWED DAY BY DAY. My Spirit is in charge of your renewal, and He is alive within you—directing your growth in grace. Find hope through trusting that I continually *hold you by your right hand*—and I am preparing you for Glory!

We do not lose heart. Though our outer self is wasting away, our inner self is being renewed day by day. —2 CORINTHIANS 4:16 ESV

Yet I am always with you; you hold me by my right hand. You guide me with your counsel, and afterward you will take me into glory. —PSALM 73:23–24

Also read:
ROMANS 8:9

Before You Turn Out the Light

Do not be weighed down by the failures and disappointments of this day. Resolve to begin tomorrow anew, seeking to walk with Me.

September 19
MORNING

THERE IS A MIGHTY BATTLE going on for control of your mind. Heaven and earth intersect in your mind; the tugs of both spheres influence your thinking. I created you with the capacity to experience foretastes of heaven. When you shut out the world and focus on My Presence, you can enjoy sitting with Me *in heavenly realms*. This is an incredible privilege reserved for precious ones who belong to Me and seek My Face. Your greatest strength is your desire to spend time communing with Me. As you concentrate on Me, *My Spirit fills your mind with Life and Peace.*

The world exerts a downward pull on your thoughts. Media bombard you with greed, lust, and cynicism. When you face these things, pray for protection and discernment. Stay in continual communication with Me whenever you walk through the wastelands of this world. Refuse to worry, because this form of worldliness will weigh you down and block awareness of My Presence. Stay alert, recognizing the battle being waged against your mind. Look forward to an eternity of strife-free living, reserved for you in heaven.

EPHESIANS 2:6; ROMANS 8:6;
1 JOHN 2:15, 17

September 19
EVENING

Although you may think you are *planning your way*, I am actually the One who *directs your steps*. However, you can choose the hard way (ignoring Me) or the right way (seeking My will). Treasure My teaching in your heart, for it is not your plans but *My counsel that will stand*.

The mind of man plans his way, but the Lord directs his steps. —Proverbs 16:9 nasb

There are many plans in a man's heart, nevertheless the Lord's counsel—that will stand. —Proverbs 19:21 nkjv

Also read:
Jeremiah 10:23; Psalm 32:8

Before You Turn Out the Light

Turn back to Me quickly when your myriad plans confuse you. I'm invested in saving you precious time and energy.

September 20
MORNING

Try to see things more and more from My perspective. Let the Light of My Presence so fully fill your mind that you view the world through Me. When little things don't go as you had hoped, look to Me lightheartedly and say, "Oh, well." This simple discipline can protect you from being burdened with an accumulation of petty cares and frustrations. If you practice this diligently, you will make a life-changing discovery: You realize that most of the things that worry you are not important. If you shrug them off immediately and return your focus to Me, you will walk through your days with lighter steps and a joyful heart.

When serious problems come your way, you will have more reserves for dealing with them. You will not have squandered your energy on petty problems. You may even reach the point where you can agree with the apostle Paul that all your troubles are *light and momentary* compared with *the eternal glory* being achieved by them.

PSALM 36:9 NKJV, PROVERBS 20:24;
2 CORINTHIANS 4:17–18

September 20
EVENING

WHENEVER YOU ARE FEELING BATTERED by life's trials, remember *the crown of righteousness* that is stored up for you. I have promised to give it to all those who love Me—who long for My return. When I, *the Chief Shepherd*, come back for you, *you will receive the crown of Glory that will never fade away*!

> *Finally, there is laid up for me the crown of righteousness, which the Lord, the righteous Judge, will give to me on that Day, and not to me only but also to all who have loved His appearing.* —2 TIMOTHY 4:8 NKJV

> *And when the Chief Shepherd appears, you will receive the crown of glory that will never fade away.* —1 PETER 5:4

Also read:
JAMES 1:12; 1 CORINTHIANS 9:25

Before You Turn Out the Light

Strive to do more than compete for an imperishable prize—endure, steadfast till the end.

September 21
MORNING

WAIT QUIETLY IN MY PRESENCE while My thoughts form silently in the depths of your being. Do not try to rush this process, because hurry keeps your heart earthbound. I am the Creator of the entire universe, yet I choose to make My humble home in your heart. It is there where you know Me most intimately; it is there where I speak to you in holy whispers. Ask My Spirit to quiet your mind so that you can hear *My still small voice* within you. I am speaking to you continually: words of Life . . . Peace . . . Love. Tune your heart to receive these messages of abundant blessing. *Lay your requests before Me, and wait in expectation.*

COLOSSIANS 1:16 NKJV;
1 KINGS 19:12 NKJV; PSALM 5:3

September 21
EVENING

YOUR PRAYERS ARE NOT CRIES IN THE DARK; on the contrary, they rise to My kingdom of eternal Light. *Call to Me, and I will answer you, and show you great and mighty things.* Only *the eyes of your heart* can see such spiritual realities.

> *"Call to Me, and I will answer you, and show you great and mighty things, which you do not know."* —JEREMIAH 33:3 NKJV

> *I pray also that the eyes of your heart may be enlightened in order that you may know the hope to which he has called you, the riches of his glorious inheritance in the saints.* —EPHESIANS 1:18

Also read:
PSALM 143:10; REVELATION 21:23

Before You Turn Out the Light

Be open to My teaching. I help you understand great mysteries at heart level.

September 22
MORNING

Trust Me and refuse to worry, for *I am your Strength and Song.* You are feeling wobbly this morning, looking at difficult times looming ahead, measuring them against your own strength. However, they are not today's tasks—or even tomorrow's. So leave them in the future and come home to the present, where you will find Me waiting for you. Since *I am your Strength*, I can empower you to handle each task as it comes. Because *I am your Song*, I can give you Joy as you work alongside Me.

Keep bringing your mind back to the present moment. Among all My creatures, only humans can anticipate future events. This ability is a blessing, but it becomes a curse whenever it is misused. If you use your magnificent mind to worry about tomorrow, you cloak yourself in dark unbelief. However, when the hope of heaven fills your thoughts, the Light of My Presence envelops you. Though heaven is future, it is also present tense. As you walk in the Light with Me, you have one foot on earth and one foot in heaven.

Exodus 15:2; 2 Corinthians 10:5;
Hebrews 10:23

September 22

EVENING

COWARDLINESS IS NOT OF MY KINGDOM. When you are feeling overwhelmed by your circumstances, remember who you are—a child of the eternal King! Invite Me into the very circumstances that are intimidating you, and let the Light of My powerful Presence strengthen you. When you choose to live courageously, I am pleased—and I respond by strengthening your heart.

Be of good courage, and He shall strengthen your heart, all you who hope in the LORD. —PSALM 31:24 NKJV

Christ is faithful as a son over God's house. And we are his house, if we hold on to our courage and the hope of which we boast. —HEBREWS 3:6

Also read:
ROMANS 8:15–17 NKJV; 1 TIMOTHY 1:17

Before You Turn Out the Light

Regain your strength by remembering who you are!

September 23

MORNING

WALK WITH ME in the freedom of forgiveness. The path we follow together is sometimes steep and slippery. If you carry a burden of guilt on your back, you are more likely to stumble and fall. At your request, I will remove the heavy load from you and bury it at the foot of the cross. When I unburden you, you are undeniably free! Stand up straight and tall in My Presence so that no one can place more burdens on your back. Look into My Face and feel the warmth of My Love-Light shining upon you. It is this unconditional Love that frees you from both fears and sins. Spend time basking in the Light of My Presence. As you come to know Me more and more intimately, you grow increasingly free.

PSALM 68:19; 1 JOHN 1:7–9;
1 JOHN 4:18

September 23
EVENING

THE GOD OF THIS AGE *has blinded the minds of unbelievers, so they search for heaven in hellish ways—excesses and perversions of every kind. However, great sinners can be transformed into exceptional Christians when they turn their passionate appetites toward Me. My Love and forgiveness satisfy soul-hunger as nothing else can.*

The god of this age has blinded the minds of unbelievers, so that they cannot see the light of the gospel of the glory of Christ, who is the image of God. —2 CORINTHIANS 4:4

"Why spend money on what is not bread, and your labor on what does not satisfy? Listen, listen to me and eat what is good, and your soul will delight in the richest of fare." —ISAIAH 55:2

Also read:
PSALM 105:4

Before You Turn Out the Light

Much of your angst is actually a longing for heaven's perfection. Seek Me for the desires of your heart.

September 24
MORNING

Live first and foremost in My Presence. Gradually you will become more aware of Me than of people and places around you. This awareness will not detract from your relationships with others. Instead, it will increase your ability to give love and encouragement to them. My Peace will permeate your words and demeanor. You will be active in the world, yet one step removed from it. You will not be easily shaken because My enveloping Presence buffers the blow of problems.

This is the path I have set before you. As you follow it wholeheartedly, you experience abundant Life and Peace.

PSALM 89:15–16; PSALM 16:8;
2 PETER 1:2; JOHN 10:28 NKJV

September 24
EVENING

AWARENESS OF YOUR NEED FOR ME is what creates a strong connection to My Presence. My Power flows into you continually: It gives you strength to take the next step, strength to resist discouragement and despair, strength to know Me in intimate dependence. Only My Power can enable you to live abundantly in the midst of your limitations.

To him who is able to keep you from falling and to present you before his glorious presence without fault and with great joy—to the only God our Savior be glory, majesty, power and authority, through Jesus Christ our Lord, before all ages, now and forevermore! Amen. —JUDE VV. 24–25

Also read:
HABAKKUK 3:17–19; PHILIPPIANS 4:7

Before You Turn Out the Light

Stay right by My side, connected with Me. The knowledge that I am with you is what keeps you from the pit of despair.

September 25
MORNING

POUR ALL OF YOUR ENERGY into trusting Me. It is through trust that you stay connected to Me, aware of My Presence. Every step on your life-journey can be a step of faith. Baby steps of trust are simple for you; you can take them with almost unconscious ease. Giant steps are another matter altogether: leaping across chasms in semidarkness, scaling cliffs of uncertainty, trudging *through the valley of the shadow of death*. These feats require sheer concentration, as well as utter commitment to Me.

Each of My children is a unique blend of temperament, giftedness, and life experiences. Something that is a baby step for you may be a giant step for another person, and vice versa. Only I know the difficulty or ease of each segment of your journey. Beware of trying to impress others by acting as if your giant steps are only baby ones. Do not judge others who hesitate in trembling fear before an act that would be easy for you. If each of My children would seek to please Me above all else, fear of others' judgments would vanish, as would attempts to impress others. Focus your attention on the path just ahead of you and on the One who never leaves your side.

PSALM 23:4; MATTHEW 7:1–2;
PROVERBS 29:25

September 25
EVENING

I rejoice in your seeking Me persistently—day in and day out. This is extremely pleasing to Me, and I reward you in numerous ways: I whet your appetite to know Me ever more intimately; I gradually change the desires of your heart so they line up more and more with the contents of My heart; I pour out upon you tender, overflowing Love.

> *And without faith it is impossible to please God, because anyone who comes to him must believe that he exists and that he rewards those who earnestly seek him.* —Hebrews 11:6

> *"And you will seek Me and find Me, when you search for Me with all your heart."* —Jeremiah 29:13 NKJV

Also read:
Hebrews 11:1 AMP; Psalm 103:14 NKJV

Before You Turn Out the Light

Seek—and you will find. Only believe.

September 26
MORNING

COME TO ME AND LISTEN! Attune yourself to My voice, and receive My richest blessings. Marvel at the wonder of communing with the Creator of the universe while sitting in the comfort of your home. Kings who reign on earth tend to make themselves inaccessible; ordinary people almost never gain an audience with them. Even dignitaries must plow through red tape and protocol in order to speak with royalty.

Though I am King of the universe, I am totally accessible to you. I am with you wherever you are. Nothing can separate you from My Presence! When I cried out from the cross, *"It is finished!" the curtain of the temple was torn in two from top to bottom.* This opened the way for you to meet Me face to Face, with no need of protocol or priests. I, the King of kings, am your constant Companion.

ISAIAH 50:4; ISAIAH 55:2–3;
JOHN 19:30; MATTHEW 27:50–51

September 26

EVENING

Because I am your Creator, I know how you function best. I designed you for rich communion with Me. Don't just talk to Me; listen to Me as well. I speak to you through My Word, My Spirit, My creation.

> *Who of you by worrying can add a single hour to his life? Since you cannot do this very little thing, why do you worry about the rest?* —Luke 12:25–26

> *An anxious heart weighs a man down, but a kind word cheers him up.* —Proverbs 12:25

Also read:
Psalm 25:4–5; 1 Thessalonians 5:17 amp

Before You Turn Out the Light

Put your energy into communicating with Me rather than reviewing your problems. As you do, you will find your worries vanishing.

September 27
MORNING

RELAX IN *MY EVERLASTING ARMS*. Your weakness is an opportunity to grow strong in awareness of My Almighty Presence. When your energy fails you, do not look inward and lament the lack you find there. Look to Me and My sufficiency; rejoice in My radiant riches that are abundantly available to help you.

Go gently through this day, leaning on Me and enjoying My Presence. Thank Me for your neediness, which is building trust-bonds between us. If you look back on your journey thus far, you can see that days of extreme weakness have been some of your most precious times. Memories of these days are richly interwoven with golden strands of My intimate Presence.

DEUTERONOMY 33:27; ROMANS 8:26;
PSALM 27:13–14

September 27
EVENING

WHEN YOU ARE GOING THROUGH PAINFUL TRIALS, it is tempting to blame Me because you know I have unlimited Power to intervene. However, I refrained from using that Power to save Myself from brutal torture and execution. Whenever I allow you to suffer, try to see it as My vote of confidence in you. Remember that I allow you to *share in My sufferings in order that you may also share in My Glory.*

> *For consider Him who endured such hostility from sinners against Himself, lest you become weary and discouraged in your souls.* —HEBREWS 12:3 NKJV

> *Now if we are children, then we are heirs—heirs of God and co-heirs with Christ, if indeed we share in his sufferings in order that we may also share in his glory.* —ROMANS 8:17

Also read:
HEBREWS 4:15

Before You Turn Out the Light

If you are doubting My Love for you, just look at all
I suffered so I could spend eternity with you.

September 28
MORNING

OPEN YOUR MIND AND HEART—your entire being—to receive My Love in full measure. So many of My children limp through their lives starved for Love because they haven't learned the art of receiving. This is essentially an act of faith: believing that I love you with boundless, everlasting Love. The art of receiving is also a discipline: training your mind to trust Me, coming close to Me with confidence.

Remember that the evil one is the *father of lies*. Learn to recognize his deceptive intrusions into your thoughts. One of his favorite deceptions is to undermine your confidence in My unconditional Love. Fight back against these lies! Do not let them go unchallenged. *Resist the devil in My Name, and he will slink away from you. Draw near to Me*, and My Presence will envelop you in Love.

EPHESIANS 3:16–19; HEBREWS 4:16;
JOHN 8:44; JAMES 4:7–8 NKJV

September 28
EVENING

BECAUSE I AM INFINITE, I can see you simultaneously as you are now and as you will be in heaven. The present view helps Me work with you on things you need to change; the heavenly vision enables Me to love you with perfect, everlasting Love. The best way to see through eyes of grace is to look through the lens of My unfailing Love.

How priceless is your unfailing love! Both high and low among men find refuge in the shadow of your wings. —PSALM 36:7

I sought the LORD, and he answered me; he delivered me from all my fears. Those who look to him are radiant; their faces are never covered with shame. —PSALM 34:4–5

Also read:
ZEPHANIAH 3:17 NASB

Before You Turn Out the Light

Though you are troubled by fear of failure, remind yourself: My Love for you will never fail.

September 29
MORNING

I AM WITH YOU and all around you, encircling you in golden rays of Light. I always behold you Face to face. Not one of your thoughts escapes My notice. Because I am infinite, I am able to love you as if you and I were the only ones in the universe.

Walk with Me in intimate Love-steps, but do not lose sight of My Majesty. I desire to be your closest Friend, yet I am also your sovereign Lord. I created your brain with capacity to know Me as Friend and Lord simultaneously. The human mind is the pinnacle of My creation, but so few use it for its primary purpose—knowing Me. I communicate continually through My Spirit, My Word, and My creation. Only humans are capable of receiving Me and responding to My Presence. You are indeed *fearfully and wonderfully made*!

PSALM 34:4–6; 2 PETER 1:16–17;
JOHN 17:3; PSALM 139:14

September 29
EVENING

It is important for you to know Me as the Initiator in our relationship. If you think it is your spiritual disciplines that keep you close to Me, you are at risk. But if you are relying on Me—what I have done, am doing, will do—you know My Love for you is always assured, so you can rest in Me.

> *Above all else, guard your heart, for it is the wellspring of life.* —PROVERBS 4:23

> *"I am the vine, you are the branches; he who abides in Me, and I in him, he bears much fruit, for apart from Me you can do nothing."* —JOHN 15:5 NASB

Also read:
PSALM 42:2; PSALM 52:8

Before You Turn Out the Light

I am the One who pursued you first. Reflect on what this says about how much I value you.

September 30
MORNING

I AM PERPETUALLY WITH YOU, taking care of you. That is the most important fact of your existence. I am not limited by time or space; My Presence with you is a forever-promise. You need not fear the future, for I am already there. When you make that quantum leap into eternity, you will find Me awaiting you in heaven. Your future is in My hands; I release it to you day by day, moment by moment. Therefore, *do not worry about tomorrow.*

I want you to live this day abundantly, seeing all there is to see, doing all there is to do. Don't be distracted by future concerns. Leave them to Me! Each day of life is a glorious gift, but so few people know how to live within the confines of today. Much of their energy for abundant living spills over the timeline into tomorrow's worries or past regrets. Their remaining energy is sufficient only for limping through the day, not for living it to the full. I am training you to keep your focus on My Presence in the present. This is how to receive abundant Life, which flows freely from My throne of grace.

MATTHEW 6:34; JOHN 10:10;
JAMES 4:13–15

September 30
EVENING

There is a vibrant kinship between us as I live in and through you. *My yoke is not harsh, hard, sharp, or pressing; on the contrary, it is comfortable, gracious, and pleasant.* As you submit to these bonds of Love, I fill you with Life and Joy in overflowing abundance.

> *Take My yoke upon you and learn of Me, for I am gentle (meek) and humble (lowly) in heart, and you will find rest (relief and ease and refreshment and recreation and blessed quiet) for your souls. For My yoke is wholesome (useful, good—not harsh, hard, sharp or pressing, but comfortable, gracious and pleasant), and My burden is light and easy to be borne.* —MATTHEW 11:29–30 AMP

Also read:
JOHN 15:11; 1 PETER 1:8–9

Before You Turn Out the Light

Say yes to Me and My ways, and I will teach you more and more about Me.

October

"Come to me, all you who are weary and burdened, and I will give you rest."

MATTHEW 11:28

October 1

MORNING

Worship Me only. *I am King of kings and Lord of lords, dwelling in unapproachable Light.* I am taking care of you! I am not only committed to caring for you, but I am also absolutely capable of doing so. Rest in Me, My weary one, for this is a form of worship.

Though self-flagellation has gone out of style, many of My children drive themselves like racehorses. They whip themselves into action, ignoring how exhausted they are. They forget that I am sovereign and that *My ways are higher* than theirs. Underneath their driven service, they may secretly resent Me as a harsh taskmaster. Their worship of Me is lukewarm because I am no longer their *First Love*.

My invitation never changes: *Come to Me, all you who are weary, and I will give you rest.* Worship Me by resting peacefully in My Presence.

1 TIMOTHY 6:15–16; ISAIAH 55:8–9;
REVELATION 2:4; MATTHEW 11:28

October 1
EVENING

Your problems feel so heavy because you have given them too much power. Each time you focus on them and forget about Me, you empower them a bit more. I want you to put your troubles down long enough to view the vast expanse of Life that is spread out before you—all the way into eternity!

> *Our light and momentary troubles are achieving for us an eternal glory that far outweighs them all.* —2 Corinthians 4:17

> *Trust in him at all times, O people; pour out your hearts to him, for God is our refuge. "Selah."* —Psalm 62:8

Also read:
2 Corinthians 4:6 AMP

Before You Turn Out the Light

Here is the best way to lay your problems down: Pour out your heart to Me.

October 2
MORNING

NEVER TAKE FOR GRANTED My intimate nearness. Marvel at the wonder of My continual Presence with you. Even the most ardent human lover cannot be with you always. Nor can another person know the intimacies of your heart, mind, and spirit. *I know everything about you—even the number of hairs on your head.* You don't need to work at revealing yourself to Me.

Many people spend a lifetime or a small fortune searching for someone who understands them. Yet I am freely available to all who call upon My Name, who open their hearts to receive Me as Savior. This simple act of faith is the beginning of a lifelong love story. I, the Lover of your soul, understand you perfectly and love you eternally.

PSALM 145:18 NKJV; LUKE 12:7;
JOHN 1:12; ROMANS 10:13

October 2

EVENING

I AM WATCHING OVER YOU CONTINUALLY. No matter what you are experiencing or how alone you feel, trust that I am with you—well aware of your circumstances. *Nothing* can separate you from My loving Presence.

> *I am convinced that neither death nor life, neither angels nor demons, neither the present nor the future, nor any powers, neither height nor depth, nor anything else in all creation, will be able to separate us from the love of God that is in Christ Jesus our Lord.* —ROMANS 8:38–39

> *The LORD has been my defense, and my God the rock of my refuge.* —PSALM 94:22 NKJV

Also read:

PROVERBS 3:5 AMP

Before You Turn Out the Light

Lean on Me for support; I am indeed your Rock.

October 3

MORNING

WHEN MANY THINGS SEEM to be going wrong, trust Me. When your life feels increasingly out of control, thank Me. These are supernatural responses, and they can lift you above your circumstances. If you do what comes naturally in the face of difficulties, you may fall prey to negativism. Even a few complaints can set you on a path that is a downward spiral, by darkening your perspective and mind-set. With this attitude controlling you, complaints flow more and more readily from your mouth. Each one moves you steadily down the slippery spiral. The lower you go, the faster you slide; but it is still possible to apply brakes. Cry out to Me in My Name! Affirm your trust in Me, regardless of how you feel. Thank Me for everything, though this seems unnatural—even irrational. Gradually you will begin to ascend, recovering your lost ground.

When you are back on ground level, you can face your circumstances from a humble perspective. If you choose supernatural responses this time—trusting and thanking Me—you will experience My unfathomable Peace.

PSALM 13:5; EPHESIANS 5:20;
PSALM 34:10

October 3
EVENING

I AM CONSTANTLY WORKING to transform your life. I stand ready to help you at all times—during stormy episodes as well as times of smooth sailing. I am not only *ever-living* but also more abundantly alive than you can possibly imagine. There are no limits to what My *great Power and Glory* can accomplish! I can change the most "hopeless" situation into outright victory.

We have this hope as an anchor for the soul, firm and secure. It enters the inner sanctuary behind the curtain, where Jesus, who went before us, has entered on our behalf. He has become a high priest forever. —HEBREWS 6:19

Then you will know that I am the Lord; those who hope in me will not be disappointed. —ISAIAH 49:23

Also read:
1 PETER 1:3 AMP; MARK 13:26 NKJV

Before You Turn Out the Light

No circumstance is too difficult for Me. Rest in My great Power and Glory, and trust Me.

October 4

MORNING

I AM THE CREATOR OF HEAVEN AND EARTH: Lord of all that is and all that will ever be. Although I am unimaginably vast, I choose to dwell within you, permeating you with My Presence. Only in the spirit realm could Someone so infinitely great live within someone so very small. Be awed by the Power and the Glory of My Spirit within you!

Though the Holy Spirit is infinite, *He deigns to be your Helper.* He is always ready to offer assistance; all you need to do is ask. When the path before you looks easy and straightforward, you may be tempted to *go it alone* instead of relying on Me. This is when you are in the greatest danger of stumbling. Ask My Spirit to help you as you go each step of the way. Never neglect this glorious Source of strength within you.

JOHN 14:16–17 NKJV;
JOHN 16:7; ZECHARIAH 4:6

October 4
EVENING

YOU TEND TO WASTE ENERGY trying to determine whether your resources are adequate for the day's demands. How much better to simply acknowledge your inadequacy when you awaken each morning! If you stay in touch with Me throughout the day, I will place enough Power at your disposal to meet your needs as they arise.

> *Your sandals shall be iron and bronze; as your days, so shall your strength be.* —DEUTERONOMY 33:25 NKJV

> *God is our refuge and strength, an ever-present help in trouble.* —PSALM 46:1

Also read:
PSALM 105:4

Before You Turn Out the Light

Turn from self-help and turn toward Me—
your ever-present Help—for strength to equal
the demands that remain of this day.

October 5
MORNING

REMEMBER THAT JOY is not dependent on your circumstances. Some of the world's most miserable people are those whose circumstances seem the most enviable. People who reach the top of the ladder career-wise are often surprised to find emptiness awaiting them. True Joy is a by-product of living in My Presence. Therefore you can experience it in palaces, in prisons . . . anywhere.

Do not judge a day as devoid of Joy just because it contains difficulties. Instead, concentrate on staying in communication with Me. Many of the problems that clamor for your attention will resolve themselves. Other matters you must deal with, but I will help you with them. If you make problem solving secondary to the goal of living close to Me, you can find Joy even in your most difficult days.

HABAKKUK 3:17–19; 1 CHRONICLES 16:27

October 5

EVENING

The more you become like Me, the more you can experience hope. Your transformed character convinces you that you do indeed belong to Me. This helps you cope with the problems you face, trusting that you and I *together* can handle them.

> *We also rejoice in our sufferings, because we know that suffering produces perseverance; perseverance, character; and character, hope. And hope does not disappoint us, because God has poured out his love into our hearts by the Holy Spirit, whom he has given us.* —Romans 5:3–5

> *I can do all things through Christ who strengthens me.* —Philippians 4:13 NKJV

Also read:
John 14:15–17 NKJV

Before You Turn Out the Light

Think of some ways to cooperate with Me as you persevere through this difficult time.

October 6
MORNING

BE WILLING TO FOLLOW wherever I lead. Follow Me wholeheartedly, with glad anticipation quickening your pace. Though you don't know what lies ahead, I know; and that is enough! Some of My richest blessings are just around the bend: out of sight, but nonetheless very real. To receive these gifts, you must *walk by faith—not by sight*. This doesn't mean closing your eyes to what is all around you. It means subordinating the visible world to the invisible Shepherd of your soul.

Sometimes I lead you up a high mountain with only My hand to support you. The higher you climb, the more spectacular the view becomes; also, the more keenly you sense your separation from the world with all its problems. This frees you to experience exuberantly the joyous reality of My Presence. Give yourself fully to these Glory-moments, awash in dazzling Light. I will eventually lead you down the mountain, back into community with others. Let My Light continue to shine within you as you walk among people again.

2 Corinthians 5:7; Psalm 96:6;
John 8:12; Psalm 36:9

October 6

EVENING

Sometimes—especially when many things are going wrong—all you can do is hold on to Me. The best thing to do at such times is *seek My Face* and *profess* your hope. Negative words will pull you down, but when you openly affirm your hope and trust in Me, you gain strength to move forward with confidence.

> *Let us hold unswervingly to the hope we profess, for he who promised is faithful.* —Hebrews 10:23

> *No temptation has overtaken you that is not common to man. God is faithful, and he will not let you be tempted beyond your ability, but with the temptation he will also provide the way of escape, that you may be able to endure it.* —1 Corinthians 10:13 esv

Also read:
Psalm 27:7–8 nkjv

Before You Turn Out the Light

Make this the basis of your confidence—that
I am faithful and I can be trusted.

October 7

MORINING

IN ORDER TO HEAR MY VOICE, you must release all your worries into My care. Entrust to Me everything that concerns you. This clears the way for you to seek My Face unhindered. Let Me free you from fear that is hiding deep inside you. Sit quietly in My Presence, allowing My Light to soak into you and drive out any darkness lodged within you.

Accept each day just as it comes to you, remembering that I am sovereign over your life. *Rejoice in this day that I have made*, trusting that I am abundantly present in it. Instead of regretting or resenting the way things are, *thank Me in all circumstances*. Trust Me and don't be fearful; thank Me and rest in My sovereignty.

1 PETER 5:6–7; PSALM 118:24;
1 THESSALONIANS 5:18

October 7
EVENING

YOU HAVE EXPERIENCED PERSONAL BENEFITS from thanking Me for hard situations, but there is more—much more! Your sacrifice of thanksgiving has divine Power to weaken spiritual strongholds of evil. Moreover, your patient endurance of suffering can strengthen and encourage My people on earth.

*Trust in the L*ORD *with all your heart and lean not on your own understanding.* —PROVERBS 3:5

For though we live in the world, we do not wage war as the world does. The weapons we fight with are not the weapons of the world. On the contrary, they have divine power to demolish strongholds. —2 CORINTHIANS 10:3–4

Also read:
PSALM 107:22; EPHESIANS 5:20

Before You Turn Out the Light

Trust deeply in My goodness, My mercy, My Love.

October 8
MORNING

I LOVE YOU WITH *an everlasting Love*. The human mind cannot comprehend My constancy. Your emotions flicker and falter in the face of varying circumstances, and you tend to project your fickle feelings onto Me. Thus you do not benefit fully from My unfailing Love.

You need to look beyond the flux of circumstances and discover Me gazing lovingly back at you. This awareness of My Presence strengthens you as you receive and respond to My Love. *I am the same yesterday, today, and forever!* Let My Love flow into you continually. Your need for Me is as constant as the outflow of My Love to you.

JEREMIAH 31:3; EXODUS 15:13;
HEBREWS 13:8

October 8

EVENING

Though I never leave you, you can leave Me by forgetting I am with you. No matter how many times you forget Me, My Love for you will never fail. Grow strong in this constant, nourishing Love.

> *But I am like an olive tree, flourishing in the house of God; I trust in God's unfailing love for ever and ever.* —Psalm 52:8

> *. . . to know the love of Christ which passes knowledge; that you may be filled with all the fullness of God.* —Ephesians 3:19 nkjv

Also read:
Deuteronomy 31:6; Romans 8:26

Before You Turn Out the Light

Set your heart on living steadfastly in My Presence, as a tree rooted in Me.

October 9

MORNING

YOU HAVE BEEN on a long, uphill journey, and your energy is almost spent. Though you have faltered at times, you have not let go of My hand. I am pleased with your desire to stay close to Me. There is one thing, however, that displeases Me: your tendency to complain. You may talk to Me as much as you like about the difficulty of the path we are following. I understand better than anyone else the stresses and strains that have afflicted you. You can ventilate safely to Me because talking with Me tempers your thoughts and helps you see things from My perspective.

Complaining to others is another matter altogether. It opens the door to deadly sins such as self-pity and rage. Whenever you are tempted to grumble, come to Me and talk it out. As you open up to Me, I will put My thoughts in your mind and My song in your heart.

JEREMIAH 31:25; PHILIPPIANS 2:14–15;
PSALM 40:3

October 9

EVENING

Sometimes you feel weighed down by My Sovereign will—trapped by circumstances you cannot change. Submit to Me and My ways in your life, even though you long to break free. Trust that I will relieve your suffering in My perfect, wisely appointed time.

> *Humble yourselves, therefore, under God's mighty hand, that he may lift you up in due time.* —1 Peter 5:6

> *[God] gives more grace. Therefore He says: "God resists the proud, but gives grace to the humble." . . . Humble yourselves in the sight of the Lord, and He will lift you up.* —James 4:6, 10 nkjv

Also read:
Micah 6:8 nkjv

Before You Turn Out the Light

Rather than growing impatient with Me in difficult circumstances, humble yourself and pray.

October 10
MORNING

Trust Me enough to let things happen without striving to predict or control them. Relax, and refresh yourself in the Light of My everlasting Love. My Love-Light never dims, yet you are often unaware of My radiant Presence. When you project yourself into the future, rehearsing what you will do or say, you are seeking to be self-sufficient: to be adequate without My help. This is a subtle sin—so common that it usually slips by unnoticed.

The alternative is to live fully in the present, depending on Me each moment. Rather than fearing your inadequacy, rejoice in My abundant supply. Train your mind to seek My help continually, even when you feel competent to handle something by yourself. Don't divide your life into things you can do by yourself and things that require My help. Instead, learn to rely on Me in every situation. This discipline will enable you to enjoy life more and to face each day confidently.

Psalm 37:3–6; Philippians 4:19 nkjv

October 10
EVENING

*S*HEEP HAVE NOTHING TO FEAR from a shepherd who is good. So it is with Me: You can feel safe and secure in My sheltering Presence. *My unfailing Love surrounds all those who trust in Me*, so your most important task as a sheep in My pasture is to keep on trusting Me—the perfect Shepherd of your soul.

> *The Lord is good, a stronghold in the day of trouble; and He knows those who trust in Him.* —NAHUM 1:7 NKJV

> *Many are the woes of the wicked, but the Lord's unfailing love surrounds the man who trusts in him.* —PSALM 32:10

Also read:
JOHN 10:14; PSALM 62:1–2

Before You Turn Out the Light

Find rest in Me alone, for I am perfectly good and infinitely strong.

October 11
MORNING

I AM THE CULMINATION of all your hopes and desires. *I am the Alpha and the Omega, the first and the last: who is and was and is to come.* Before you knew Me, you expressed your longing for Me in hurtful ways. You were ever so vulnerable to the evil around you in the world. But now My Presence safely shields you, enfolding you in My loving arms. *I have lifted you out of darkness into My marvelous Light.*

Though I have brought many pleasures into your life, not one of them is essential. Receive My blessings with open hands. Enjoy My good gifts, but do not cling to them. Turn your attention to *the Giver of all good things*, and rest in the knowledge that you are complete in Me. The one thing you absolutely need is the one thing you can never lose: My Presence with you.

PSALM 62:5–8; REVELATION 1:8;
1 PETER 2:9 NKJV; JAMES 1:17

October 11

EVENING

Since I am your Savior-God, you have every reason to *watch in hope for Me*! I always hear your prayers—and also the Spirit's *intercession for you with groanings that cannot be uttered. I am He who will sustain you. I have made you and I will carry you; I will sustain you and I will rescue you.*

> *The Spirit also helps in our weaknesses. For we do not know what we should pray for as we ought, but the Spirit Himself makes intercession for us with groanings which cannot be uttered.* —Romans 8:26 nkjv

> *"Even to your old age and gray hairs I am he, I am he who will sustain you. I have made you and I will carry you; I will sustain you and I will rescue you."* —Isaiah 46:4

Also read:
Micah 7:7

Before You Turn Out the Light

Search carefully for My work in your circumstances.
I am rescuing you in this very moment.

October 12

MORNING

Beware of seeing yourself through other people's eyes. There are several dangers to this practice. First of all, it is nearly impossible to discern what others actually think of you. Moreover, their views of you are variable: subject to each viewer's spiritual, emotional, and physical condition. The major problem with letting others define you is that it borders on idolatry. Your concern to please others dampens your desire to please Me, your Creator.

It is much more real to see yourself through *My eyes*. My gaze upon you is steady and sure, untainted by sin. Through My eyes you can see yourself as one who is deeply, eternally loved. Rest in My loving gaze, and you will receive deep Peace. Respond to My loving Presence by *worshiping Me in spirit and in truth*.

Hebrews 11:6; Romans 5:5;
John 4:23–24

October 12
EVENING

IT IS YOUR SOUL I LOVE rather than your appearance or performance. Sometimes you are so dissatisfied with both of these that they become your focus. To break free from this self-preoccupation, relax in My loving Presence, and let the Light of My Love soak into your entire being.

"Though the mountains be shaken and the hills be removed, yet my unfailing love for you will not be shaken nor my covenant of peace be removed," says the L*ord, who has compassion on you.* —Isaiah 54:10

"Cease striving and know that I am God; I will be exalted among the nations, I will be exalted in the earth." —Psalm 46:10 nasb

Also read:
Psalm 63:1–5

Before You Turn Out the Light

Reorient yourself around this truth: I created you to know Me and to center your life in Me.

October 13

MORNING

Take time to be still in My Presence. The more hassled you feel, the more you need this sacred space of communion with Me. Breathe slowly and deeply. Relax in My holy Presence while *My Face shines upon you*. This is how you receive My Peace, which I always proffer to you.

Imagine the pain I feel when My children tie themselves up in anxious knots, ignoring My gift of Peace. I died a criminal's death to secure this blessing for you. Receive it gratefully; hide it in your heart. My Peace is an inner treasure, growing within you as you trust in Me. Therefore, circumstances cannot touch it. Be still, enjoying Peace in My Presence.

PSALM 46:10; NUMBERS 6:25–26;

JOHN 14:27

October 13
EVENING

When you are weary, you find it easier to lean on Me than to enjoy My company, but it is possible for you to *be joyful in Me—Your Savior*—even in desperate circumstances. Remember that *I am your strength*. Rejoice in Me, and relax while I speak to you in *gentle whispers*.

> *Though the fig tree does not bud and there are no grapes on the vines, though the olive crop fails and the fields produce no food, though there are no sheep in the pen and no cattle in the stalls, yet I will rejoice in the Lord, I will be joyful in God my Savior. The Sovereign Lord is my strength; he makes my feet like the feet of a deer, he enables me to go on the heights.* —Habakkuk 3:17–19

> *After the earthquake came a fire, but the Lord was not in the fire. And after the fire came a gentle whisper.* —1 Kings 19:12

Also read:
Romans 8:38–39

Before You Turn Out the Light

Lean on Me as much as you like, but
don't forget to enjoy Me as well.

October 14
MORNING

BE PREPARED TO SUFFER FOR ME, in My Name. All suffering has meaning in My kingdom. Pain and problems are opportunities to demonstrate your trust in Me. Bearing your circumstances bravely—even thanking Me for them—is one of the highest forms of praise. This sacrifice of thanksgiving rings golden-toned bells of Joy throughout heavenly realms. On earth also, your patient suffering sends out ripples of good tidings in ever-widening circles.

When suffering strikes, remember that I am sovereign and that I can bring good out of everything. Do not try to run from pain or hide from problems. Instead, accept adversity in My Name, offering it up to Me for My purposes. Thus your suffering gains meaning and draws you closer to Me. Joy emerges from the ashes of adversity through your trust and thankfulness.

JAMES 1:2–4; PSALM 107:21–22;
PSALM 33:21

October 14

EVENING

Stay close to Me as I work on mending your broken heart. Of course, your repaired heart will not be exactly as it was before, but in some ways it will be much better. Your renewed heart—stripped of its cherished hopes—will have more space for Me.

> *As the eyes of slaves look to the hand of their master, as the eyes of a maid look to the hand of her mistress, so our eyes look to the Lord our God, till he shows us his mercy.* —Psalm 123:2

> *Create in me a clean heart, O God, and renew a steadfast spirit within me.* —Psalm 51:10 NKJV

Also read:
Isaiah 61:1 nkjv; Lamentations 3:22–23

Before You Turn Out the Light

Sit still in My holy Light while I cleanse you from the wounds of disappointment.

October 15

MORNING

Try to stay conscious of Me as you go step by step through this day. My Presence with you is both a promise and a protection. My final statement just before I ascended into heaven was: *Surely I am with you always.* That promise was for all of My followers, without exception.

The promise of My Presence is a powerful protection. As you journey through your life, there are numerous pitfalls along the way. Many voices clamor for your attention, enticing you to go their way. A few steps away from your true path are pits of self-pity and despair, plateaus of pride and self-will. If you take your eyes off Me and follow another's way, you are in grave danger. Even well-meaning friends can lead you astray if you let them usurp My place in your life. The way to stay on the path of Life is to keep your focus on Me. Awareness of My Presence is your best protection.

MATTHEW 28:20; HEBREWS 12:1–2

October 15
EVENING

THERE IS AN OPEN ROAD AHEAD OF YOU—all the way to heaven. The challenge before you is to stop focusing on your problems and limitations—and to believe that the way ahead really is an *open* road, in spite of how it looks. When you are struggling, simply take the next step and thank Me for clearing the way.

We walk by faith, not by sight. —2 CORINTHIANS 5:7 NKJV

You have made known to me the path of life; you will fill me with joy in your presence, with eternal pleasures at your right hand. —PSALM 16:11

Also read:
1 CORINTHIANS 10:13; JOHN 14:6 NKJV

Before You Turn Out the Light

I endured what I did to open up the path of
Life for you. Now have faith to believe that
I am *the* Way to the Father in heaven.

October 16
MORNING

Look to Me continually for help, comfort, and companionship. Because I am always by your side, the briefest glance can connect you with Me. When you look to Me for help, it flows freely from My Presence. This recognition of your need for Me, in small matters as well as in large ones, keeps you spiritually alive.

When you need comfort, I love to enfold you in My arms. I enable you not only to feel comforted but also to be a channel through whom I comfort others. Thus you are doubly blessed, because a living channel absorbs some of whatever flows through it.

My constant Companionship is the *pièce de résistance*: the summit of salvation blessings. No matter what losses you experience in your life, no one can take away this glorious gift.

PSALM 34:4–6; PSALM 105:4;
2 CORINTHIANS 1:3–4

October 16
EVENING

WAIT IN MY PRESENCE while I reveal Myself to you. Put aside thoughts of upcoming tasks as you focus pleasurably on Me. Allow awareness of My Presence to become imprinted on your consciousness. Then move gently from this contemplative time into your routine duties. The more you include Me in your awareness, the more your routines will sparkle with the liveliness of My company.

I wait for the Lord, my soul waits, and in his word I put my hope. My soul waits for the Lord. —PSALM 130:5–6

The Lord has compassion on those who fear him; for he knows how we are formed. —PSALM 103:13–14

Also read:
ACTS 17:28

Before You Turn Out the Light

As you close your eyes, think about how you
can invite Me into tomorrow's tasks.

October 17

MORNING

ANXIETY IS A RESULT OF envisioning the future without Me. So the best defense against worry is staying in communication with Me. When you turn your thoughts toward Me, you can think much more positively. Remember to listen as well as to speak, making your thoughts a dialogue with Me.

If you must consider upcoming events, follow these rules: 1) Do not linger in the future, because anxieties sprout up like mushrooms when you wander there. 2) Remember the promise of My continual Presence; include Me in any imagery that comes to mind. This mental discipline does not come easily because you are accustomed to being god of your fantasies. However, the reality of My Presence with you, now and forevermore, outshines any fantasy you could ever imagine.

LUKE 12:22–26; EPHESIANS 3:20–21

October 17
EVENING

I REALIZE THAT STRIVING TO ACHIEVE comes almost as naturally to you as breathing. When a goal grabs your attention, your instinct is to "go for it" without really thinking it through. But when you take the time to first discuss matters with Me, you experience much more satisfaction.

Blessed are those who have learned to acclaim you, who walk in the light of your presence, O Lord. They rejoice in your name all day long; they exult in your righteousness. —PSALM 89:15–16

There are many plans in a man's heart, nevertheless the Lord's counsel—that will stand. —PROVERBS 19:21 NKJV

Also read:
PSALM 37:5 NASB; PHILIPPIANS 4:13 NASB

Before You Turn Out the Light

Rather than chasing dead ends tomorrow, talk with Me first. Let's consult together right now.

October 18

MORNING

Go gently through this day, keeping your eyes on Me. I will open up the way before you as you take steps of trust along your path. Sometimes the way before you appears to be blocked. If you focus on the obstacle or search for a way around it, you will probably go off course. Instead, focus on Me, the Shepherd who is leading you along your life-journey. Before you know it, the "obstacle" will be behind you and you will hardly know how you passed through it.

That is the secret of success in My kingdom. Although you remain aware of the visible world around you, your primary awareness is of Me. When the road before you looks rocky, you can trust Me to get you through that rough patch. My Presence enables you to face each day with confidence.

JOHN 10:14–15; ISAIAH 26:7;
PROVERBS 3:25–26

October 18
EVENING

Trust Me in times of confusion—when things don't make sense and nothing you do seems to help. Invite Me to enter into your struggles—to be ever so close to you. Though others may not understand what you're going through, I understand perfectly, and *I am with you, watching over you* continually.

> *"I am with you and will watch over you wherever you go, and I will bring you back to this land. I will not leave you until I have done what I have promised you."* —Genesis 28:15

> *My soul clings to you; your right hand upholds me.* —Psalm 63:8

> *Also read:*
> John 15:26 nkjv

Before You Turn Out the Light

Rest assured that there is a way forward, even though you can't yet see it. Take My hand—and trust.

October 19
MORNING

Come to Me with your defenses down, ready to be blessed and filled with My Presence. Relax and feel the relief of being totally open and authentic with Me. You have nothing to hide and nothing to disclose because I know everything about you already. You can have no other relationship like this one. Take time to savor its richness, basking in My golden Light.

One of the worst consequences of the Fall is the elaborate barriers people erect between themselves and others. Facades abound in the world, even in My body, the church. Sometimes, church is the last place where people feel free to be themselves. They cover up with Sunday clothes and Sunday smiles. They feel relief when they leave because of the strain of false fellowship. The best antidote to this artificial atmosphere is practicing My Presence at church. Let your primary focus be communing with Me, worshiping Me, glorifying Me. Then you will be able to smile at others with My Joy and love them with My Love.

1 JOHN 1:5–7; EXODUS 33:14;
PHILIPPIANS 4:8

October 19
EVENING

Anyone who has seen Me has seen the Father; therefore, as you get to know Me better, you simultaneously come to know the Father more fully. The better you know Us, the more Our sacred Love dwells in you. There are no limits to the depth of intimacy you and I can experience.

> *For now we are looking in a mirror that gives only a dim (blurred) reflection [of reality as in a riddle or enigma], but then [when perfection comes] we shall see in reality and face to face! Now I know in part (imperfectly), but then I shall know and understand fully and clearly, even in the same manner as I have been fully and clearly known and understood [by God].* —1 Corinthians 13:12 AMP

Also read:
John 14:9; Psalm 42:7; John 17:26

Before You Turn Out the Light

One day you will know and understand Me fully, just as you are known. Until then, persist in your blessed pursuit of Me and your study of My Word.

October 20

MORNING

I AM YOUR LIVING GOD, far more abundantly alive than the most vivacious person you know. The human body is wonderfully crafted, but gravity and the inevitable effects of aging weigh it down. Even the most superb athlete cannot maintain his fitness over many decades. Lasting abundant life can be found in Me alone. Do not be anxious about the weakness of your body. Instead, view it as the prelude to My infusing energy into your being.

As you identify more and more fully with Me, My Life becomes increasingly intertwined with yours. Though the process of aging continues, inwardly you grow stronger with the passing years. Those who live close to Me develop an inner aliveness that makes them seem youthful in spite of their years. Let My Life shine through you as you *walk in the Light* with Me.

REVELATION 1:18; PSALM 139:14;
COLOSSIANS 1:29; ISAIAH 2:5

October 20
EVENING

YOU DON'T HAVE TO CHOOSE between enjoying Me or enjoying the many good gifts I provide. It is simply a matter of priorities: I want you to treasure Me above all else. If you keep Me first in your life, My good gifts will not become idols. Delight yourself in Me, and *I will give you the desires and secret petitions of your heart.*

Every good and perfect gift is from above, coming down from the Father of the heavenly lights, who does not change like shifting shadows. —JAMES 1:17

*Delight yourself also in the L*ORD*, and He will give you the desires and secret petitions of your heart.* —PSALM 37:4 AMP

Also read:
2 CHRONICLES 16:9; ACTS 2:28

Before You Turn Out the Light

Your yearning for an awakened soul brings me pleasure. Keep seeking Joy in My Presence.

October 21

MORNING

To live in My Presence consistently, you must expose and expel your rebellious tendencies. When something interferes with your plans or desires, you tend to resent the interference. Try to become aware of each resentment, however petty it may seem. Don't push those unpleasant feelings down; instead, let them come to the surface where you can deal with them. Ask My Spirit to increase your awareness of resentful feelings. Bring them boldly into the Light of My Presence so that I can free you from them.

The ultimate solution to rebellious tendencies is submission to My authority over you. Intellectually, you rejoice in My sovereignty, without which the world would be a terrifying place. But when My sovereign will encroaches on your little domain of control, you often react with telltale resentment.

The best response to losses or thwarted hopes is praise: *The Lord gives and the Lord takes away. Blessed be the name of the Lord.* Remember that all good things—your possessions, your family and friends, your health and abilities, your time—are gifts from Me. Instead of feeling entitled to all these blessings, respond to them with gratitude. Be prepared to let go of anything I take from you, but never let go of My hand!

Psalm 139:23–24; 1 Peter 5:6;
Job 1:21 nkjv

October 21

EVENING

Y OU LIVE IN AN AGE OF ENTITLEMENT, so you need to counteract the barrage of propaganda proclaiming you deserve more. My Word is *sharper than any double-edged sword*; I use it to perform spiritual surgery on *the thoughts and attitudes of your heart.* As Scripture lights up your perspective and your path, I set you free from the prison of ingratitude, releasing you to enjoy the pleasures of a thankful heart.

> *. . . to open eyes that are blind, to free captives from prison and to release from the dungeon those who sit in darkness.* —ISAIAH 42:7

> *For the word of God is living and active. Sharper than any double-edged sword, it penetrates even to dividing soul and spirit, joints and marrow; it judges the thoughts and attitudes of the heart.* —HEBREWS 4:12

Also read:

PSALM 119:105

Before You Turn Out the Light

Beseech Me to raise your perspective and secure your release from the dungeon of ungratefulness.

October 22
MORNING

No matter what your circumstances may be, you can find Joy in My Presence. On some days, Joy is generously strewn along your life-path, glistening in the sunlight. On days like that, being content is as simple as breathing the next breath or taking the next step. Other days are overcast and gloomy; you feel the strain of the journey, which seems endless. Dull gray rocks greet your gaze and cause your feet to ache. Yet Joy is still attainable. *Search for it as for hidden treasure.*

Begin by remembering that I have created this day; it is not a chance occurrence. Recall that I am present with you whether you sense My Presence or not. Then, start talking with Me about whatever is on your mind. Rejoice in the fact that I understand you perfectly and I know exactly what you are experiencing. As you continue communicating with Me, your mood will gradually lighten. Awareness of My marvelous Companionship can infuse Joy into the grayest day.

PSALM 21:6; PROVERBS 2:4;
COLOSSIANS 1:16 NKJV

October 22

EVENING

Glorifying and enjoying Me is a higher priority than maintaining a tidy, structured life. Even if you succeed in creating a tidy life for a time, you will not be able to maintain it. Instead of wasting your energy on an impossible task, endeavor to *walk more consistently in the Light of My Presence.*

> *"I have brought you glory on earth by completing the work you gave me to do. And now, Father, glorify me in your presence with the glory I had with you before the world began."* —John 17:4–5

> *Blessed are those who have learned to acclaim you, who walk in the light of your presence, O Lord. They rejoice in your name all day long; they exult in your righteousness.* —Psalm 89:15–16

Also read:

Psalm 139:1–2

Before You Turn Out the Light

Examine each of your endeavors to ensure that
I will be glorified in your every action.

October 23
MORNING

As you turn your attention to Me, feel the Light of My Presence shining upon you. Open your mind and heart to receive My heavenly smile of approval. Let My gold-tinged Love wash over you and soak into the depths of your being. As you are increasingly filled with My Being, you experience joyous union with Me: *I in you and you in Me.* Your Joy-in-Me and My Joy-in-you become intertwined and inseparable. I suffuse your soul with Joy in My Presence; *at My right hand there are pleasures forevermore.*

NUMBERS 6:26 AMP; JOHN 17:20–23;
PSALM 16:11 NKJV

October 23
EVENING

PONDER THE STRENGTH OF MY LOVE. This Love is the most powerful force in the universe, and it will ultimately prevail—in your current life (as you trust Me) and throughout eternity. Remember that you are *My beloved*. This is your forever-identity. Rejoice in this intimate security, for it is worth more than all the wealth in the world!

> *Many waters cannot quench love; rivers cannot wash it away. If one were to give all the wealth of his house for love, it would be utterly scorned.* —SONG OF SONGS 8:7

> *And so we know and rely on the love God has for us. God is love. Whoever lives in love lives in God, and God in him. In this way, love is made complete among us so that we will have confidence on the day of judgment, because in this world we are like him. There is no fear in love. But perfect love drives out fear.* —1 JOHN 4:16–18

Also read:
1 JOHN 1:7 NASB; JAMES 4:8 NKJV

Before You Turn Out the Light

Where can My strong Love reinforce your courage? Your perseverance?

October 24
MORNING

LIE DOWN IN GREEN PASTURES of Peace. Learn to unwind whenever possible, resting in the Presence of your Shepherd. This electronic age keeps My children "wired" much of the time, too tense to find Me in the midst of their moments. I built into your very being the need for rest. How twisted the world has become when people feel guilty about meeting this basic need! How much time and energy they waste by being always on the go rather than taking time to seek My direction for their lives.

I have called you to walk with Me down *paths of Peace*. I want you to blaze a trail for others who desire to live in My peaceful Presence. I have chosen you less for your strengths than for your weaknesses, which amplify your need for Me. Depend on Me more and more, and I will shower Peace on all your paths.

PSALM 23:1–3; GENESIS 2:2–3;
LUKE 1:79

October 24

EVENING

To live at peace with everyone, you need to control not only what you say and do but also what you think. When you indulge in negative thinking about someone, your relationship with that person is damaged. Those hurtful thoughts also affect your relationship with Me, and they may have a depressive effect on you. The remedy lies in seeking My forgiveness, then asking My Spirit to help you think *My* thoughts. This is the way of *Life and Peace*.

> *If it is possible, as far as it depends on you, live at peace with everyone.* —Romans 12:18

> *"Therefore, if you are offering your gift at the altar and there remember that your brother has something against you, leave your gift there in front of the altar. First go and be reconciled to your brother; then come and offer your gift."* —Matthew 5:23–24

Also read:
Romans 8:6

Before You Turn Out the Light

Attempt to mend your thoughts and ways in any relationship that is currently disrupted, and then freely worship Me.

October 25

MORNING

I AM GOD WITH YOU, for all time and throughout eternity. Don't let the familiarity of that concept numb its impact on your consciousness. My perpetual Presence with you can be a continual source of Joy, springing up and flowing out in streams of abundant Life. Let your mind reverberate with meanings of My Names: Jesus, *the Lord saves*; and Immanuel, *God with us*. Strive to remain conscious of My Presence even in your busiest moments. Talk with Me about whatever delights you, whatever upsets you, whatever is on your mind. These tiny steps of daily discipline, taken one after the other, will keep you close to Me on the path of Life.

MATTHEW 1:21, 23; JOHN 10:10 NKJV;
ACTS 2:28

October 25
EVENING

REMEMBER THAT THE EVIL ONE attacks you continually with burning arrows of accusation. Even if some of the arrows wound you, do not despair. I am the Great Physician: My loving Presence can both heal your wounds and train you to trust Me more.

> *But as for you, you meant evil against me; but God meant it for good, in order to bring it about as it is this day, to save many people alive.* —GENESIS 50:20 NKJV

> *In addition to all this, take up the shield of faith, with which you can extinguish all the flaming arrows of the evil one.* —EPHESIANS 6:16

Also read:
2 PETER 3:18

Before You Turn Out the Light

Use your shield of faith to stop the enemy's weapons and extinguish their flames.

October 26
MORNING

Come to Me when you are hurting, and I will soothe your pain. Come to Me when you are joyful, and I will share your Joy, multiplying it many times over. I am All you need, just when you need it. Your deepest desires find fulfillment in Me alone.

This is the age of self-help. Bookstores abound with books about "taking care of number one," making oneself the center of all things. The main goal of these methodologies is to become self-sufficient and confident. You, however, have been called to take a "road less traveled": continual dependence on Me. True confidence comes from knowing you are complete in My Presence. Everything you need has its counterpart in Me.

ISAIAH 49:13; JOHN 15:5;
JAMES 1:4

October 26

EVENING

Do not despair when hard times come your way, and do not try to escape them prematurely—timing is My prerogative! When you are grieving, you may feel as if sorrow will accompany you the rest of your days, but remember that I have promised to show compassion. Look up to Me, and see My Face shining down upon you.

> *There is a time for everything, and a season for every activity under heaven.* —ECCLESIASTES 3:1

> *Through the LORD's mercies we are not consumed, because His compassions fail not. They are new every morning; great is Your faithfulness. "The LORD is my portion," says my soul, "therefore I hope in Him!"* —LAMENTATIONS 3:22–24 KJV

Also read:
LAMENTATIONS 3:32; NUMBERS 6:25 NKJV

Before You Turn Out the Light

In your suffering, search for signs of My merciful Presence. I never run out of compassion.

October 27
MORNING

As you become increasingly aware of My Presence, you find it easier to discern the way you should go. This is one of the practical benefits of living close to Me. Instead of wondering about what is on the road ahead or worrying about what you should do if . . . or when . . . , you can concentrate on staying in communication with Me. When you actually arrive at a choice-point, I will show you which direction to go.

Many people are so preoccupied with future plans and decisions that they fail to see choices they need to make today. Without any conscious awareness, they make their habitual responses. People who live this way find a dullness creeping into their lives. They sleepwalk through their days, following well-worn paths of routine.

I, the Creator of the universe, am the most creative Being imaginable. I will not leave you circling in deeply rutted paths. Instead, I will lead you along fresh trails of adventure, revealing to you things you did not know. Stay in communication with Me. Follow My guiding Presence.

PSALM 32:8; GENESIS 1:1;
ISAIAH 58:11 NKJV

October 27
EVENING

Your mind so easily slips into the future, where worries abound. You also spend way too much time analyzing the past. Meanwhile, splendors of the present moment parade before you, and you don't even notice. I will help you learn to rest in *My* sufficiency, depending on Me more and more.

> *But he said to me, "My grace is sufficient for you, for my power is made perfect in weakness." Therefore I will boast all the more gladly about my weaknesses, so that Christ's power may rest on me.* —2 CORINTHIANS 12:9

> *And my God will meet all your needs according to his glorious riches in Christ Jesus.* —PHILIPPIANS 4:19

Also read:
PSALM 34:5; MATTHEW 6:34

Before You Turn Out the Light

Abide in My grace. Moment by moment,
I'll give you everything you need.

October 28

MORNING

Do not expect to be treated fairly in this life. People will say and do hurtful things to you, things that you don't deserve. When someone mistreats you, try to view it as an opportunity to grow in grace. See how quickly you can forgive the one who has wounded you. Don't be concerned about setting the record straight. Instead of obsessing about other people's opinions of you, keep your focus on Me. Ultimately, it is My view of you that counts.

As you concentrate on relating to Me, remember that I have clothed you in My righteousness and holiness. I see you attired in these radiant garments, which I bought for you with My blood. This also is not fair; it is pure gift. When others treat you unfairly, remember that My ways with you are much better than fair. My ways are Peace and *Love, which I have poured out into your heart by My Spirit.*

Colossians 3:13; Isaiah 61:10;
Ephesians 1:7–8; Romans 5:5

October 28

EVENING

*S*INCE I LIVE IN YOUR HEART, My Peace is accessible to you there. Ask Me to increase your awareness of My peaceful Presence. Keep returning your thoughts to Me by whispering, "Jesus."

*My help comes from the L*ORD*, the Maker of heaven and earth.* —PSALM 121:2

*The name of the L*ORD *is a strong tower; the righteous run to it and are safe.* —PROVERBS 18:10

Also read:
JOHN 16:33

Before You Turn Out the Light

Did a messy day interrupt your Peace? Call a time-out from the confusion, and turn to Me before you return to problem-solving.

October 29
MORNING

Linger in My Presence a while. Rein in your impulses to plunge into the day's activities. Beginning your day alone with Me is essential preparation for success. A great athlete takes time to prepare himself mentally for the feat ahead of him before he moves a muscle. Similarly, your time of being still in My Presence equips you for the day ahead of you. Only I know what will happen to you this day. I have arranged the events you will encounter as you go along your way. If you are not adequately equipped for the journey, you will *grow weary and lose heart*. Relax with Me while I ready you for action.

ZECHARIAH 2:13; EPHESIANS 2:10;
HEBREWS 12:3

October 29
EVENING

Be careful not to confuse *being* holy with trying to *appear* holy. The more you know Me and love Me, the easier it is for you to let Me live through you. Without your even realizing it, intimacy with Me transforms you into My likeness—My holy image.

> *But just as he who called you is holy, so be holy in all you do; for it is written: "Be holy, because I am holy."* —1 Peter 1:15–16

> *You, however, are controlled not by the sinful nature but by the Spirit, if the Spirit of God lives in you. And if anyone does not have the Spirit of Christ, he does not belong to Christ.* —Romans 8:9

Also read:
Colossians 1:27 nkjv

Before You Turn Out the Light

Welcome My Spirit to live and love through you as a defense against old habits and unholy ways.

October 30
MORNING

I AM WITH YOU. I am with you. I am with you. Heaven's bells continually peal with that promise of My Presence. Some people never hear those bells because their minds are earthbound and their hearts are closed to Me. Others hear the bells only once or twice in their lifetimes, in rare moments of seeking Me above all else. My desire is that My "sheep" hear My voice continually, for *I am the ever-present Shepherd.*

Quietness is the classroom where you learn to hear My voice. Beginners need a quiet place in order to still their minds. As you advance in this discipline, you gradually learn to carry the stillness with you wherever you go. When you step back into the mainstream of life, strain to hear those glorious bells: *I am with you. I am with you. I am with you.*

ISAIAH 41:10 NKJV; JEREMIAH 29:12–13;
JOHN 10:14, 27–28

October 30
EVENING

WHEN PEOPLE ARE AFRAID, they long to feel protected by someone who is bigger and stronger. Be assured that I am always watching over you—*like a shepherd watching over his flock*. Expressing yourself freely to Me will help you become aware of My loving Presence.

> *Hear the word of the Lord, O nations; proclaim it in distant coastlands: "He who scattered Israel will gather them and will watch over his flock like a shepherd."* —Jeremiah 31:10

> *Trust in Him at all times, you people; pour out your heart before Him; God is a refuge for us.* —Psalm 62:8 nkjv

Also read:
Psalm 145:20; 1 John 4:19 nkjv

Before You Turn Out the Light

Let the promise of My watchcare comfort you this night.

October 31

MORNING

LEARN TO LISTEN TO ME even while you are listening to other people. As they open their souls to your scrutiny, *you are on holy ground*. You need the help of My Spirit to respond appropriately. Ask Him to think through you, live through you, love through you. My own Being is alive within you in the Person of the Holy Spirit. If you respond to others' needs through your unaided thought processes, you offer them dry crumbs. When the Spirit empowers your listening and speaking, *My streams of living water flow* through you to other people. Be a channel of My Love, Joy, and Peace by listening to Me as you listen to others.

EXODUS 3:5; 1 CORINTHIANS 6:19;
JOHN 7:38–39

October 31
EVENING

Do not usurp My role in people's lives, no matter how much you long to help them. Learn from Me: Because I have *all authority in heaven and on earth*, I could rescue or control anyone at will, yet I wanted them to be free to love Me—or not. Restrain your urges to solve people's problems; instead, use your time and energy to listen to them and pray for them.

Then Jesus came to them and said, "All authority in heaven and on earth has been given to me." —Matthew 28:18

Let the morning bring me word of your unfailing love, for I have put my trust in you. Show me the way I should go, for to you I lift up my soul. —Psalm 143:8

Also read:
Ephesians 3:20–21

Before You Turn Out the Light

Entrust your loved ones to Me. They are much safer in My hands than anywhere else.

November

And my God will meet all your needs according to his glorious riches in Christ Jesus.

PHILIPPIANS 4:19

November 1

MORNING

Do not be discouraged by the difficulty of keeping your focus on Me. I know that your heart's desire is to be aware of My Presence continually. This is a lofty goal; you aim toward it but never fully achieve it in this life. Don't let feelings of failure weigh you down. Instead, try to see yourself as I see you. First of all, I am delighted by your deep desire to walk closely with Me through your life. I am pleased each time you initiate communication with Me. In addition, I notice the progress you have made since you first resolved to live in My Presence.

When you realize that your mind has wandered away from Me, don't be alarmed or surprised. You live in a world that has been rigged to distract you. Each time you plow your way through the massive distractions to communicate with Me, you achieve a victory. Rejoice in these tiny triumphs, and they will increasingly light up your days.

ROMANS 8:33–34; HEBREWS 4:14–16

November 1
EVENING

THOUGH MANY THINGS can affect your ability to think clearly—poor sleep, health, or nutrition; lack of fresh air and exercise; worries of the world; excessive busyness—it is still possible to exert much control over your thinking. Ask My Spirit to help you in this endeavor. As you persevere in making good thought-choices, you will enjoy My refreshing Presence more and more.

> *Therefore, holy brothers, who share in the heavenly calling, fix your thoughts on Jesus, the apostle and high priest whom we confess.* —HEBREWS 3:1

> *Be self-controlled and alert. Your enemy the devil prowls around like a roaring lion looking for someone to devour.* —1 PETER 5:8

Also read:
PSALM 141:3; ACTS 3:19

Before You Turn Out the Light

Don't let your thoughts run freely; set a guard over them, being self-controlled and alert.

November 2
MORNING

GROW STRONG in the Light of My Presence. Your weakness does not repel Me. On the contrary, it attracts My Power, which is always available to flow into a yielded heart. Do not condemn yourself for your constant need of help. Instead, come to Me with your gaping neediness; let the Light of My Love fill you.

A yielded heart does not whine or rebel when the going gets rough. It musters the courage to thank Me even during hard times. Yielding yourself to My will is ultimately an act of trust. *In quietness and trust is your strength.*

PSALM 116:5–7; EPHESIANS 5:20;
ISAIAH 30:15

November 2
EVENING

I AM TRAINING YOU IN THE DISCIPLINE OF perseverance. Your ongoing struggle is *not* a mistake or a punishment. Try to view it, instead, as a rich opportunity: Your uphill journey keeps you aware of your neediness, so you look to Me for help.

> *Consider Him who endured such hostility from sinners against Himself, lest you become weary and discouraged in your souls.* —HEBREWS 12:3 NKJV

> *The LORD appeared to us in the past, saying: "I have loved you with an everlasting love; I have drawn you with loving-kindness."* —JEREMIAH 31:3

Also read:
ISAIAH 61:1 NKJV; PHILIPPIANS 3:20–21

Before You Turn Out the Light

Be careful to avoid the sinful snare of self-pity. Trustingly whisper My Name instead, and feel the embrace of My everlasting Love.

November 3
MORINING

Every time something thwarts your plans or desires, use that as a reminder to communicate with Me. This practice has several benefits. The first is obvious: Talking with Me blesses you and strengthens our relationship. Another benefit is that disappointments, instead of dragging you down, are transformed into opportunities for good. This transformation removes the sting from difficult circumstances, making it possible to be joyful in the midst of adversity.

Begin by practicing this discipline in all the little disappointments of daily life. It is often these minor setbacks that draw you away from My Presence. When you reframe *setbacks as opportunities*, you find that you gain much more than you have lost. It is only after much training that you can accept major losses in this positive way. But it is possible to attain the perspective of the apostle Paul, who wrote: *Compared to the surpassing greatness of knowing Christ Jesus, I consider everything I once treasured to be as insignificant as rubbish.*

Proverbs 19:21; Colossians 4:2;

Philippians 3:7–8

November 3
EVENING

You will continue to sin till you leave this world, but I have provided an effective way of dealing with sin—*godly sorrow*, a growth-promoting sorrow motivated by love and concern for all those whom you have hurt (including Me). It is a work of the Holy Spirit, and it brings real repentance that *leaves no regret*. When your heart condemns you, remember that *I am greater than your heart and I know all things*.

For if our heart condemns us, God is greater than our heart, and knows all things. —1 John 3:20 NKJV

Godly sorrow brings repentance that leads to salvation and leaves no regret, but worldly sorrow brings death. —2 Corinthians 7:10

Also read:
Ephesians 6:16; Revelation 12:10

Before You Turn Out the Light

Try heeding your conscience less and My Spirit and My Word more. There's no better time than now.

November 4
MORNING

WALK PEACEFULLY WITH ME through this day. You are wondering how you will cope with all that is expected of you. You must traverse this day like any other: one step at a time. Instead of mentally rehearsing how you will do this or that, keep your mind on My Presence and on taking the next step. The more demanding your day, the more help you can expect from Me. This is a training opportunity, since I designed you for deep dependence on your Shepherd-King. Challenging times wake you up and amplify your awareness of needing My help.

When you don't know what to do, wait while I open the way before you. Trust that I know what I'm doing, and be ready to follow My lead. *I will give strength to you, and I will bless you with Peace.*

EXODUS 33:14; DEUTERONOMY 33:25;
HEBREWS 13:20–21; PSALM 29:11

November 4
EVENING

Do you really believe My grace is sufficient for you? If so, then it makes sense to stop your anxious striving. Don't worry about tomorrow's needs—My sufficiency is for one day at a time.

> *Those who look to him are radiant; their faces are never covered with shame.* —Psalm 34:5

> *"Therefore do not worry about tomorrow, for tomorrow will worry about itself. Each day has enough trouble of its own."* —Matthew 6:34

Also read:
2 Corinthians 12:9; Philippians 4:19

Before You Turn Out the Light

Live in the present! Look to Me for your every need in this moment.

November 5
MORNING

You can live as close to Me as you choose. I set up no barriers between us; neither do I tear down barriers that you erect.

People tend to think their circumstances determine the quality of their lives. So they pour their energy into trying to control those situations. They feel happy when things are going well and sad or frustrated when things don't turn out as they'd hoped. They rarely question this correlation between their circumstances and feelings. Yet it is possible *to be content in any and every situation*.

Put more energy into trusting Me and enjoying My Presence. Don't let your well-being depend on your circumstances. Instead, connect your joy to My precious promises:

> *I am with you and will watch over you wherever you go. I will meet all your needs according to My glorious riches. Nothing in all creation will be able to separate you from My Love.*

PHILIPPIANS 4:12; GENESIS 28:15;
PHILIPPIANS 4:19; ROMANS 8:38–39

November 5

EVENING

You have tasted My goodness, and you want more. I have responded to this desire in several ways: I've allowed suffering in your life, so that you can learn to trust Me more; also, I have blessed you with intimate experiences of My Presence to boost your confidence in My perfection. My goal is for you to become so convinced of My goodness that nothing can shake your trust in Me.

> *Oh, taste and see that the Lord is good; blessed is the man who trusts in Him!* —Psalm 34:8 nkjv

> *"You will seek me and find me when you seek me with all your heart."* —Jeremiah 29:13

> *Also read:*
> Psalm 63:5

Before You Turn Out the Light

Give Me your whole heart, which opens the way for genuine intimacy between us.

November 6

MORNING

SEEK TO PLEASE ME above all else. As you journey through today, there will be many choice-points along your way. Most of the day's decisions will be small ones you have to make quickly. You need some rule of thumb to help you make good choices. Many people's decisions are a combination of their habitual responses and their desire to please themselves or others. This is not My way for you. Strive to please Me in everything, not just in major decisions. This is possible only to the extent that you are living in close communion with Me. When My Presence is your deepest delight, you know almost instinctively what will please Me. A quick *glance* at Me is all you need to make the right choice. *Delight yourself in M*e more and more; seek My pleasure in all you do.

JOHN 8:29; HEBREWS 11:5–6;
PSALM 37:4

November 6
EVENING

IN ORDER TO DO SOMETHING WELL, you need to feel at peace about the many other things you could be doing but are not. When you have set your priorities according to My will, you can relax and focus on accomplishing what *I* deem important. As you seek to please Me above all else, you will grow more and more into the *workmanship*—the masterpiece—I created you to be.

> *How sweet are your words to my taste, sweeter than honey to my mouth! I gain understanding from your precepts; therefore I hate every wrong path. Your word is a lamp to my feet and a light for my path.* —PSALM 119:103–105

> *We are His workmanship, created in Christ Jesus for good works, which God prepared beforehand that we should walk in them.* —EPHESIANS 2:10 NKJV

Also read:
PSALM 105:4 NKJV

Before You Turn Out the Light

As you look at all of tomorrow's possibilities before you, seek My Face and My will.

November 7
MORNING

WORSHIP ME *in the beauty of holiness.* All true beauty reflects some of who I AM. I am working My ways in you: the divine Artist creating loveliness within your being. My main work is to clear out debris and clutter, making room for My Spirit to take full possession. Collaborate with Me in this effort by being willing to let go of anything I choose to take away. I know what you need, and I have promised to provide all of that—abundantly!

Your sense of security must not rest in your possessions or in things going your way. I am training you to depend on Me alone, finding fulfillment in My Presence. This entails being satisfied with much or with little, accepting *either* as My will for the moment. Instead of grasping and controlling, you are learning to release and receive. Cultivate this receptive stance by trusting Me in every situation.

PSALM 29:2 NKJV; PSALM 27:4;
PSALM 52:8

November 7
EVENING

I WANT YOU TO BE ALL MINE—filled to overflowing with My Love, Joy, and Peace. Because these Glory-gifts leak out of you, you need Me continually for renewal. As I fill you with My Glory-gifts, let My wondrous Light shine through you into other people's lives.

> *However, we possess this precious treasure [the divine Light of the Gospel] in [frail, human] vessels of earth, that the grandeur and exceeding greatness of the power may be shown to be from God and not from ourselves.* —2 CORINTHIANS 4:7 AMP

> *"In the same way, let your light shine before men, that they may see your good deeds and praise your Father in heaven."* —MATTHEW 5:16

Also read:
GALATIANS 5:22; COLOSSIANS 1:27

Before You Turn Out the Light

Even though you are a frail earthen jar, I am eager to fill you with My Love, Joy, and Peace. Stay with Me a while; don't rush our time together.

November 8
MORNING

Learn to appreciate difficult days. Be stimulated by the challenges you encounter along your way. As you journey through rough terrain with Me, gain confidence from your knowledge that together we can handle anything. This knowledge is comprised of three parts: your relationship with Me, promises in the Bible, and past experiences of coping successfully during hard times.

Look back on your life, and see how I have helped you through difficult days. If you are tempted to think, "Yes, but that was then, and this is now," remember who I AM! Although you and your circumstances may change dramatically, *I remain the same* throughout time and eternity. This is the basis of your confidence. In My Presence *you live and move and have your being.*

ISAIAH 41:10; PSALM 102:27;
ACTS 17:27–28

November 8
EVENING

PEOPLE ARE ALWAYS TRYING to diminish Me, to cut Me down to a god who is understandable and predictable. Whenever you find yourself struggling to accept My ways with you or My ways with the world, stop and remember who I am. Bow your mind and heart before My infinite intelligence, and worship Me—the mysterious, majestic holy One who suffered and died for you.

> *Seek the LORD while he may be found; call on him while he is near. . . . "For my thoughts are not your thoughts, neither are your ways my ways," declares the LORD. "As the heavens are higher than the earth, so are my ways higher than your ways and my thoughts than your thoughts."* —ISAIAH 55:6, 8–9

> *Trust in the LORD with all your heart and lean not on your own understanding.* —PROVERBS 3:5

Also read:
GENESIS 1:3, 9

Before You Turn Out the Light

Surrender your thoughts and ways to Mine.
I will show you things you've never seen!

November 9

MORNING

SIT QUIETLY WITH ME, letting all your fears and worries bubble up to the surface of your consciousness. There, in the Light of My Presence, the bubbles pop and disappear. However, some fears surface over and over again, especially fear of the future. You tend to project yourself mentally into the next day, week, month, year, decade; and you visualize yourself coping badly in those times. What you are seeing is a false image, because it doesn't include Me. Those gloomy times that you imagine will not come to pass, since My Presence will be with you at *all* times.

When a future-oriented worry assails you, capture it and disarm it by suffusing the Light of My Presence into that mental image. Say to yourself, "Jesus will be with me then and there. With His help, I can cope!" Then, come home to the present moment, where you can enjoy Peace in My Presence.

LUKE 12:22–25; DEUTERONOMY 31:6;
2 CORINTHIANS 10:5

November 9

EVENING

YOU ARE ON AN ADVENTUROUS TRAIL with Me. This is not an easy time, but it is nonetheless good—full of blessings as well as struggles. Be open to learning all that I want to teach you as you journey through challenging terrain, and be willing to let go of familiar comforts so you can say a wholehearted "Yes!" to this adventure.

For He shall give His angels charge over you, to keep you in all your ways. In their hands they shall bear you up, lest you dash your foot against a stone. —PSALM 91:11–12 NKJV

A man's mind plans his way, but the Lord directs his steps and makes them sure. —PROVERBS 16:9 AMP

Also read:
DEUTERONOMY 29:29 NKJV; 1 THESSALONIANS 5:17

Before You Turn Out the Light

Pray continually as you make decisions on this journey. I will make your steps sure.

November 10

MORNING

Focus your entire being on My living Presence. I am most assuredly with you, enveloping you in My Love and Peace. While you relax in My Presence, I am molding your mind and cleansing your heart. I am re-creating you into the one I designed you to be.

As you move from stillness into the activities of your day, do not relinquish your attentiveness to Me. If something troubles you, talk it over with Me. If you get bored with what you are doing, fill the time with prayers and praise. When someone irritates you, don't let your thoughts linger on that person's faults. Gently nudge your mind back to Me. Every moment is precious if you keep your focus on Me. Any day can be a good day because My Presence permeates all time.

Psalm 89:15–16; 1 John 3:19–20;
Jude vv. 24–25; Psalm 41:12

November 10

EVENING

Small matters can lead to major consequences, so it's wise to entrust to Me even things that seem unimportant. One way of doing this is through seeking to please Me in every aspect of your life. When you do so, I surprise you in several ways: I answer your prayers bountifully, and I awaken your heart to the radiant pleasure of living in union with Me.

So we make it our goal to please him, whether we are at home in the body or away from it. —2 Corinthians 5:9

You are my lamp, O Lord; the Lord turns my darkness into light. —2 Samuel 22:29

Also read:
John 10:10 nasb; Matthew 11:30 amp

Before You Turn Out the Light

Delegate even the details of tomorrow to Me, and wait with expectation.

November 11
MORNING

Do not let any set of circumstances intimidate you. The more challenging your day, the more of My Power I place at your disposal. You seem to think that I empower you equally each day, but this is not so. Your tendency upon awakening is to assess the difficulties ahead of you, measuring them against your average strength. This is an exercise in unreality.

I know what each of your days will contain, and I empower you accordingly. The degree to which I strengthen you on a given day is based mainly on two variables: the difficulty of your circumstances, and your willingness to depend on Me for help. Try to view challenging days as opportunities to receive more of My Power than usual. Look to Me for all that you need, and watch to see what I will do. *As your day, so shall your strength be.*

EPHESIANS 1:18–20; PSALM 105:4;
DEUTERONOMY 33:25 NKJV

November 11
EVENING

I CREATED THE WORLD gloriously beautiful, and I want you to appreciate beauty when you see it. However, even more beneficial than sight is hope, which is itself a kind of vision. It enables you to see—through the eyes of your heart—things that are *not yet*.

Practice hoping for things you do not see—both for this life and the next.

> *If we hope for what we do not see, we eagerly wait for it with perseverance.* —ROMANS 8:25 NKJV

> *Now faith is the assurance (the confirmation, the title deed) of the things [we] hope for, being the proof of things [we] do not see and the conviction of their reality [faith perceiving as real fact what is not revealed to the senses].* —HEBREWS 11:1 AMP

Also read:
JOHN 17:22 NKJV

Before You Turn Out the Light

Train the eyes of your heart on Me. I offer you the hope of heaven as My Promise to you.

November 12

MORNING

This is a time of abundance in your life. *Your cup runneth over* with blessings. After plodding uphill for many weeks, you are now traipsing through lush meadows drenched in warm sunshine. I want you to enjoy to the full this time of ease and refreshment. I delight in providing it for you.

Sometimes My children hesitate to receive My good gifts with open hands. Feelings of false guilt creep in, telling them they don't deserve to be so richly blessed. This is nonsense-thinking because no one deserves anything from Me. My kingdom is not about earning and deserving; it's about believing and receiving.

When a child of Mine balks at accepting My gifts, I am deeply grieved. When you receive My abundant blessings with a grateful heart, I rejoice. My pleasure in giving and your pleasure in receiving flow together in joyous harmony.

PSALM 23:5 KJV; JOHN 3:16;
LUKE 11:9–10; ROMANS 8:32

November 12

EVENING

REMEMBER WHO I AM: *King of kings and Lord of lords, dwelling in dazzlingly unapproachable Light.* I am also your Shepherd, tenderly leading you step by step through your life. I want you to realize how precious you are to Me—how much I delight in you. I long for you to reciprocate by delighting in Me.

> *. . . God, the blessed and only Ruler, the King of kings and Lord of lords, who alone is immortal and who lives in unapproachable light, whom no one has seen or can see. To him be honor and might forever. Amen.* —1 TIMOTHY 6:15–16

> *Delight yourself in the LORD and he will give you the desires of your heart.* —PSALM 37:4

> *Also read:*
> REVELATION 1:14–16; HEBREWS 4:16

Before You Turn Out the Light

Relish the privilege you have to commune with Me. I am listening to your heart as well as your words.

November 13

MORNING

I AM *CHRIST IN YOU, the hope of Glory.* The One who walks beside you, holding you by your hand, is the same One who lives within you. This is a deep, unfathomable mystery. You and I are intertwined in an intimacy involving every fiber of your being. The Light of My Presence shines within you, as well as upon you. I am in you, and you are in Me; therefore nothing in heaven or on earth can separate you from Me!

As you sit quietly in My Presence, your awareness of My Life within you is heightened. This produces the *Joy of the Lord, which is your strength. I, the God of hope, fill you with all Joy and Peace as you trust in Me, so that you may bubble over with hope by the power of the Holy Spirit.*

COLOSSIANS 1:27; ISAIAH 42:6;
NEHEMIAH 8:10; ROMANS 15:13 AMP

November 13

EVENING

Throw Me your cares—your anxieties and concerns—with abandon. As soon as you release those worrisome things, you can breathe a sigh of relief and refresh yourself in My loving Presence. It doesn't matter if you have to do this many times each day—and sometimes during the night too. I am always awake, ready to catch your cares and bear your burdens.

> *[Cast] all your care upon Him, for He cares for you.* —1 Peter 5:7 nkjv

> *The Lord watches over you—the Lord is your shade at your right hand; the sun will not harm you by day, nor the moon by night. The Lord will keep you from all harm—he will watch over your life; the Lord will watch over your coming and going both now and forevermore.* —Psalm 121:5–8

Also read:
Psalm 139:23 nkjv; Psalm 68:19

Before You Turn Out the Light

Fling your cares—every one of them—into My strong, waiting hands. I never miss!

November 14
MORNING

BASK IN THE LUXURY of being fully understood and unconditionally loved. Dare to see yourself as I see you: radiant in My righteousness, cleansed by My blood. I view you as the one I created you to be, the one you will be in actuality when heaven becomes your home. It is My Life within you that is changing you *from glory to glory.* Rejoice in this mysterious miracle! Thank Me continually for the amazing gift of My Spirit within you.

Try to depend on the help of the Spirit as you go through this day of life. Pause briefly from time to time so you can consult with this Holy One inside you. He will not force you to do His bidding, but He will guide you as you give Him space in your life. Walk along this wondrous way of collaboration with My Spirit.

PSALM 34:5; 2 CORINTHIANS 5:21;
2 CORINTHIANS 3:18 NKJV; GALATIANS 5:25

November 14

EVENING

The best way to face yourself is to remember that you are constantly clothed in My robe of righteousness. I have no illusions about what lies beneath that pristine garment of salvation. Nonetheless, what you most feared to expose is no match for the Power of My radiant Presence. Collaborate with Me as I work on growing the gifts I planted in your soul.

The Lord your God is with you, he is mighty to save. He will take great delight in you, he will quiet you with his love, he will rejoice over you with singing. —Zephaniah 3:17

But I trust in your unfailing love; my heart rejoices in your salvation. I will sing to the Lord, for he has been good to me. —Psalm 13:5–6

Also read:
Isaiah 61:10

Before You Turn Out the Light

Entrust yourself into My capable care, asking Me to transform you according to My plan.

November 15

MORNING

APPROACH PROBLEMS with a light touch. When your mind moves toward a problem area, you tend to focus on that situation so intensely that you lose sight of Me. You pit yourself against the difficulty as if you had to conquer it immediately. Your mind gears up for battle, and your body becomes tense and anxious. Unless you achieve total victory, you feel defeated.

There is a better way. When a problem starts to overshadow your thoughts, bring this matter to Me. Talk with Me about it and look at it in the Light of My Presence. This puts some much-needed space between you and your concern, enabling you to see from My perspective. You will be surprised at the results. Sometimes you may even laugh at yourself for being so serious about something so insignificant.

You will always face trouble in this life. But more importantly, you will always have Me with you, helping you to handle whatever you encounter. Approach problems with a light touch by viewing them in My revealing Light.

LUKE 12:25 ESV; PSALM 89:15; JOHN 16:33

November 15

EVENIN G

WHEN YOU WORSHIP ME, you connect with Me in a powerful way that transcends time and circumstances. Praising Me draws you into the depths of My Presence, where you can glimpse My Power and Glory. No matter how difficult your day may seem, the Light of My Presence will shine through the darkness as you worship Me.

Thou art holy, O thou that inhabitest the praises of Israel. —PSALM 22:3 KJV

Then I looked and heard the voice of many angels, numbering thousands upon thousands, and ten thousand times ten thousand. They encircled the throne and the living creatures and the elders. In a loud voice they sang: "Worthy is the Lamb, who was slain, to receive power and wealth and wisdom and strength and honor and glory and praise!" —REVELATION 5:11–12

Also read:
ACTS 17:28 NKJV

Before You Turn Out the Light

You vanquish the enemy and bring Me glory when you worship Me. How did praise get you victoriously through this day?

November 16

MORNING

As you look at the day before you, you see a twisted, complicated path, with branches going off in all directions. You wonder how you can possibly find your way through that maze. Then you remember the One who is *with you always, holding you by your right hand*. You recall My promise to *guide you with My counsel*, and you begin to relax. As you look again at the path ahead, you notice that a peaceful fog has settled over it, obscuring your view. You can see only a few steps in front of you, so you turn your attention more fully to Me and begin to enjoy My Presence.

The fog is a protection for you, calling you back into the present moment. Although I inhabit all of space and time, you can communicate with Me only here and now. Someday the fog will no longer be necessary, for you will have learned to keep your focus on Me and on the path just ahead of you.

PSALM 73:23–24; PSALM 25:4–5;
1 CORINTHIANS 13:12

November 16

EVENING

I WILL NEVER LIMIT MYSELF to doing only what you can anticipate and understand—to do so would be to cease being God! So expect your life to become increasingly surprising as you grow closer to Me. You will discover traces of My vibrant Presence in unusual places.

> *"As the heavens are higher than the earth, so are my ways higher than your ways and my thoughts than your thoughts."* —ISAIAH 55:9

> *With your help I can advance against a troop; with my God I can scale a wall.* —PSALM 18:29

Also read:
1 PETER 1:8 NASB

Before You Turn Out the Light

Start expecting each new day to contain surprises. In this, you'll view unforeseen events not as something wrong but as something from Me.

November 17

MORNING

THERE IS *NO CONDEMNATION* for those who are in Me. *The law of the Spirit of Life has set you free from the law of sin and death.* Not many Christians know how to live in this radical freedom, which is their birthright. I died to set you free; live freely in Me!

To walk along the path of freedom, you must keep your mind firmly fixed on Me. Many voices proclaim, "This is the way for you to go," but only My voice tells you the true way. If you follow the way of the world with all its glitter and glamour, you will descend deeper and deeper into an abyss. Christian voices also can lead you astray: "Do this!" "Don't do that!" "Pray this way!" "Don't pray that way!" If you listen to all those voices, you will become increasingly confused.

Be content to be a simple sheep, listening for My voice and following Me. *I will lead you into restful green pastures and guide you along paths of righteousness.*

ROMANS 8:1–2; ISAIAH 30:21;
JOHN 10:27; PSALM 23:1–3

November 17
EVENING

GIVE ME YOUR SADNESS and your problems. Sorrow shared with Me is permeated with brilliant sparkles of Joy—like numerous Christmas lights glittering in the darkness. I am your devoted Friend and also your King of kings, accomplishing My divine transformation in you.

> *He has sent Me to bind up the brokenhearted . . . and provide for those who grieve in Zion—to bestow on them a crown of beauty instead of ashes, the oil of gladness instead of mourning, and a garment of praise instead of a spirit of despair. They will be called oaks of righteousness, a planting of the LORD for the display of his splendor.* —ISAIAH 61:1–3

> *Jesus looked at them and said, "With man this is impossible, but with God all things are possible."* —MATTHEW 19:26

Also read:
JOHN 14:27

Before You Turn Out the Light

Give Me your broken dreams, and I will not only heal your brokenness but also supply you with a better dream.

November 18
MORNING

COME TO ME, and rest in My Peace. My Face is shining upon you, in rays of *Peace transcending understanding*. Instead of trying to figure things out yourself, you can relax in the Presence of the One who knows everything. As you lean on Me in trusting dependence, you feel peaceful and complete. This is how I designed you to live: in close communion with Me.

When you are around other people, you tend to cater to their expectations—real or imagined. You feel enslaved to pleasing them, and your awareness of My Presence grows dim. Your efforts to win their approval eventually exhaust you. You offer these people dry crumbs rather than the *living water* of My Spirit flowing through you. This is not My way for you! Stay in touch with Me, even during your busiest moments. Let My Spirit give you words of grace as you live in the Light of My Peace.

PHILIPPIANS 4:6–7; JOHN 7:38;
EPHESIANS 5:18–20

November 18
EVENING

THE VERY THINGS that trouble you most—your weaknesses and wounds—are of greatest use to Me in helping others. By letting these humble, hurting parts of you be exposed, you bless others, My Light shining through you into their lives. Thus your weakness and woundedness, consecrated to Me, become treasures in My kingdom.

*For God, who said, "Let light shine out of darkness,"
made his light shine in our hearts to give us the
light of the knowledge of the glory of God in
the face of Christ.* —2 CORINTHIANS 4:6

*But we have this treasure in jars of clay to show that this
all-surpassing power is from God and not from us. We are
hard pressed on every side, but not crushed; perplexed,
but not in despair; persecuted, but not abandoned; struck
down, but not destroyed.* —2 CORINTHIANS 4:7–9

Also read:
PSALM 89:15

Before You Turn Out the Light

Receive My healing and then turn outward: Who can you minister to by revealing your wounds?

November 19
MORNING

LEAVE OUTCOMES UP TO ME. Follow Me wherever I lead, without worrying about how it will all turn out. Think of your life as an adventure, with Me as your Guide and Companion. Live in the now, concentrating on staying in step with Me. When our path leads to a cliff, be willing to climb it with My help. When we come to a resting place, take time to be refreshed in My Presence. Enjoy the rhythm of life lived close to Me.

You already know the ultimate destination of your journey: your entrance into heaven. So keep your focus on the path just before you, leaving outcomes up to Me.

JOHN 10:4; PSALM 27:13–14; EXODUS 15:13

November 19

EVENING

YOU MUST LEAVE ROOM in your worldview for *mystery*—accepting the limitations of your understanding and knowledge. I will never be predictable or controllable, but I am trustworthy. When adversity strikes you or your loved ones, remember the words of Job: *The LORD gave, and the LORD has taken away. Blessed be the name of the LORD.*

> *Beyond all question, the mystery of godliness is great: He appeared in a body, was vindicated by the Spirit, was seen by angels, was preached among the nations, was believed on in the world, was taken up in glory.* —1 TIMOTHY 3:16

> *[Job] said: "Naked I came from my mother's womb, and naked shall I return there. The LORD gave, and the LORD has taken away; blessed be the name of the LORD." In all this Job did not sin nor charge God with wrong.* —JOB 1:21–22 NKJV

Also read:

JOB 42:3

Before You Turn Out the Light

Even when you do not understand My ways,
bless My Name as an act of faith.

November 20
MORNING

I AM PLEASED WITH YOU, MY CHILD. Allow yourself to become fully aware of My pleasure shining upon you. You don't have to perform well in order to receive My Love. In fact, a performance focus will pull you away from Me, toward some sort of Pharisaism. This can be a subtle form of idolatry: worshiping your own good works. It can also be a source of deep discouragement when your works don't measure up to your expectations.

Shift your focus from your performance to My radiant Presence. The Light of My Love shines on you continually, regardless of your feelings or behavior. Your responsibility is to be receptive to this unconditional Love. Thankfulness and trust are your primary receptors. Thank Me for everything; *trust in Me at all times*. These simple disciplines will keep you open to My loving Presence.

EPHESIANS 2:8–9; EPHESIANS 3:16–19;
PSALM 62:8

November 20
EVENING

As your Love for Me grows stronger, so does your desire to please Me. Whenever you seek to please Me, think about Me as the Lover of your soul, the One who loves you perfectly every nanosecond of your existence. Let your budding desire to please Me flourish in the Light of My unfailing Love.

> *Therefore, holy brothers, who share in the heavenly calling, fix your thoughts on Jesus, the apostle and high priest whom we confess.* —HEBREWS 3:1

> *But I am like an olive tree flourishing in the house of God; I trust in God's unfailing love for ever and ever.* —PSALM 52:8

Also read:
JOHN 15:9–11

Before You Turn Out the Light

To increase your passion for Me, take steps to discover how passionately I love you. What will you do toward that goal?

November 21

MORNING

Thank Me throughout this day for My Presence and My Peace. These are gifts of supernatural proportions. Ever since the resurrection, I have comforted My followers with these messages: *Peace be with you*, and *I am with you always*. Listen as I offer you My Peace and Presence in full measure. The best way to receive these glorious gifts is to thank Me for them.

It is impossible to spend too much time thanking and praising Me. I created you first and foremost to glorify Me. Thanksgiving and praise put you in proper relationship with Me, opening the way for My riches to flow into you. As you thank Me for My Presence and Peace, you appropriate My richest gifts.

LUKE 24:36; MATTHEW 28:20;
HEBREWS 13:15; 2 CORINTHIANS 9:15 NKJV

November 21
EVENING

You receive encouragement as a free gift from Me when you make the effort to hold on to your hope—focusing on what I've *already* done (died for your sins), what I *am* doing (living in you), and what I *will* do (take you home to heaven). I love to give good gifts in generous proportions. So cling to hope, beloved, and you will be *greatly* encouraged.

By two unchangeable things in which it is impossible for God to lie, we who have fled to take hold of the hope offered to us may be greatly encouraged. —HEBREWS 6:18

I press on toward the goal to win the prize for which God has called me heavenward in Christ Jesus. All of us who are mature should take such a view of things. And if on some point you think differently, that too God will make clear to you. Only let us live up to what we have already attained. —PHILIPPIANS 3:14–16

Also read:
GALATIANS 2:20 NKJV

Before You Turn Out the Light

Prayerfully lay claim to the hope of heaven.
It is your birthright as a Christian.

November 22
MORNING

A THANKFUL ATTITUDE opens windows of heaven. Spiritual blessings fall freely onto you through those openings into eternity. Moreover, as you look up with a grateful heart, you get glimpses of Glory through those windows. You cannot yet live in heaven, but you can experience foretastes of your ultimate home. Such samples of heavenly fare revive your hope. Thankfulness opens you up to these experiences, which then provide further reasons to be grateful. Thus your path becomes an upward spiral: ever increasing in gladness.

Thankfulness is not some sort of magic formula; it is the language of Love, which enables you to communicate intimately with Me. A thankful mind-set does not entail a denial of reality with its plethora of problems. Instead, it *rejoices in Me, your Savior*, in the midst of trials and tribulations. *I am your refuge and strength, an ever-present and well-proved help in trouble.*

EPHESIANS 1:3; HABAKKUK 3:17–18;
PSALM 46:1 AMP

November 22

EVENING

You may be feeling cramped in your current situation, but your salvation is an ever-expanding gift. My Spirit lives inside you, and He is always working to sanctify you—making you more like Me. This is an inner expansion, and it will continue till I call you home *to Glory*.

> *He brought me out into a spacious place; he rescued me because he delighted in me.* —2 Samuel 22:20

> *And I heard a loud voice from heaven saying, "Behold, the tabernacle of God is with men, and He will dwell with them, and they shall be His people. God Himself will be with them and be their God. And God will wipe away every tear from their eyes; there shall be no more death, nor sorrow, nor crying. There shall be no more pain, for the former things have passed away."* —Revelation 21:3–4 nkjv

Also read:

Psalm 73:24 esv

Before You Turn Out the Light

Write this on your heart: If you belong to Me,
you are in a spacious place of salvation.

November 23

MORNING

As you sit quietly in My Presence, let Me fill your heart and mind with thankfulness. This is the most direct way to achieve a thankful stance. If your mind needs a focal point, gaze at My Love poured out for you on the cross. Remember that *nothing in heaven or on earth can separate you from that Love*. This remembrance builds a foundation of gratitude in you, a foundation that circumstances cannot shake.

As you go through this day, look for tiny treasures strategically placed along the way. I lovingly go before you and plant little pleasures to brighten your day. Look carefully for them, and pluck them one by one. When you reach the end of the day, you will have gathered a lovely bouquet. Offer it up to Me with a grateful heart. Receive My Peace as you lie down to sleep, with thankful thoughts playing a lullaby in your mind.

Romans 8:38–39; 1 Corinthians 3:11;
Psalm 4:7–8

November 23

EVENING

IT IS POSSIBLE to be *sorrowful, yet always rejoicing.* The Holy Spirit empowered Paul to find Joy in the midst of adversity, and He can do the same for you. You must be willing, though, to let go of anything, trusting that I will never let go of *you.*

> *Be strong and courageous. Do not be afraid or terrified because of them, for the L*ORD *your God goes with you; he will never leave you nor forsake you.* —DEUTERONOMY 31:6

> *In all things we commend ourselves as ministers of God . . . as sorrowful, yet always rejoicing; as poor, yet making many rich; as having nothing, and yet possessing all things.* —2 CORINTHIANS 6:4, 10 NKJV

Also read:
PSALM 73:23–24

Before You Turn Out the Light

Grieve your losses, even as you learn to focus on the good things that remain.

November 24

MORNING

THANKFULNESS takes the sting out of adversity. That is why I have instructed you to *give thanks for everything*. There is an element of mystery in this transaction: You give Me thanks (regardless of your feelings), and I give you Joy (regardless of your circumstances). This is a spiritual act of obedience—at times, blind obedience. To people who don't know Me intimately, it can seem irrational and even impossible to thank Me for heartrending hardships. Nonetheless, those who obey Me in this way are invariably blessed, even though difficulties may remain.

Thankfulness opens your heart to My Presence and your mind to My thoughts. You may still be in the same place, with the same set of circumstances, but it is as if a light has been switched on, enabling you to see from My perspective. It is this *Light of My Presence* that removes the sting from adversity.

EPHESIANS 5:20; PSALM 118:1;
PSALM 89:15

November 24

EVENING

It is natural that you want to minimize pain. However, in My Word I continually call you to transcendent living, to go beyond what is natural to what is supernatural. Though My ways may entail sacrifice and pain, I accomplish through them not just what is good for you—but what is best.

> *As for God, his way is perfect. . . . He is a shield for all who take refuge in him.* —2 Samuel 22:31

> *We live by faith, not by sight.* —2 Corinthians 5:7

Also read:
Deuteronomy 33:27 AMP

Before You Turn Out the Light

Will you heed My call to push through your fear into the unknown depths of living by faith instead of sight? Underneath you are My everlasting arms.

November 25

MORNING

Thank Me frequently as you journey through today. This practice makes it possible to *pray without ceasing*, as the apostle Paul taught. If you are serious about learning to pray continually, the best approach is to thank Me in every situation. These thankful prayers provide a solid foundation on which you can build all your other prayers. Moreover, a grateful attitude makes it easier for you to communicate with Me.

When your mind is occupied with thanking Me, you have no time for worrying or complaining. If you practice thankfulness consistently, negative thought patterns will gradually grow weaker and weaker. *Draw near to Me* with a grateful heart, and My Presence will *fill you with Joy and Peace*.

1 Thessalonians 5:16–18 kjv;
James 4:8; Romans 15:13

November 25
EVENING

I AM PLEASED by your desire to rely on Me in your small moments as well as in the big events of your life. When you whisper My Name, I respond not only to your neediness but also to your love. As you look to Me, My Face shines upon you in radiant approval—brightening your day and helping you feel secure.

> *Come near to God and he will come near to you.* —JAMES 4:8

> *And everyone who calls on the name of the Lord will be saved.* —ACTS 2:21

Also read:
ACTS 4:12; NUMBERS 6:25–26 AMP

Before You Turn Out the Light

Reflect on how often you looked to Me today.
I will go with you tomorrow as well.

November 26
MORNING

This is the day that I have made! As you rejoice in this day of life, it will yield up to you precious gifts and beneficial training. Walk with Me along the high road of thanksgiving, and you will find all the delights I have made ready for you.

To protect your thankfulness, you must remember that you reside in a fallen world, where blessings and sorrows intermingle freely. A constant focus on adversity defeats many Christians. They walk through a day that is brimming with beauty and brightness, seeing only the grayness of their thoughts. Neglecting the practice of giving thanks has darkened their minds. How precious are My children who remember to thank Me at all times. They can walk through the darkest days with Joy in their hearts because they know that the Light of My Presence is still shining on them. *Rejoice in this day that I have made*, for I am your steadfast Companion.

PSALM 118:24; PSALM 116:17;

PSALM 118:28

November 26

EVENING

I LONG TO FILL YOU WITH JOY, but you must collaborate with Me in this process. Do not be like a spoiled child on Christmas Day—hastily tearing open all the presents and then saying, "Is that all?" Every single day is a precious gift from Me!

The Lord has done great things for us, and we are filled with joy. —Psalm 126:3

In this you greatly rejoice, though now for a little while you may have had to suffer grief in all kinds of trials. These have come so that your faith—of greater worth than gold, which perishes even though refined by fire—may be proved genuine and may result in praise, glory and honor when Jesus Christ is revealed. Though you have not seen him, you love him; and even though you do not see him now, you believe in him and are filled with an inexpressible and glorious joy. —1 Peter 1:6–8

Also read:

Deuteronomy 33:27 nkjv; Jeremiah 29:13 nkjv

Before You Turn Out the Light

Did you rejoice in My goodness today?
How did you receive My Joy?

November 27

MORNING

LET THANKFULNESS RULE in your heart. As you thank Me for blessings in your life, a marvelous thing happens. It is as if *scales fall off your eyes*, enabling you to see more and more of My glorious riches. With your eyes thus opened, you can help yourself to whatever you need from My treasure house. Each time you receive one of My golden gifts, let your thankfulness sing out praises to My Name. "Hallelujahs" are the language of heaven, and they can become the language of your heart.

A life of praise and thankfulness becomes a life filled with miracles. Instead of trying to be in control, you focus on Me and what I am doing. This is the power of praise: centering your entire being in Me. This is how I created you to live, for I made you in My own image. Enjoy abundant life by overflowing with praise and thankfulness.

COLOSSIANS 3:15; ACTS 9:18;
REVELATION 19:3–6; PSALM 100:4

November 27

EVENING

IT IS IMPOSSIBLE to have a happy heart when your mind is full of negative thoughts. This is why you need to exert control over your thinking. Invite the Holy Spirit to control your mind; look at your thoughts in His holy Light, and reject those that are unfitting for a child of the King.

> *"And I will pray the Father, and He will give you another Helper, that He may abide with you forever."* —JOHN 14:16 NKJV

> *The mind of sinful man is death, but the mind controlled by the Spirit is life and peace.* —ROMANS 8:6

Also read:
PROVERBS 17:22 AMP; JOHN 14:2 NKJV

Before You Turn Out the Light

Which lies and partial truths do you need to replace with My absolute truth? The Holy Spirit will faithfully reveal them.

November 28
MORNING

Rest in the deep assurance of My unfailing Love. Let your body, mind, and spirit relax in My Presence. Release into My care anything that is troubling you so that you can focus your full attention on Me. Be awed by the vast dimensions of My Love for you: *wider, longer, higher, and deeper* than anything you know. Rejoice that this marvelous Love is yours forever!

The best response to this glorious gift is a life steeped in thankfulness. Every time you thank Me, you acknowledge that I am your Lord and Provider. This is the proper stance for a child of God: receiving with thanksgiving. Bring Me the sacrifice of gratitude, and watch to see how much I bless you.

1 Peter 5:7; Ephesians 3:16–19;
Psalm 107:21–22

November 28

EVENING

YOU ARE OFTEN SUBJECT to a slumbering soul: taking for granted your life with all its blessings, being overly focused on negative things, buying into the world's version of the good life. I want to help you break free from these worldly weights so your soul can soar in the heights with Me.

Every good and perfect gift is from above, coming down from the Father of the heavenly lights, who does not change like shifting shadows. —JAMES 1:17

You have made known to me the paths of life; you will fill me with joy in your presence. —ACTS 2:28

Also read:
PSALM 37:4 AMP; 2 CHRONICLES 16:9

Before You Turn Out the Light

Keep Me first in all things. This frees Me to bless you bountifully and prevents My gifts from becoming idols.

November 29

MORNING

Let Me infuse My Peace into your innermost being. As you sit quietly in the Light of My Presence, you can sense Peace growing within you. This is not something that you accomplish through self-discipline and willpower; it is opening yourself to receive My blessing.

In this age of independence, people find it hard to acknowledge their neediness. However, I have taken you along a path that has highlighted your need for Me, placing you in situations where your strengths were irrelevant and your weaknesses were glaringly evident. Through the aridity of those desert marches, I have drawn you closer and closer to Myself. You have discovered flowers of Peace blossoming in the most desolate places. You have learned to thank Me for hard times and difficult journeys, trusting that through them I accomplish My best work. You have realized that needing Me is the key to knowing Me intimately, which is the gift above all gifts.

JOHN 14:27 NKJV; ISAIAH 58:11;
ISAIAH 40:11

November 29
EVENING

Come to Me with all your neediness. You can cry out, "Help me, Jesus!" Then wait patiently in My Presence. Your weariness will eventually give way to new strength as you trustingly wait upon Me.

Though youths grow weary and tired, and vigorous young men stumble badly, yet those who wait for the Lord will gain new strength; they will mount up with wings like eagles, they will run and not get tired, they will walk and not become weary. —Isaiah 40:30–31 nasb

[We are] sorrowful, yet always rejoicing; poor, yet making many rich; having nothing, and yet possessing everything. —2 Corinthians 6:10

Also read:
Psalm 118:24 nkjv; John 15:5

Before You Turn Out the Light

Let Me show you what it means to rejoice and
be renewed, even in your troubles.

November 30
MORNING

PROBLEMS ARE PART OF LIFE. They are inescapable, woven into the very fabric of this fallen world. You tend to go into problem-solving mode all too readily, acting as if you have the capacity to fix everything. This is a habitual response, so automatic that it bypasses your conscious thinking. Not only does this habit frustrate you, it also distances you from Me.

Do not let fixing things be your top priority. You are ever so limited in your capacity to correct all that is wrong in the world around you. Don't weigh yourself down with responsibilities that are not your own. Instead, make your relationship with Me your primary concern. Talk with Me about whatever is on your mind, seeking My perspective on the situation. Rather than trying to fix everything that comes to your attention, ask Me to show you what is truly important. Remember that you are *en route* to heaven, and let your problems fade in the Light of eternity.

PSALM 32:8; LUKE 10:41–42;
PHILIPPIANS 3:20–21

November 30

EVENING

The combination of My image and My Spirit in you is powerful—making you fit for greatness. When you are engaged in combat, keep looking to Me for strength and guidance. Abandon yourself to the challenges I have chosen for you. Then you will find your days increasingly devoted to sacred adventures shared with Me—your King!

And if the Spirit of him who raised Jesus from the dead is living in you, he who raised Christ from the dead will also give life to your mortal bodies through his Spirit, who lives in you. —Romans 8:11

Therefore put on the full armor of God, so that when the day of evil comes, you may be able to stand your ground, and after you have done everything, to stand. —Ephesians 6:13

Also read:
1 Timothy 6:15–16

Before You Turn Out the Light

View yourself as a chosen warrior with your mind and armor prepared for battle. Together we will handle any difficulties to come.

December

"For to us a child is born. . . . And he will be called Wonderful Counselor, Mighty God, Everlasting Father, Prince of Peace."

Isaiah 9:6

December 1

MORNING

I LOVE YOU with an everlasting Love, which flows out from the depths of eternity. Before you were born, I knew you. Ponder the awesome mystery of a Love that encompasses you from before birth to beyond the grave.

Modern man has lost the perspective of eternity. To distract himself from the gaping jaws of death, he engages in ceaseless activity and amusement. The practice of being still in My Presence is almost a lost art, yet it is this very stillness that enables you to experience My eternal Love. You need the certainty of My loving Presence in order to weather the storms of life. During times of severe testing, even the best theology can fail you if it isn't accompanied by experiential knowledge of Me. The ultimate protection against sinking during life's storms is devoting time to develop your friendship with Me.

JEREMIAH 31:3; LAMENTATIONS 3:22–26

December 1

EVENING

Y OUR YEARNING for permanence is good because it is a longing for eternal, invisible reality. That reality is primarily about Me, and I draw near in response to your seeking heart. I am able to give you a firm place to stand, *setting your feet on a rock.*

> *He lifted me out of the slimy pit, out of the mud and mire; he set my feet on a rock and give me a firm place to stand.* —PSALM 40:2

> *The LORD is my rock, my fortress and my deliverer; my God is my rock, in whom I take refuge. He is my shield and the horn of my salvation, my stronghold.* —PSALM 18:2

Also read:
REVELATION 21:6; 1 TIMOTHY 1:17

Before You Turn Out the Light

Ponder what it means to hide yourself in Me—your Rock, your Fortress, your Stronghold, your Refuge.

December 2
MORNING

I AM THE PRINCE OF PEACE. As I said to My disciples, I say also to you: *Peace be with you.* Since I am your constant Companion, My Peace is steadfastly with you. When you keep your focus on Me, you experience both My Presence and My Peace. Worship Me as King of kings, Lord of lords, and Prince of Peace.

You need My Peace each moment to accomplish My purposes in your life. Sometimes you are tempted to take shortcuts in order to reach your goal as quickly as possible. But if the shortcut requires turning your back on My peaceful Presence, you must choose the longer route. Walk with Me along paths of Peace; enjoy the journey in My Presence.

ISAIAH 9:6; JOHN 20:19–21;
PSALM 25:4 NKJV

December 2

EVENING

I AM TEACHING YOU THE SECRET OF BEING CONTENT in any and every situation. This secret is all about *Me*—who I am and what I offer you. I am your Creator and King, your Savior and Shepherd. I offer you Myself in all My Power and Glory. Trust in Me and in My infinite riches and generous Love.

I know what it is to be in need, and I know what it is to have plenty. I have learned the secret of being content in any and every situation, whether well fed or hungry, whether living in plenty or in want. I can do everything through him who gives me strength. —PHILIPPIANS 4:12–13

And my God shall supply all your need according to His riches in glory by Christ Jesus. —PHILIPPIANS 4:19 NKJV

Also read:
ISAIAH 55:8–9 NKJV

Before You Turn Out the Light

Content yourself in Me.

December 3

MORNING

Do not be surprised by the fiery attacks on your mind. When you struggle to find Me and to live in My Peace, don't let discouragement set in. You are engaged in massive warfare, spiritually speaking. The evil one abhors your closeness to Me, and his demonic underlings are determined to destroy our intimacy. When you find yourself in the thick of battle, call upon My Name: "Jesus, help me!" At that instant, the battle becomes Mine; your role is simply to trust Me as I fight for you.

My Name, properly used, has unlimited Power to bless and protect. At the end of time, *every knee will bow (in heaven, on earth, and under the earth) when My Name is proclaimed*. People who have used "Jesus" as a shoddy swear word will fall down in terror on that awesome day. But all those who have drawn near Me through trustingly uttering My Name will be filled with *inexpressible and glorious Joy*. This is your great hope as you await My return.

Ephesians 6:12; Philippians 2:9–10;
1 Peter 1:8–9

December 3
EVENING

WHAT YOU DO WITH YOUR BODY can help or hinder what goes on in your soul. When you realize you are grasping for control, intentionally open your hands, releasing the matter to Me and inviting Me to take charge. You are now in a good position to receive many blessings from Me, not the least of which is awareness of My Presence.

> *I want men everywhere to lift up holy hands in prayer, without anger or disputing.* —1 TIMOTHY 2:8

> *"For I am the LORD, your God, who takes hold of your right hand and says to you, Do not fear; I will help you."* —ISAIAH 41:13

> *Also read:*
> JOHN 20:19; MATTHEW 18:4 NKJV

Before You Turn Out the Light

Physically position your heart, your mind, and your hands to receive My Peace.

December 4
MORNING

MY THOUGHTS *are not your thoughts; neither are your ways My ways. As the heavens are higher than the earth, so are My ways and thoughts higher than yours.* Remember who I AM when you spend time with Me. Marvel at the wonder of being able to commune with the King of the universe—any time, any place. Never take this amazing privilege for granted!

Though I am vastly higher and greater than you, I am training you to think My thoughts. As you spend time in My Presence, My thoughts gradually form in your mind. My Spirit is the Director of this process. Sometimes He brings Bible verses to mind. Sometimes He enables you to hear Me "speak" directly to you. These communications strengthen you and prepare you for whatever is before you on your life-path. Take time to listen to My voice. Through your sacrifice of precious time, I bless you far more than you dare to ask.

ISAIAH 55:8–9; COLOSSIANS 4:2;
PSALM 116:17

December 4

EVENING

My unshakable kingdom is for all people who love Me, who know Me as Savior. This everlasting kingdom consists of things that *no eye has seen, no ear has heard, no mind has conceived.* Let these precious promises ignite your thankfulness until you are aglow with My living Presence—shining brightly in this dark world.

> *However, as it is written: "No eye has seen, no ear has heard, no mind has conceived what God has prepared for those who love him."* —1 Corinthians 2:9

> *"And if I go and prepare a place for you, I will come back and take you to be with me that you also may be where I am."* —John 14:3

> *Also read:*
> Exodus 24:17 nkjv

Before You Turn Out the Light

Stand firm in My promises; be generous with your praise.

December 5

MORNING

Let My Presence override everything you experience. Like a luminous veil of Light, I hover over you and everything around you. I am training you to stay conscious of Me in each situation you encounter.

When the patriarch Jacob ran away from his enraged brother, he went to sleep on a stone pillow in a land that seemed desolate. But after dreaming about heaven and angels and promises of My Presence, he awoke and exclaimed: "Surely the Lord is in this place, and I was not aware of it." His discovery was not only for him but for all who seek Me. Whenever you feel distant from Me, say, "Surely the Lord is in this place!" Then ask Me to give you awareness of My Presence. This is a prayer that I delight to answer.

Psalm 31:20; Genesis 28:11–16

December 5
EVENING

WHEN YOU REALIZE you have lost your way, there is only one remedy: Admit that you are directionless, and ask for My help. Let the peacefulness of My Presence revive you. As My Peace settles over your mind and soul, the way before you will open up step by step.

> *Commit to the LORD whatever you do, and your plans will succeed.* —PROVERBS 16:3

> *Direct me in the path of your commands, for there I find delight.* —PSALM 119:35

Also read:
EXODUS 33:14; EPHESIANS 2:10

Before You Turn Out the Light

Pause with Me . . . let Me soothe your frazzled nerves.

December 6
MORNING

STAY EVER SO CLOSE TO ME, and you will not deviate from the path I have prepared for you. This is the most efficient way to stay on track; it is also the most enjoyable way. Men tend to multiply duties in their observance of religion. This practice enables them to give Me money, time, and work without yielding up to Me what I desire the most—their hearts. Rules can be observed mechanically. Once they become habitual, they can be followed with minimal effort and almost no thought. These habit-forming rules provide a false sense of security, lulling the soul into a comatose condition.

What I search for in My children is an awakened soul that thrills to the Joy of My Presence! I created mankind to glorify Me and enjoy Me forever. I provide the Joy; your part is to glorify Me by living close to Me.

DEUTERONOMY 6:5; COLOSSIANS 3:23;
PSALM 16:11; PSALM 86:12 NKJV

December 6
EVENING

I AM YOUR LIVING REDEEMER. Since *you were bought* at such an immeasurable price, I want you to *glorify Me in your body and in your spirit*. You glorify Me in your body by taking good care of yourself and abstaining from immorality; you glorify Me in your spirit by delighting in Me above all else. The world contains much beauty and many sources of enjoyment, but I outshine them all.

> *I know that my Redeemer lives, and that in the end he will stand upon the earth. And after my skin has been destroyed, yet in my flesh I will see God; I myself will see him with my own eyes.* —JOB 19:25–27

> *For you were bought at a price; therefore glorify God in your body and in your spirit, which are God's.* —1 CORINTHIANS 6:20 NKJV

Also read:
JOHN 8:34; ZEPHANIAH 3:17

Before You Turn Out the Light

In My Name, joyfully engage in the healthy pleasures of this life! Your life is a gift from Me.

December 7

MORNING

I AM WITH YOU IN ALL THAT YOU DO, even in the most menial task. I am always aware of you, concerned with every detail of your life. Nothing escapes My notice—not even *the number of hairs on your head*. However, your awareness of My Presence falters and flickers; as a result, your life experience feels fragmented. When your focus is broad enough to include Me in your thoughts, you feel safe and complete. When your perception narrows so that problems or details fill your consciousness, you feel empty and incomplete.

Learn to look steadily at Me in all your moments and all your circumstances. Though the world is unstable and in flux, you can experience continuity through your uninterrupted awareness of My Presence. *Fix your gaze on what is unseen*, even as the visible world parades before your eyes.

MATTHEW 10:29–31; HEBREWS 11:27;
2 CORINTHIANS 4:18

December 7
EVENING

I AM INDEED THE FIRM FOUNDATION on which you can build your life. Though I want you to enjoy the material blessings I provide, you must not depend on them to feel safe. Real security rests in Me alone—not in Me plus favorable circumstances.

> *Jesus Christ is the same yesterday and today and forever.* —HEBREWS 13:8

> *Trust in the LORD forever, for the LORD, the LORD, is the Rock eternal.* —ISAIAH 26:4

Also read:
HEBREWS 13:5; JEREMIAH 29:13 AMP

Before You Turn Out the Light

Construct your life on the Rock of My Presence. Nothing can destroy that foundation!

December 8
MORNING

Y*OUR NEEDS AND MY RICHES* are a perfect fit. I never meant for you to be self-sufficient. Instead, I designed you to need Me not only for daily bread but also for fulfillment of deep yearnings. I carefully crafted your longings and feelings of incompleteness to point you to Me. Therefore, do not try to bury or deny these feelings. Beware also of trying to pacify these longings with lesser gods: people, possessions, power.

Come to Me in all your neediness, with defenses down and with desire to be blessed. As you spend time in My Presence, your deepest longings are fulfilled. Rejoice in your neediness, which enables you to find intimate completion in Me.

PHILIPPIANS 4:19; COLOSSIANS 2:2–3;
PSALM 84:11–12 NKJV

December 8

EVENING

The more frequently you look to Me for help, the more you will find Me faithful. I sustain you moment by moment, so there is never a time when you don't need Me. Awareness of your neediness is actually a rich blessing—connecting you to Me and My abundant supply!

> *"The Lord does not look at the things man looks at. Man looks at the outward appearance, but the Lord looks at the heart."* —1 Samuel 16:7

I have set the Lord continually before me; because He is at my right hand, I shall not be moved. —Psalm 16:8 amp

Also read:
Genesis 3:4–5

Before You Turn Out the Light

Rely on Me now and in whatever may come.
This is the way I want you to live.

December 9
MORNING

Be willing to go out on a limb with Me. If that is where I am leading you, it is the safest place to be. Your desire to live a risk-free life is a form of unbelief. Your longing to live close to Me is at odds with your attempts to minimize risk. You are approaching a crossroads in your journey. In order to follow Me wholeheartedly, you must relinquish your tendency to play it safe.

Let Me lead you step by step through this day. If your primary focus is on Me, you can walk along perilous paths without being afraid. Eventually, you will learn to relax and enjoy the adventure of our journey together. As long as you stay close to Me, My sovereign Presence protects you wherever you go.

Psalm 23:4; Psalm 9:10;
John 12:26

December 9

EVENING

You can call upon Me to help you live courageously—facing adversity or danger with confidence and determination. Stand firm in My strength, beloved, refusing to give in or give up. I take pleasure in you always, but especially when you are bravely *hoping in My steadfast Love*.

> *Be strong and of good courage, do not fear nor be afraid of [the nations in the Promised Land]; for the Lord your God, He is the One who goes with you. He will not leave you nor forsake you.* —Deuteronomy 31:6 nkjv

> *The Lord takes pleasure in those who fear him, in those who hope in his steadfast love.* —Psalm 147:11 esv

Also read:
Ephesians 1:18–19

Before You Turn Out the Light

Consider the ways you can actively maintain
your hope in Me, no matter what.

December 10
MORNING

Make Me the focal point of your search for security. In your private thoughts, you are still trying to order your world so that it is predictable and feels safe. Not only is this an impossible goal, but it is also counterproductive to spiritual growth. When your private world feels unsteady and you grip My hand for support, you are living in conscious dependence on Me.

Instead of yearning for a problem-free life, rejoice that trouble can highlight your awareness of My Presence. In the darkness of adversity, you are able to see more clearly the radiance of My Face. Accept the value of problems in this life, *considering them pure joy*. Remember that you have an eternity of trouble-free living awaiting you in heaven.

Isaiah 41:10; Psalm 139:10;
James 1:2

December 10
EVENING

My PRESENCE AND PEACE are inseparable: When your mind is stayed on Me, I keep you in perfect Peace. Understanding that your ability to stay focused on Me is limited, I do not expect perfection from you—only perseverance. Never give up!

> *Do not be anxious about anything, but in everything, by prayer and petition, with thanksgiving, present your requests to God. And the peace of God, which transcends all understanding, will guard your hearts and your minds in Christ Jesus.* —PHILIPPIANS 4:6–7

> *You will keep him in perfect peace, whose mind is stayed on You, because he trusts in You.* —ISAIAH 26:3 NKJV

Also read:
PROVERBS 20:24

Before You Turn Out the Light

Take all that I've taught you about directing your thoughts to Me—whispering My Name to remind you of My Presence, giving thanks, offering up brief praises and petitions—and keep practicing.

December 11
MORNING

I AM WORKING ON YOUR BEHALF. Bring Me all your concerns, including your dreams. Talk with Me about everything, letting the Light of My Presence shine on your hopes and plans. Spend time allowing My Light to infuse your dreams with life, gradually transforming them into reality. This is a very practical way of collaborating with Me. I, the Creator of the universe, have deigned to co-create with you. Do not try to hurry this process. If you want to work with Me, you have to accept My time frame. Hurry is not in My nature. Abraham and Sarah had to wait many years for the fulfillment of My promise, a son. How their long wait intensified their enjoyment of this child! *Faith is the assurance of things hoped for, perceiving as real fact what is not revealed to the senses.*

PSALM 36:9; GENESIS 21:1–7;
HEBREWS 11:1 AMP

December 13
EVENING

GROWING IN GRACE is all about transformation—becoming more like Me. This is a glorious adventure and an awesome privilege, yet it is also painful at times. Cling to My hand—walking with Me in trusting dependence along the path I've prepared for you—*for My Word is a lamp to your feet and a light for your path.*

The word of God is living and powerful, and sharper than any two-edged sword, piercing even to the division of soul and spirit, and of joints and marrow, and is a discerner of the thoughts and intents of the heart. —HEBREWS 4:12 NKJV

Those God foreknew he also predestined to be conformed to the likeness of his Son, that he might be the firstborn among many brothers. —ROMANS 8:29

Also read:
HEBREWS 13:8 NKJV; PSALM 119:105

Before You Turn Out the Light

Take My Word with you as your lamp in the darkness.

December 14

MORNING

Rest in Me, My child, forgetting about the worries of the world. Focus on Me—Immanuel—and let My living Presence envelop you in Peace. Tune in to My eternal security, for *I am the same yesterday, today, and forever.* If you live on the surface of life by focusing on ever-changing phenomena, you will find yourself echoing the words of Solomon: *"Meaningless! Meaningless! Everything is meaningless!"*

Living in collaboration with Me is the way to instill meaning into your days. Begin each day alone with Me so that you can experience the reality of My Presence. As you spend time with Me, the way before you opens up step by step. Arise from the stillness of our communion, and gradually begin your journey through the day. Hold My hand in deliberate dependence on Me, and I will smooth out the path before you.

MATTHEW 1:22–23; HEBREWS 13:8;
ECCLESIASTES 1:2; PROVERBS 3:6

December 14

EVENING

Though I'm pleased by your willingness to depend on Me in tough situations, I desire much more from you: I want you to rely on Me even when you feel competent to handle a situation yourself. When you utilize your talents and abilities, remember to do so thankfully, asking Me to help you use them wisely, according to My will. This collaborative way of doing things will not only help you accomplish more; it will also keep you close to Me, communing with Me, delighting in Me, enjoying Me.

> *I have strength for all things in Christ Who empowers me [I am ready for anything and equal to anything through Him Who infuses inner strength into me].* —Philippians 4:13 amp

> *Because of the Lord's great love we are not consumed, for his compassions never fail. They are new every morning; great is your faithfulness.* —Lamentations 3:22–23

Before You Turn Out the Light

In both uncertain and "sure" situations, announce your trust in Me as often as you need to. Your fears will diminish as you acknowledge My faithfulness time after time.

December 15

MORNING

Your longing for heaven is good because it is an extension of your yearning for Me. The hope of heaven is meant to strengthen and encourage you, filling you with wondrous Joy. Many Christians have misunderstood this word *hope*, believing that it denotes wishful thinking. Nothing could be farther from the truth! As soon as I became your Savior, heaven became your ultimate destination. The phrase *hope of heaven* highlights the benefits you can enjoy even while remaining on earth. This hope keeps you spiritually alive during dark times of adversity; it brightens your path and heightens your awareness of My Presence. My desire is *that you may overflow with hope by the power of the Holy Spirit.*

ROMANS 8:23–25; HEBREWS 6:18–19;
ROMANS 15:13

December 15

EVENING

That cry of your heart is a prayer I am eager to answer. Intentionally release your worries into My care and keeping; then rest in the knowledge that I am taking care of you and all that concerns you. As you trustingly relax in My Presence, find refreshment in the refuge of My everlasting arms.

> *The eternal God is your refuge, and underneath are the everlasting arms.* —Deuteronomy 33:27

> *Immediately the boy's father exclaimed, "I do believe; help me overcome my unbelief!"* —Mark 9:24

Also read:
Psalm 37:5–6

Before You Turn Out the Light

Decide on how you can symbolize leaving your worries with Me—and then do this very thing.

December 16

MORNING

I AM SPEAKING in the depths of your being. Be still so that you can hear My voice. I speak in the language of Love; My words fill you with Life and Peace, Joy and hope. I desire to talk with all of My children, but many are too busy to listen. The "work ethic" has them tied up in knots. They submit wholeheartedly to this taskmaster, wondering why they feel so distant from Me.

Living close to Me requires making Me your *First Love*—your highest priority. As you seek My Presence above all else, you experience Peace and Joy in full measure. I also am blessed when you make Me first in your life. While you journey through life in My Presence, *My Glory brightens the world around you.*

PSALM 119:64; ISAIAH 50:4;
REVELATION 2:4; ISAIAH 60:2

December 16
EVENING

As you come to know Me more intimately, you grow increasingly aware of your sins. This presents you with a continual choice—to focus on your flaws and failures or to rejoice in My glorious gift of salvation. When My ultimate sacrifice is your focus, you live in joyful assurance of being wondrously loved.

> *But I trust in your unfailing love; my heart rejoices in your salvation. I will sing to the LORD, for he has been good to me.* —PSALM 13:5–6

> *"Greater love has no one than this, than to lay down one's life for his friends."* —JOHN 15:13 NKJV

Also read:
LUKE 7:47; JOHN 8:12

Before You Turn Out the Light

There is no greater Love than Mine. Let it in—
and then let it flow through you to others.

December 17

MORNING

COME TO ME with your gaping emptiness, knowing that in Me you are complete. As you rest quietly in My Presence, My Light within you grows brighter and brighter. Facing the emptiness inside you is simply the prelude to being filled with My fullness. Therefore, rejoice on those days when you drag yourself out of bed, feeling sluggish and inadequate. Tell yourself that this is a perfect day to depend on Me in childlike trust. If you persevere in this dependence as you go through the day, you will discover at bedtime that Joy and Peace have become your companions. You may not realize at what point they joined you on your journey, but you will feel the beneficial effects of their presence. The perfect end to such a day is a doxology of gratitude. I am He from whom all blessings flow!

2 CORINTHIANS 4:6; MATTHEW 5:3, 6;
COLOSSIANS 2:9–10; PSALM 150:6

December 17
EVENING

IT IS POSSIBLE to feel isolated even when you are with other people because of the privacy of your thoughts and unspoken needs. The only thing that can adequately fill the gaps of isolation is awareness of My abiding Presence. Come to Me with your ever-so-human emptiness, and My divine Presence will fill you with Life to the full!

The LORD is righteous in all his ways and loving toward all he has made. The LORD is near to all who call on him, to all who call on him in truth. —PSALM 145:17–18

"The thief comes only to steal and kill and destroy; I have come that they may have life, and have it to the full." —JOHN 10:10

Also read:
PSALM 41:12

Before You Turn Out the Light

Notice My abiding Presence with you as you seek My Face. My knowledge of you is picture-perfect and framed in unconditional Love.

December 18
MORNING

WHEN YOU ARE PLAGUED by a persistent problem—one that goes on and on—view it as a rich opportunity. An ongoing problem is like a tutor who is always by your side. The learning possibilities are limited only by your willingness to be teachable. In faith, thank Me for your problem. Ask Me to open your eyes and your heart to all that I am accomplishing through this difficulty. Once you have become grateful for a problem, it loses its power to drag you down. On the contrary, your thankful attitude will lift you up into heavenly places with Me. From this perspective, your difficulty can be seen as *a slight, temporary distress that is producing for you a transcendent Glory never to cease*!

ISAIAH 30:20–21; EPHESIANS 5:19–20;
2 CORINTHIANS 4:17 AMP

December 19
EVENING

Your limitations actually provide a solid structure within which you can make choices about your life. Significantly, as you say yes to the boundaries I have placed around you, you can look up and see Me smiling upon you. You realize that *up* is the only direction where you face no limitations.

And God raised us up with Christ and seated us with him in the heavenly realms in Christ Jesus. —Ephesians 2:6

Now the Lord is the Spirit, and where the Spirit of the Lord is, there is freedom. —2 Corinthians 3:17

Also read:
Psalm 34:18

Before You Turn Out the Light

What will you choose: the weight of self-pity
or the wings of My limitations?

December 20
MORNING

WHEN I JOINED THE RANKS of humanity, born into the humblest conditions, My Glory was hidden from all but a few people. Occasionally, streaks of Glory shone out of Me, especially when I began to do miracles. Toward the end of My life, I was taunted and tempted to display more of My awesome Power than My Father's plan permitted. I could have called down legions of angels to rescue Me at any point. Imagine the self-control required of a martyr who could free Himself at will! All of this was necessary to provide the relationship with Me that you now enjoy. Let your life become a praise song to Me by proclaiming My glorious Presence in the world.

JOHN 2:11; LUKE 23:35–36;
PSALM 92:1–5

December 20
EVENING

As you exert your will to abstain from ungodly behavior, there is abundant help available to you in this battle. *Faith, hope, and love* all work together to shield you as you journey through this world. They also keep you close to Me.

> *Since we belong to the day, let us be self-controlled, putting on faith and love as a breastplate, and the hope of salvation as a helmet.* —1 Thessalonians 5:8

> *Stand therefore, having fastened on the belt of truth, and having put on the breastplate of righteousness, and, as shoes for your feet, having put on the readiness given by the gospel of peace.* —Ephesians 6:14–15 esv

Also read:
Galatians 5:22–23 nkjv; 1 Corinthians 13:13

Before You Turn Out the Light

Suit up tonight so that you may go forth
with self-control tomorrow.

M Y PLAN FOR YOUR LIFE is unfolding before you. Sometimes the road you are traveling seems blocked, or it opens up so painfully slowly that you must hold yourself back. Then, when time is right, the way before you suddenly clears—through no effort of your own. What you have longed for and worked for I present to you freely, as pure gift. You feel awed by the ease with which I operate in the world, and you glimpse *My Power and My Glory.*

Do not fear your weakness, for it is the stage on which My Power and Glory perform most brilliantly. As you persevere along the path I have prepared for you, depending on My strength to sustain you, expect to see miracles—and you will. Miracles are not always visible to the naked eye, but those who *live by faith* can see them clearly. *Living by faith, rather than sight,* enables you to see My Glory.

PSALM 63:2–5; 2 CORINTHIANS 5:7;
JOHN 11:40

December 21
EVENING

Ask Me to help you think My thoughts and see things from My perspective. As you wait in My Presence, I not only unscramble your thinking; I also straighten your path, removing obstacles, giving insights that save time, and so on. When you spend precious time with Me, I compensate you generously, smoothing out the circumstances of your day.

O LORD, you have searched me and you know me. You know when I sit and when I rise; you perceive my thoughts from afar. —PSALM 139:1–2

We wait in hope for the LORD; he is our help and our shield. In him our hearts rejoice, for we trust in his holy name. May your unfailing love rest upon us, O LORD, even as we put our hope in you. —PSALM 33:20–22

Also read:
GENESIS 1:27

Before You Turn Out the Light

Recall how I smoothed the way for you today—and thank Me for it.

December 22

MORNING

COME TO ME, and rest in My Presence. As you ponder the majestic mystery of the Incarnation, relax in My everlasting arms. I am the only Person who was ever *sired* by the Holy Spirit. This is beyond your understanding. Instead of trying to comprehend My Incarnation intellectually, learn from the example of the wise men. They followed the leading of a spectacular star, then fell down in humble worship when they found Me.

Praise and worship are the best responses to the wonder of My Being. Sing praises to My holy Name. Gaze at Me in silent adoration. Look for a star of guidance in your own life, and be willing to follow wherever I lead. *I am the Light from on high that dawns upon you, to guide your feet into the way of Peace.*

LUKE 1:35; JOHN 1:14; MATTHEW 2:10–11 NKJV;
LUKE 1:78–79 AMP